PRINCIPLES OF AYURVEDIC THERAPEUTICS

Indian Medical Science Series No : 39

Source for Students Practitioners and Student - I

PRINCIPLES OF AYURVEDIC THERAPEUTICS

By

ATMAKURI VINAYA KUMAR

M.B.B.S., M.D., M.M.N., Ph.D., D.Sc.

SRI SATGURU PUBLICATIONS

A Division of

INDIAN BOOKS CENTRE

Delhi • India

Published by :
SRI SATGURU PUBLICATIONS
Indological and Oriental Publishers
A Division of
INDIAN BOOKS CENTRE
40/5, Shakti Nagar,
Delhi-110007
(INDIA)

First Edition : Delhi, 1995

ISBN 81-7030-463-6

Printed at :
Mehra Offset Press, Delhi.

PRINTED IN INDIA

Contents

	Foreword	vii
	Preface	xi
	Acknowledgements	xv
1.	Introduction	1
2.	Fundamentals of Ayurveda	9
3.	Health and Disease	61
4.	Causation of Disease	71
5.	Clinical Manifestations of Disease	83
6.	Case-taking and Examination of the Patient and the Disease	109
7.	Investigation of the Patient	137
8.	Principles of Diagnosis	173
9.	Classification of Disease	181
10.	Principles of Treatment	207
11.	Pharmaco Therpeutics in Ayurveda	227
12.	Principles of Drug (Dravya) Administration	251
13.	Ayurveda and Yoga	263
14.	Appendix	293
	Subject Index	299

Foreword

The term Ayurveda connotes science of life. It is the science which deals with the life of human beings. It deals in particular with the maintenance of the body and to promote long life without any ailments. Apart from this, Ayurveda is a science that bestows the knowledge on us to maintain the body and mind in a state of equilibrium by adopting the basic principles of it as enshrined in "Asthanga Ayurveda".

Understanding, assimilation, and putting into practice the basic principles is the first and foremost approach for upliftment and progress of a person or a country or any science. Hence, Charaka, Sushruta, and Vaghbhatta practiced and advocated Ayurveda from philosophical state to metaphysical state.

Bringing up a person in a positive and promotive way is an investment for the future of mankind in terms of human resources. Person needs proper programming for the development in terms of physical, physiological, psychological, sociological and moral values. A society with ill equipped persons either physical or moral could weaken the society. Ayurveda can contribute to the society in such a calamity.

At this present juncture, Dr. Atmakuri Vinaya Kumar, is bringing out his book on "Principles of Ayurvedic Therapeutics", produced in collaboration with the Society for Advancement of Research and Development of Integrated Medicine (SARDIM), a registered organization, under Hyderabad Public societies Act (AP).

I feel it is a great honour conferred on me to write the foreword to this excellently brought out volume. This book is the result of strenuous efforts of the author in referring and collecting vast matter from the scattered scientific sources on Ayurveda. The author, is the Director to Matrusri Medical Centre and Centre for Alternative Medicine Therapy, Hyderabad. He is well qualified practitioner and consultant of Modern school of Medicine and is one of the best clinicians I have known. However, whenever allopathy fails to help the patient, he advises and uses alternative therapies like Ayurveda, Homeopathy, and Acupuncture. He has also taken deep interest in the literary and clinical aspects of alternative medicines and is carrying out clinical research for the past two decades. It is beyond doubt that Ayurveda has attained the status of the best alternative therapy among all other systems of medicine. That is why "World Health Organization" has opened a separate cell on alternative systems of medicine and is seriously searching for therapeutic clues with the help of these systems.

The present book has been divided into three parts: the first part dealing with the basic principles of Ayurveda, health, and disease; the second part with the principles of investigation, diagnosis of disease; and the third part with the principles of pharmacotherapeutics and drug administration and yoga.

In this treaties like volume, he surveyed Ayurvedic literature to the greatest extent and also incorporated some of the articles of eminent and distinguished authors of Ayurveda. It is an essence of Ayurvedic therapapeutic principles to the practitioners, research scholars as well as student community of all systems of medicine. The treaties is in accordance with the principles laid down in Ayurveda, and is well presented with inclusion of the latest scientific data. For example: the objective correlation of the three physiological neurohumors-acetylocholine, adrenaline and histamine, with the tridoshas-vata, pitta, and kapha respectively; their seasonal variations; the well recognised concept of the microbes (Krimi) in disease causation in Ayurveda; the technique of diagnosing a specific disease in the incubation period itself; the inclusion of an article on the standardisation of Proforma for assessment of Constitution (Prakriti) of an individual; and the importance of Rasa Panchaka siddhanta and its utility in the evaluation of drug effects. Under each section, a number of tables have been included wherever necessary to make the text easily understandable along with inclusion of bibliography.

This book gives immense pleasure to the reader and is a good companion to the students and research scholars alike.

I would like to conclude with an appreciation and advise the author to bring out some more useful works of this kind in future.

I once again express my happiness to associate myself with this work by writing the foreword to it.

"I wish him all success in all walks of his life".

Date : 04.05.1994
Hyderabad (AP)

Dr. I.V. Prahlad Rao
B.Sc., D.Ay. M. (B.H.U.), Dip. in Yoga, and S.T.D. (Safdarjung Hospital Delhi)
C.M.O. Govt. Ayurvedic Hospital;
Reader, Govt. Ayurvedic College,
Hyderabad (AP)

Preface

This is the first book in the proposed 20 Volume Series on Ayurveda, produced under the Students and Practitioners Series by the Research Foundation of the Society for Advancement of Research and Development of Integrated Medicine (SARDIM) (a registered organisation under the Hyderabad Public Societies Act 1360F 1860, Government of Andhra Pradesh, India 1987).

The present book titled **"Principles of Ayurvedic Therapeutics"** has a total of 14 chapters, 39 tables, 2 figures, and contributions made by 26 authors from renowned institutions and hospitals, through their publications and personal communications.

The first chapter begins with Introduction dealing with the importance of Traditional Medicine and especially Ayurveda in the present day health care needs of the community. The succeeding chapters deal with Fundamental of Ayurveda, Health and Disease, Causation of Disease, Clinical Manifestations of Disease, Case-taking and Examination of the Patient and the Disease, Investigation of the Patient, Principles of Diagnosis, Classification of Diseases, Principles of Treatment, Pharmacotherapeutics in Ayurveda, Principles of Drug Administration, and Ayurveda and Yoga, and concludes with a chapter on Appendix and subject Index.

The main features in the description of the subject matter include: Role of Ayurveda in the present day health care and Management of illness; Understanding the principles of Ayurvedic Philosophy in the light of modern science; an objective evaluation of the principles of Tridosha with relation to the physiological and pathological states of the body, largely conducted at Banaras Hindu University, Varanasi (India); Clinical manifestations of illness and the importance of diagnosing an illness in the pre-pathogenesis period of disease which is possible in Ayurveda; the importance of Samprapti (pathogenesis) in disease and diagnosis of illness; the Kriyakala (the stages of evolution of disease and the time of treatment) and management of disease; Ojas—the Ayurvedic concept of energy in human body; the origin of disease and its causation; the traditional and systemic classification of diseases in Ayurveda; the passive role of naming of diseases; the secondary role of microbes in disease causation and the importance of maintenance of Dosha-Dhatu-Mala equilibrium in the overall metabolism of the body; the importance of Prakriti (constitution and temperament) and its objective evaluation; the importance of examination of the patient and the disease in the diagnosis of patient and the disease for proper treatment to be instituted; the principles of treatment and the role of Pancha-Karma therapy especially in the management of Chronic disorders, the clinico-pharmacological characteristics of Dravyas (drugs) in Ayurvedic chikitsa (treatment); and the role of Yoga and its therapeutic value both in the prevention, promotion and cure of disease along with Ayurveda. Chapter on Appendix gives a list of Ayurvedic terms and its modern medicine equivalents of diseases described for an easy understanding of the subject even by non-Ayurvedic students and practitioners of various systems of medicine.

The book in its present form helps the students and practitioners from undergraduate to postgraduate levels and research scholars for a study of the Principles of Ayurvedic Therapeutics in the light of recent advances made in medicine. The book helps to a large extent in understanding the Ayurvedic therapeutics by non-Ayurvedic students and practitioners alike from various healing-arts.

The book has been written after due consultation of many students and physicians of various schools of Medicine and the day to day problems they encounter in the study and practice of Ayurvedic Therapeutic Medicine.

It is really heartening to me to keep on record that the present book has been completed with the active contribution of the eminent teachers and physicians—Dr. T.N. Pande, BIMS, Ph.D, FRAS (Lond.), Central Research Institute and Hospital (Ayurveda), Ministry of Health and Family Welfare, Govt. of Indial; Dr. K.D. Sharma. Bhishgacharya, Ayurvedacharya, MSAIM (Jam); Dr. M. Paramkush Rao, MD (Ayu), Lecturer, Department of Dravyaguna and R.S.S.V. Ayurvedic College, Tirupati (AP); Formerly, Professor of Ayurveda with the Brazilian Government through M.A.P. India; and Dr.A.R. Vasudeva Murthy, MD (Ayu), Dip. Yoga, Lecturer, Department of Kayachikitsa, S.V. Ayurvedic College, Tirupati (AP).

In spite of thorough scrutiny of the subject matter before submitting it for publication, some mistakes and omissions might be present for which I request the readers to excuse me for the same.

If the present volume advances the art and science of/ healing through Ayurvedic system of Medicine in however a small measure, the author will deem that his efforts have not been in vain; on the contrary he will have the satisfaction that his pains have been enormously rewarded. As it is, the book fulfils a long cherished desire of the author to render his iota of service to the suffering humanity.

Any suggestions and advice for the improvement in the form and content of this book would be greatly welcome to the author.

Atmakuri Vinaya Kumar

Acknowledgements

I am very much indebted to the following authors, publishers, and Health Care Organizations and Institutions whose works, publications have been referred to by the author in preparation of the present book. If any omissions are present, it is not intentional and the readers are requested to pardon me for the same.

Authors

1. Dr. T.N. Pande
2. Dr. K.D. Sharma
3. Dr. M. Paramkush Rao
4. Dr. A.R.V. Murthy
5. Dr. Narayana Swamy
6. Dr. T. Seshagiri Rao
7. Mrs. Kanchana Srinivasan
8. Mrs. K. Janaki
9. Dr. L.D. Dwivedi
10. Prof. L.V. Guru
11. Dr. G.V. Satyavati
12. Dr. V.B. Athavale
13. Dr. T.L. Devaraj
14. Dr. D.P. Sahu

15. Dr. D.V. Sandu
16. Dr. Keim Gertrud
17. Dr. N.V.K. Varrier
18. Dr. K.R.L. Gupta
19. Dr. R. Dwivedi
20. Dr. G. Singh
21. Dr. P.S. Varier
22. Dr. G.G. Pandey
23. Dr. Sri Kanta Murthy
24. Dr. K.L. Sharma
25. Dr. D.L. Narayana
26. (Mrs.) Dr. Vaishali N. Dadkar

Publishers

1. Indian Council of Medical Research, Delhi.
2. Central Council for Research in Ayurveda and Siddha, Delhi.
3. Sterling Publishers, Delhi.
4. Himalaya Drug Co., Bombay
5. Arya Vaidya Sala, Kottakkal, Kerala
6. Sri Satguru Publications, Delhi
7. Chowkamba Sanskrit Series Office, Varanasi
8. Chowkamba Surbharathi Prakashan, Varanasi
9. Krishnadas Academy, Varanasi
10. Banaras Hindu University, Varanasi.

Health Care Organisations and Institutions

1. World Health Organization
2. Indian Council of Medical Research
3. Central Council for Research in Ayurveda and Siddha

4. Banaras Hindu University
5. Rengarajan Siddha Tutorial College, Madurai
6. Arya Vaidya Sala, Kottakkal

Journals

1. Journal of Research and Education in Indian Medicine
2. Journal of Research in Ayurveda and Siddha
3. Aryavaidyan
4. Probe
5. Ayurveda Samachar
6. Indian Council of Medical Research
7. The Hindu

CHAPTER 1

Introduction

The declaration of the International Conference on Primary Health Care in Alma Ata, USSR, 1978 (WHO/ UNICEF-1978) marked a turning point in global health strategy. It is no coincidence that this document started out with a critical appraisal of modern technological medicine, its concentration of complex and costly technology on limited segments of the population, and its doubtful relevance to four fifths of the world people. From this premise the concept of primary health care were formulated, including positive acknowledgement of the role of traditional indigenous practitioners.

Much interest in Traditional Medicine has been generated with the adoption of the resolution WHA-30.49 on "Promotion and Development of Training and Research in Traditional Medicine" and WHA-31.33 on "Drug Policies and Management-Medicinal Plants" by the Thirtieth and Thirty First World Health Assemblies. These resolutions have assumed added importance with the Alma Ata Declaration on Primary Health Care.

What are the reasons for this universal and positive interest in traditional medicine, a subject matter that only 30-years ago had attracted but a few historians of medicine and ethnologists, and that medical and health authorities had considered as an impediment rather than an asset to health care? The reasons are to be found in growing dissatisfaction with modern medical institutions as critiqued in the Alma Ata Declaration. Today, the once glorious Western self image has been deflated and the once dominant Eurocentric World view is being abandoned by which the Western image of non-Western cultures has been upgraded. These are possible changes in the idealogical climate that have to be seen against the historical background of global decolonization and geo-political retreat of the European powers. It is in the wake of these historical events that a worldwide positive assessment of the non-Western healing arts has taken place.

Thus, the importance of the traditional systems of medicine and of certain traditional medical practices has now been recognised all over the world. Since time immemorial some of the traditional medical practices have become an integral part of the social culture particularly in the countries of the third world.

A highly comprehensive definition of traditional medicine has been arrived at by a group of WHO experts :

"... the sum total of all the knowledge and practises whether explicable or not, used in diagnosis, prevention and elimination of physical, mental or social imbalance and relying exclusively on practical experience and observation handed down from generation to generation whether verbally or in writing."

"... Traditional Medicine might also be considered as a solid amalgamation of dynamic medical know-how and ancestral experience."

While there exist a number of traditional systems of medicine as well as traditional practises all over the world, for practical purposes, we might identify a few of them as of global importance, depending on their long experience, authenticity as also current applicability to and acceptability by population groups. These are summarised in the table 1-1.

(G.V. Satyavati 1982)

AYURVEDA

Among the various systems of Traditional Medicine, Ayurveda stands out distinctly as not only a system of great antiquity but an organised system with distinct aims and objectives. Ayurveda is known to date back to the Vedic Period (7000 B.C. - 3000 B.C.). In fact, the Atharvaveda, one of the four Vedas (Rig Veda, Yajur Veda, Sama Veda and Atharva Veda) mentions many a plant and their medicinal uses, as also a number of traditional practises of therapeutic importance.

It is important to realise however, that Ayurveda is not just curative in approach but reveals a deeper insight into the various problems of human life.

The principal aim of any system of medicine is to maintain and promote positive health as well as ensure the prevention of diseases on the other. Its scope is not limited to any geographical region but is universal in its approach. The absence of any physical ailment is not health, but only such a person can be called healthy who, apart from freedom of morbidity, is happy mentally, sexually, psychologically and spiritually. This approach is very relevant especially in today's stress-filled world as the individual is considered as being composed of his or her physique, mind, intellect and soul. This is the approach of Ayurveda to health and disease in simple terms.

The philosophy of Ayurveda bear testimony to the value of our ancient tradition in providing effective health care. The approach of the Indian Traditional Systems of Medicine (ITSM) is of a holistic nature which interprets life as a synergy of several factors—mental, physical and spiritual. Instead of concentrating on treating a specific disease or ailment as is the case with modern medicine, the ITSM try to promote and strengthen the health and resistance of the individual so as to withstand the strain of the disease. With the building up of resistance, the disease vanishes leaving a healthy body and mind.

As the physical state of the universe depends on the perfect balance amongst the elements constituting it, the biological state of the human body depends on the balance between all its constituents and the outside environment. Disease is a result of imbalance and many manifest in certain organs depending on their state or function. The therapy is therefore, to be directed at correcting the basic imbalance rather than aiming at correcting some organ function. In very simple terms, this is the approach of Ayurveda to the treatment of diseases.

The environment influences the bodily functions to a great extent. Most of the contacts of man with the environment are through air, water and food. The characteristics of air, and water changes relatively slowly and are responsible for seasonal variations in the atmosphere and consequently in body functions—the so called 'Biological Rhythms.' But variability in food is tremendous. Since food could have a profound influence on biological functions, the food we eat and find agreeable should be in a balanced state compatible with the human body.

In the treatment of diseases, Ayurveda predominantly uses herbs, many of which are the same as those used as food normally. Some of the herbs used are, however, decidedly toxic in their natural form. Therefore, in order to accentuate a particular activity to influence body function in a particular manner, the herbs need to be processed in a particular way. The pharmaceutical processing of herbs is a very sophisticated and advanced method of accentuating the desired biological activities and eliminating harmful activities from plants. Thus, there is a great distinction between herbal medicines and traditional medicines on the one hand and properly processed Ayurvedic medicines on the other.

The concept of imbalance in biological processes as described in Ayurveda may apparently be unintelligible to modern scientists and physicians. However, since past few decades, Modern Medicine has progressed to certain extent to understand and accept some concepts which are fundamental to Ayurvedic teachings. These include, the biologic rhythms, the importance of the time of administration of drugs and doing Surgery (The Hindu, May 25, 1991), the predisposition to disease, the influence of the mind on health and disease, the need for total treatment of body and mind etc., are only recent revelations to Modern Medicine.

Ayurvedic treatment aims at correcting the imbalance in biological function and also supporting the psyche and the immune functions. It is therefore, essential to carefully select the necessary ingredients, combine them judiciously to obtain the desirable qualities and process them scientifically so that appropriate doses may be given for optimum effects without any harm. When such a treatment is aimed at a particular patient depending on his/her constitution, habits and ailment, it becomes perfect Ayurvedic treatment.

However, in clinical practice, it is obvious that this is not possible today. The diagnosis is often made according to modern medicine but modern physicians are not conversant with Ayurvedic diagnostic criteria. But it does not mean that, the wealth of the Ayurvedic knowledge cannot be denied to the patients. It is therefore, necessary to strike a balance between the knowledge of useful herbs and necessities of modern medical practice. In other words, it is necessary to make remedies in modern form without compromising the basic techniques of Ayurvedic Pharmacy, as far as possible, from the basic knowledge of Ayurveda and demonstrate the biological activities by modern standards (Editorial, Probe, Jan-Mar. 1991).

A deeper study of Ayurveda can suggest the activities which can be tested by modern methodologies. When biological activities are demonstrated, the therapeutic uses in modern terms become obvious. When such products are contemplated, the standards of efficacy and safety as applicable to any modern drug should be applied and if found acceptable, then only they become real Ayurvedic remedies which can be used by any modern medical practitioner of any healing art.

In these times of iatrogenic (drug-induced) diseases and drug prices causing economic catastrophies in families and to the country, it is necessary to take recourse to Ayurvedic not merely herbal remedies, for the wider benefit of ailing humanity and the living beings in the world.

In the succeeding chapters, the basic principles of Ayurvedic Management of Illness have been described.

Table 1-1 Some of the Major Traditional Medical Systems and Practises in the World

Major Traditional Medical Systems

1. Ayurveda—widely practised in India, Pakistan, Sri Lanka, Nepal, Tibet, Burma, and other countries.
2. Siddha—a variant of Ayurveda being practised in sections of southern parts of India.
3. Unani Tibb or Greco—Arabian Medicine - being practised in India, Pakistan, Bangladesh, Iran, the Middle-East, and a number of other countries.
4. Yoga—practised for a long time all over India, Tibet China and a few other countries and now spread to the Western countries.

5. Homoeopathy—widely practised all over the world.
6. Chinese, Tibetan and related systems of Medicine.

Major Traditional Practises or Techniques

1. Acupuncture—a significant contribution of the Chinese Medicine, along with its variants like Japanese Shiatsu, Finger massages etc.
2. Naturopathy or Nature Cure including various techniques like Hydrotherapy, Magnetotherapy, Electrotherapy, Osteopathy, and Psychotherapy.
3. Folk Medicine (including tribal medical practises) of different parts of the world.
4. Herbal remedies of various countries (China, Japan, Africa, India, etc.).
5. Marginal or Fringe Medicine—including faith healing, specialised therapies like treatments of snake bites (by drugs and charm); Tantric medicine including medico-religious practises in different parts of the globe; Occult Medicine including astrology, parapsychology, hypnosis, etc.).

Courtesy: Satyavati, G.V., Some Traditional Medical Systems and Practises of Global Importance, Indian J. Med. Res. 76 (Suppl.) December, 1982.

NOTES AND REFERENCES

1. Satyavati G.V., Some Traditional Medical Systems and Practises of Global Importance Ind. J. Med. Res., 76 (Suppl.) December, 1982.
2. Time of Administration of Drugs and Doing Surgery, The Hindu, May 25, 1991.

CHAPTER 2

Fundamentals of Ayurveda

1. Definition of Ayurveda

As the word Ayurveda implies, it has been formed by the combination of two words—Ayu and Veda meaning thereby the knowledge which deals about Ayu or life. Thus, the word Ayurveda has got a wide range of meaning i.e., to know about life, to obtain advantages from life and to maintain the life.

The following comprehensive definition of Ayurveda is given by Acharya Charaka (1000 B.C.):

"That is named the science of life (Ayurveda), wherein is laid down the good and the bad life, the happy and the unhappy life, and what is wholesome and what is unwholesome in relation to life, as also the measure of life." (Charaka Samhita Sutrasthana 1:41 (Shree Gulabkunverba Ayurvedic Society, Jamnagar, 1949, p.9) cited by G.V. Satyavati, 1982).

Therefore it is evident from the above that Charaka has defined Ayurveda as the knowledge which deals about the happiness and misery of life, advantages and disadvantages of life, and life spanor measurement of life span.

Thus, the common impression that Ayurveda is only a system of medicine does not give proper justification to wide ranging meaning of Ayurveda, because it deals with promotive and curative aspects of health as propounded by ancient Ayurvedic Physicians.

Ayurveda thus expounds a whole way of life embodying not only the physical and psychological aspects but also the philosophical, ethical and moral aspects on the one hand, and the individual and universal health, on the other. This wholistic and universal concept of health must be considered as a contribution of Ayurveda.

2. Aims and Objectives of Ayurveda

As mentioned by Acharaya Charaka, there are two main aims of Ayurvedic System of Medicine. First aim is to preserve the health of healthy individual and second is to get rid of ailing individuals from different ailments. To achieve these goods, different means, methods and regimens have been described elaborately. The first objective is achieved by means of Rasayana (Geriatrics) and Vajikarana (Aphrodisiacs). The second aim is achieved by Samshodhana (Purificative measures) and Sanhsaman Chikitsa (Alleviating measures).

3. The Source Materials of Ayurvedic Study

These are derived mostly from ancient literature on medicine and are shown below:

I. **Brihat-trayi** (The three great classical texts)

1. Charaka Samhita—Acharya Charaka (1000 B.C.) deals with Kayachikitsa (Internal Medicine).
2. Sushruta Samhita—Acharya Sushruta (1000 B.C.) deals with Shalya-Shalakya (Surgery and Ear, Nose and Throat).
3. Ashtanga Hridaya—Acharya Vaghbhatta (400 A.D.) deals with subject matter of above two classics with some additions.

II. **Laghu-trayi** (The three famous texts)

1. Madhava Nidan—Acharya Madhavakar (800 A.D.) a compendium of etiopathogenesis and signs and symptoms of all diseases mentioned in classics.

2. Sarangdhar Samhita—Acharya Sarangdhar (1400 A.D.) lucid and brief exposition with many newer additions and alterations.

3. Bhavaprakasha—In addition to description of Ayurvedic Medicine, deals with Ayurvedic Pharmacopea.

III. Others

Kashyap Samhita—deals with Balaroga (Paediatrics) together with other Ayurvedic Medicine topics.

4. Branches of Ayurveda

The science of Ayurveda had attained a stage of specialisation early, with various branches despite its 'holistic' approach. Dhanwantari (1000 B.C.) the famous exponent of Ayurveda has classified Ayurveda into eight well defined branches :

i. Kaya Chikitsa—Internal Medicine.

ii. Balachikitsa or Kaumarabhritya—Paediatrics.

iii. Grahachiktisa—Psychiatry.

iv. Shalyatantra—Surgery, major and minor.

v. Shalakya tantra or Urdhvangachikitsa—Otorhinoloaryngology (ENT).

vi. Agada tantra—Toxicology.

vii. Rasayana tantra—Geriatrics.

viii. Vajikaranatantra or Vrishya Chikitsa—Science of eugenics and aphrodisiacs.

In addition, a basic knowledge of Shareera (Anatomy), Dosha, Dhatu-Mala-Vignana (Physiology including metabolic processes). Swasthavritta (Preventive Medicine), Prasutitantra (Midwifery and obstetrics and an exhaustive knowledge of Dravyaguna (i.e. Materia Medica) and pharmacy form essential parts of Ayurveda.

PURUSHA VICHAYA SHARIRAM

According to Indian philosophy, there is complete similarity in the characters and structures of universe and of the body of the individual. The subject matter of this similarity between the cosmos and the body of the individual has been termed as purusha vichaya. The chapter dealing with this subject has been named as "Purusha Vichaya Shariram" by Acharya Charaka which is the 5th Chapter of Sharira Sthana of Charaka Samhita.

Now to mention the importance and application of the subject "Purusha Vichaya Shariram" it may be said that by equalling the Purusha (individual) to Loka (Universe), a very judicious conclusion may be drawn that whatever innumerable things of various kind and character are found in the universe in a very large quantity, the same innumerable things of various kind and character are also found in the individual in a very small quantity meaning thereby that qualitatively there is no difference between individual and universe. The difference is only quantitative. This fact has been also pointed out in the Vedic literature as "Yatha Pinda Tatha Brahmanda" meaning thereby that whatever is found in the pinda (Purusha) the same is found in Brahmanda (Cosmos).

As we are aware and careful about the balanced state of our body to maintain the life, in the same way, we should be aware and careful about the balanced state of our environment and ecology. In other words, it can be said that there is direct relationship between the individual and environment around him. Both of them are affected by each other. The importance of environment and ecology has been recognised in these days by scientists but this fact appears to be known to ancient Indian seers several thousands years before. To lay stress on this fact, the principle of Purusha Vichaya Shariram has been evolved by ancient Ayurvedists. Moreover by realising this principle, individual is always aware of the fact that he/she is responsible for all types of pain and pleasure. By knowing this fact, individual avoids all those things whatever are harmful to him and at the same time follows the regimens beneficial to him as Acharya Charaka has stated in the following citation.

"Loka Vitatmatmanam Lokam Chatmani Pashyatah Paravardrishsh Shantirgyanmulans Nashyati"
"Pashyatah Sarvabhavan hi Sarvavasthasu Sarvada Brahmabhutasaya Samyogo na Shudhsyopapadyate."

Ch. Sharir. 5/20-21.

Above mentioned citations mean that the individual seeing similarity in universe identical to him along with regarding himself similar to the universe does not cease to lose his mental peace based on proper knowledge. One who always sees similarity believes him and all things of universe does not liable to be affected by wordly affairs because mentally he is pure and thus remain happy and healthy.

Acharya Charaka has also mentioned about the innumerable parts of the body which he refers as Paramanu (cell) in the 7th Chapter of Sharira Sthana. In this context, he mentioned that at the Paramanu (Cell) level, the parts of the body are innumerable due to their multiplicity in numbers, subtleness and due to their perceptibility beyond senses. (Ch. Sharir 7/17). In the scientific perspective this fact which was known in ancient times (3000-2000 B.C.) is very important and affirms the authenticity to the principle mentioned above. According to cellular biology, now it has become clear that all of these functions occurring in human body at macro level are also occurring in the cell at micro level.

PRINCIPLES OF AYURVEDIC SYSTEM OF MEDICINE

As every science has got some of its basic fundamentals on which the entire science is based, in alike manner, Ayurveda has got few of its basic principles on which the entire Ayurvedic System of Medicine rests. Among these the following are important:

1. Panchabhuta Principle
2. Tridosha Principle
3. Sapta Dhatu Principle
4. Malas Principle
5. Srotas Principle
6. Principle of Agni
7. Principle of Rasaguna, Veerya and Vipaka

PANCHABHUTA PRINCIPLE

The Panchamahabhutas (five great bhutas) are: Akasha (space, ether), Vayu (air or gas), Agni (Heat or Tej), Jala (water or moisture or liquid) and Prithvi (earth, solid). These five bhutas or elements or particles are derived from the all pervading Brahma (Energy) in the Universe (see table 2-1). The panchabhutas, thus in various combinations and permutations tend to form the different states of matter (solid, liquid, gas, fluid etc.).

A pertinent question may be raised here that only by these five bhutas how an infinite number of objects are formed? This is a controversial matter spanning all branches of science. However, the Ayurvedists propounded that by the combination and permutation of the five bhutas— infinite number of objects are formed as only by 9 numbers including 0, infinite numbers are formed and used for all practical purposes. This fact of interaction of bhutas or basic elements leading to the formation of infinite number of objects both animate and inaminate, has been clearly mentioned by Acharya Sushruta in 42nd Chapter Sutra Sthana of Sushruta Samhita. In this context he has mentioned that all of the objects contain all of the Bhutas by means of 'paraspara sansargata.' The degree of quantum combined physically by their interactions 'Parasparanugrahata' and by means of their degree of quantum combined chemically; 'Parasparanupraveshat.' The objects are termed specific according to the predominance (Utkarsha) and diminution (Apakarsha) of the Bhutas contained in them. Due to different type of combinations and perumutations of five basic elements in different objects, there is difference of form and qualities in them.

It is also to be noted that the five Bhutas are activated (or inherently contained) during their origin—by Trigunas (the three inherent characters of nature) i.e. Satva, Rajas and Tamas. Though all of the Bhutas are embraced by Trigunas, still each of them have predominance and diminution of either of Trigunas thereby making these of different qualities and actions. Thus, Akasha being predominant of Satva Guna, Vayu being predominant of Rajoguna, Agni being predominant of Satva and Rajoguna, Jala being predominant of Satva and Tamoguna and Prithvi being predominant of Tamoguna. Hence all of the objects composed of five Bhutas have the impact of Trigunas. The same principle of presence of all gunas is applicable to all of the objects also. All these facts are indispensable for an Ayurvedic student and practitioner to understand the Panchabhuta principle and Tridosha principle (Table 2-2).

Table - 2-1 : Evolution of Panchabhutas (Subtle to Gross forms)

Brahma—	Akasha —	Vayu —	Agni —	Jala —	Prithvi
(Energy)	(Space)	(Air) or Gas	(Heat) or Tej	(Water) or Moisture liquid	(Earth) Solid

(Order of disintegration : in the reverse order). (author's view)

Table - 2-2 : Qualities of Panchabhutas Based on Trigunas

Bhuta	*Predominant quality (Guna)*
Akasha	Satwa
Vayu	Rajas
Agni	Satwa, Rajas
Jala	Satwa, Tamas
Prithvi	Tamas

Depending on the combination of Bhutas in the formation of an object, Trigunas will also be present in the same manner. Body is also composed of five Bhutas and whatever diet we take, those are also composed of five Bhutas. Therefore, it is also very necessary to know the nature of the body so that we take food according to the necessity of our body in order to keep healthy.

CORRELATION OF THE PANCHAMAHABHUTA THEORY WITH SCIENCE

Ancient physical sciences recognises five basic elements viz. earth, water, energy, air and space constituting all the objects (animate and inanimate) in the universe. Modern physics believes in about 100 basic elements like Sodium,

Potassium, Carbon, Hydrogen, Oxygen etc., which constitute the entire universe. The Modern Physics believes in Protons, Neutrons, Electrons, Positron etc., which are the basic elements constituting the entire universe including man.

When we consider the composition of man, it will be seen that Water and Earth (i.e. solids) are responsible for 55 per cent and 45 per cent of his/her mass respectively and occupies about 2.7 cubic feet of space. Air (i.e. gases) and energy are responsible for very minute fraction of his mass. The basic elemental composition of a man weighing 70 kg. is shown in Table 2-3.

Table - 2-3 : Elemental Composition of Man Weighing 70 Kg.

Element	*Kilo Gram (Kg.)*
Oxygen	43.50
Carbon	12.59
Hydrogen	06.58
Nitrogen	01.81
Calcium	01.70
Phosphorus	00.68
Chloride	00.11
Sulphur	00.10
Sodium	00.07
Potassium	00.07
Magnesium	00.04
Iron	00.07
Other Elements	traces

Courtesy: Athavale V.B., Tridosha Theory and Modern Science, PROBE, Vol: XXVII, No. 4, 1988.

Thus it appears that the classification of basic elements which constitute the entire universe will keep on changing over a period of time as scientific advances are made in understanding the universe. So, as long as the basic elements constitute a complete list and cover the composition of all objects in the universe either living or non-living, it does not matter which language one uses to express them.

TRIDOSHA PRINCIPLE

The Tridosha theory is a derivation of Panchabhautic Principle described above. The Tridosha Principle forms the foundation of Ayurveda. It has been postulated that whatever Physiological and Pathological processes occurring in the body, they are under the influence of three basic elements or particles or humours known as Vata, Pitta and Kapha. Despite of the fact that Tridoshas are also Panchabhautic (i.e. made of five basic elements, Panchabhutas), still there is predominance of Vayu and Akasha in Vata, predominance of Agni in Pitta and predominance of Jala and Prithvi in Kapha (Table - 2-4).

Table - 2-4 : Table Shows the Composition of Tridoshas

Doshas	*Composition of bhutas*	*Predominant of bhutas*
Vata	Vayu	Vayu, Akasha
Pitta	Agni	Agni, Jala
Kapha	Jala	Jala, Prithvi

Seeing the dominant role of Vayu, Agni and Jala in the life of an organism, ancient Ayurvedists evolved the Tridosha Principle. As Akasha bhuta is all pervasive and nothing can remain apart from it, and Prithvi bhuta—forms the basis of every object and being only the basis for the different actions and reactions to be acted upon, these have been deleted in Tridosha Principle, thereby making the Tridosha Principle more applied and practical. This fact should be borne in mind that Panchabhutas form the structural entity of the body while Tridoshas are responsible for maintaining the functional entity of man.

Elaborating the same act Acharya Sushruta in 21st chapter of Sutra Sthana has mentioned that all of the animate objects have their origin from Vata, Pitta and Kapha. These three doshas maintain the body when they are normal and balanced and if there is imbalance and abnormality in these three doshas, individual becomes diseased. In this context this fact must be borne in mind that Acharya Sushruta has used the word Deha (Body of the individual) meaning thereby that the role of Tridoshas is only limited to the animate objects only and not in inanimate objects. Hence, as soon as the life process starts (fertilisation of ovum) in individual, Tridosha begin their role to maintain the individual till death. After the end of life, there is no role of Tridosha, the body remains as Panchabhautic: hence the term Panchatva (death) is given to dead man. Due to the absence of balanced activity of Tridoshas, the putrefaction starts in dead body. Thus, Tridoshas are only active during the life to maintain the life of the individual.

It is to be noted that the three biologic elements (i.e. Tridoshas) are treated as dosha because they despite of being responsible to produce the body along with the life process, have the potentiality to vitiate. Hence Acharya Vijai Rakshit, commentator of Madhava Nidan (A treatise) said Katva sati dushti kartitwan doshatwam." Meaning thereby that the doshas despite of being responsible to maintain the continuity of normalcy have the potentiality to vitiate the dhatus of the body to produce diseases.

As already pointed out that there is active role of Tridoshas during the life of the individual, hence Tridoshas are responsible for all bio-chemical and physiological functions and transformations going on in the body. Even though Tridoshas are composed of Panchabhutas, anatomical structures of Tridoshas cannot be found in the body (however, see later section) though all of the functions of the bodily structures are being performed under the influence of Tridoshas. In other words, Tridoshas are physiological units rather than anatomical structures. Therefore, morphological descriptions of Tridoshas are not met in entire Ayurvedic literature: only their qualities, character, and functions have been described (Dwivedi—1988).

Every substance has some kind of Guna (character) and functions according to the principle of physical sciences. The corollary is that functions and characters are present or observed in the presence of matter only. That means Tridoshas can not remain apart from dravyas (matter). Hence, the bodily structures, which are of Panchabhautic nature, have got anatomical entity as well as support physiological entity of Tridoshas, which are also Panchabhautic nature. However because of lack of advanced knowledge at that time, only qualities and functions of different doshas have been mentioned in all of the classical texts of Ayurveda. Thus, by simply, ascertaining the nature of Tridoshas in different situations of health and disease, and by various diagnostic techniques available in Ayurveda, one can come to a reasonable physiological and pathological diagnosis of tissue or organ or system of the body affected in most of the cases. It has been found that, this mode of enquiry helps clinician to diagnose an abnormal stage of health of an individual even in the Incubation period of illness (in this stage of illness, at present, modern medicine does not offer a diagnostic procedure).

CHARACTERISTICS OF TRIDOSHAS

Acharya Charaka has mentioned about the qualities and functions of Tridoshas in the first chapter of Sutra Sthana and 18th chapter of Sutra Sthana respectively. The characteristics of Tridoshas are shown in the Table 2-5.

TRIDOSHA PRINCIPLE IN THE LIGHT OF MODERN SCIENCE

Recently, some authors opined Tridoshas as biological elements derived from the biochemical combination of the five basic elements (Panchabhutas) mentioned already. Thus Vata molecules have been described as originating from a combination of space and air and possess their qualities. That is why Vata molecules are cold, dry, light and mobile in nature.

Pitta molecules are mainly derived from the energy elements with the addition of water element. So, these molecules are hot and smooth.

Kapha molecules are formed by combination of water and earth and they are heavy, smooth, steady, less mobile and cold in nature.

Vata, Pitta and Kapha molecules are the basic constituents of life and exist in various cells of the body. They form the basic structural and functional units of the body and are described as the three pillars of life or Tridoshas. They exist together and try to dominate each other.

Vata molecules control the movements of the molecules and the division of cells. These molecules are responsible for smooth and co-ordinated movements. Activities ascribed to central, autonomic and peripheral nervous systems are identified with functions of Vata.

Table - 2-5 : Characteristics of Tridoshas in Normal State of Well Being

Character	*Vata*	*Pitta*	*Kapha*
Qualities	Ruksha (dry)	Sasneha (unctuous)	Mridu (soft)
	Sheeta (cold)	Ushna (hot)	Sheeta (cold)
	Laghu (light)	Tikshna (sharp)	Snigdha (unctuous)
	Sukshma (subtle)	Drava (liquid)	Guru (heavy)
	Chala (mobile)	Amla (sour)	Madhur (sweet)
	Vishada and Khar (rough)	Katu (pungent)	Sthira (immobile)
			Pichila (slimy)
Functions	Utsatha (enthusiasm)	Darshana (vision)	Sneha (unctuous)
	Vuchhwasa (expiration)	Pakti (digestion)	Bandha (well knitting of the body)
	Nihswasa (inspiration)	Ushma (heat production in the body.)	Sthiratva (stability of the body.)
	Chesta (movement)	Kshudra (hunger)	Gaurava (heaviness)
	Dhatugati (balanced regulation	Dehmardana (softness of the body)	Vrishya (aphrodisiac property)

	of transportation of bodily elements)		
	Gatimalam Mokshah (excretion of different excreta from the body)	Prasada (cheerfullness of the body)	Bala (strength)
		Medha (intelligence	Kshama (forgiveness)
			Dhriti (patience)
			Alobha (non-greediness)
Anatomical sites	Bladder	Sweat	Thorax
	Rectum (in particular)		(in particular)
	Joints	Body sap	Head
	Legs	Lymph	Neck
	feet	Blood	Joints
	Bones	Stomach	Stomach
	(lower part of trunk and lower	(in particular) (Lower part of	Face (chest and head)

	extremity)	stomach and mid part of body)	
Volume in healthy body	Not known	5 Anjas (volume of a fist approx.)	6 Anjas
Composition and Functions according to modern Physiology.	Oxygen, Carbon dioxide; nervous impulses, Muscular impulses, Hormones like parathyroid, Vitamind-D, Controls calcium, Phosphorus, minerals.	Enzymes, Hormones like thyroid, Vitamin B-Complex.	Water, Proteins (major part), Fats, Carbohydrates.
Neuro-humoral relationship	Acetylcholine	Catecholamines (adrenaline etc.)	Histamine

Composition according to Ayurvedic Philosophy.	Vayu (air)-predominant, Akash (space)	Agni (fire)-Predominant Jala (water)	Jala (water) Predominant Prithvi (earth)
Other characters of doshas	Clearness, fornlessness	Acuteness moderate action, white colour tendency to flow.	Stability

In the Pitta molecules, energy is the active principle where water acts as a vehicle, (because energy in pure form can destroy the body). All metabolic activities of the body and mind are considered as activities of pitta molecules. Hence, they are referred to as chemical units. They control various chemical reactions in the body like enzymes and hormonal activities, including digestion, sensory information and mental activities. Thus emotions like joy, anger, courage are influenced by pitta molecules.

Kapha is the third member of the dosha trinity. It is derived from earth and water and their combination results in the formation of various body tissues, e.g. muscle is mainly earth whereas bone is earth plus air. Kapha molecules are structural units and are responsible for the shape and form of the body. Growth, development and healing of wounds are functions of kapha molecules. The fluid component of Kapha molecules is responsible for the formation and maintenance of fluids in the intra cellular, interstitial and intravascular body compartments.

The Ayurvedic theme is thus based upon the Law of the Universe. Each object exists in a precursor form—It is born, it grows, it matures, it degenerates and dies. Thus, Kapha, Pitta and Vata molecules exists as the fine basic elements. They are formed by biological combination of the basic elements. They grow by the addition of more and more molecules to form bigger, mature molecules with specific functions. So, Kapha imparts structure and stability to the body, Pitta controls digestive, and metabolic activities and Vata directs various movements. Then they slowly degenerate and ultimately cease to function and merge into the five basic elements from which they originate.

In the last two decades, basic research has shown that the three doshas are comparable objectively to three neurohumors physiologically present in the body. These three neurohumors are : Acetylcholine, Catecholamines

(Adrenaline etc.) and Histamine which are found to correspond to the Vata, Pitta and Kapha doshas respectively. Extensive research carried out at Banaras Hindu University, Varanasi (Uttar Pradesh), India by Udupa et al has shown that the three neurohumors had alterations in body fluids when measured biochemically in accordance to the three doshas of Ayurvedic doctrine. The observations carried out in many controlled studies showed that by measuring the three nurohumors in a particular altered condition of the body, one can ascertain which dosha or doshas have been affected. Thus it appears this is the first time that the Tridosha principle of Ayurveda has been demonstrated objectively in modern scientific parlance.

An Example for Illustration of Tridoshas

A skin eruption, which exudes transparent liquid or is dry; which is prominently sensitive and painful, characterised by ruffness—is a *Vatik group*. It does not heal or mature quickly. Another eruption, which exudes yellow fluid is hot, shining, red, suppurating. It matures rapidly and has burning type of pain - It is a *Paittic* eruption. The *Kaphaja group* would be the one, which exudes thick, white, viscid secretion, is cold and slowly maturing: almost painless.

Swellings in each case will be characterised by more pain and rough surface is *Vatic Group*; more heat, redness is Paittic group, and shining and oily surface is the *Kapha group*.

It is to be noted, however that combined symptoms and signs of more than one of these governing factors are also easily distinguishable and guide clinical diagnosis.

The Tridoshas residing mostly in Amashaya (Stomach) and Pakvashaya (Intestine) move along with the Rasadhatu (Plasma) in various places of the body. In this way, in healthy state each cell and tissue of the body are protected by Tridoshas. In unhealthy state, the same Tridoshas alter the functions of the dhatus (tissues). They not only act at their normal sites of localisation but also at distant sites producing abnormal reactions and thereby causing ill-health.

Classification of Tridoshas

Depending on the functions of Tridoshas in human body, they have been divided into five types for each dosha. They are summarised in Table -2.6.

Normal Functions of Tridoshas

Vata: *Prana vayu* is a source of life without which one cannot live and which is also responsible for swallowing food, breathing, spitting, sneezing and belching. It not only regulates the heart and other vital organs including the senses of the body, but also, makes them work life long. *Udana vayu* is the main source for the strength of the body and mind. It moves from nose upto the umbilicus and it is also responsible for the production of various sounds. The strength of the mind and its functions like memory and intellect and speech are controlled by it as well. *Vyana vayu* is situated in the heart and moves all over the body. It carries the Rasa (food juice) and blood throughout the body and nourishes the entire system of the body. It not only helps in the opening and closing of the eyelids and other movements of the body, but it also aids in the secretion of perspiration. *Samana vayu* is situated near the digestive fire and moves all over the alimentary tract. It helps in the digestion, assimilation and differentiation of food from nutrients and excreta and propels the contents of the intestines forward. In other words, it controls the digestive tract and it moves in the pelvis, bladder and external genitalia. It helps in the expulsion of urine, faeces, flatus and foetus, menses and semen.

Table 2-6 : Table Shows Classification of Tridoshas According to Their Location and Functions

Dosha	No.	Type		Function
Vata :	1.	Prasapandana (Vyana)	-	Body movement.
	2.	Udvahana (Udana)	-	Making senses able to perceive their objects.
	3.	Purana (Prana)	-	Supply of nutrient materials in the entire body.
	4.	Viveka (Samana)	-	Separation of rasa from ahar rasa and separation of excreta like urine and stool from the body.
	5.	Dharana (Apana)	-	Emission of semen, urine etc., during the period of ejaculation and micturition and to retain them at resting time.
Pitta :	1.	Ragakrit (Ranjaka)	-	Colouration of blood
	2.	Paktikrit (Pachaka)	-	Digestion
	3.	Ojokrit	-	Developing resistance
	4.	Tejakrit (Alochaka)	-	Vision
	5.	Medhakrit (Sadhaka)	-	Intelligence
	6.	Ushmakrit (Brhajaka)	-	Maintaining heat of the body

Kapha :	1.	Sandhikrit	-	Well knitting and moistening of joints.
	2.	Snehanakrit	-	Keeping body moistened
	3.	Ropankrit	-	Healing of injuries
	4.	Purankrit	-	Nourishing of body by means of its property of being saumya nutrient
	5.	Sthryakrit	-	Keeping the body stable.
Types of of Kaphas :	1.	Avalambaka (supporter)	-	Kapha located in heart and by the irrigating function (ambu karma), it supports the heart along with other sites of kapha (Ast. Hrid. Sutra—12)
	2.	Kledaka (moistener)	-	Located in Amashaya (stomach) and moistens the bolus of food (Ast. Harid. Sutra—12)
	3.	Bodhaka (arouses taste sensation)	-	Located in tongue and causes feeling of taste sensation.
	4.	Tarpaka (nourisher)	-	Located in head and nourishes the eye (Ast. Hrid. Sutra—12).

5.	Sleshka (lubricator)	-	Located in all joints and lubricates all of the joints of the body to give free movements to them (Ast. Hrid. Sutra—12)

Notes :

1. The five names of vata are mentioned by the author of Charaka Samhita, whereas functions are described in Sushruta Samhita (Sushruta Sutra—15/4).
2. The five names of Pitta are given first of all by Sushruta though pitta and kapha were divided each into five according to functions and chief place of location by Charaka but names were given later on. Functions were described by Sushruta (Sushruta Sutra—15/5).
3. The five names of kapha are given by Vagbhatta where as descriptions are first seen in Sushruta Sutra—15/6.

Pitta: *Pachaka pitta* is situated in between the stomach and the intestines and it is mainly responsible for the digestion of the food that we eat. It can be correlated to digestive juices—Hydrochloric acid and enzymes secreted in the stomach and small intestine. It also regulates the functions of other pitta in the body. *Ranjaka pitta* gives colour to the food juice before it goes from the stomach to the liver. *Sadhaka pitta* is situated in the heart and helps in the normal functioning of the mind and its activities. It helps in acquiring knowledge and memory. *Bhrajaka pitta* is situated in the skin and regulates the tint of the skin. *Alochaka pitta* is situated in the eyes and is mainly responsible for regulating the normal vision size and colour of objects.

Kapha: *Kledaka kapha* is situated in the stomach and helps in moistening the food in the stomach. It nourishes other kaphas. *Avalambaka kapha* is situated in the thorax and protects the heart from excessive heat by its cooling effect. *Bhedaka kapha* is situated in the tongue and aids in detecting the taste of food which is swallowed. Thus its place is from the root of the tongue to the throat. It helps in increasing the appetite. *Tarpaka kapha* is situated in the head and cools the eyes and nose. *Sleshaka kapha* is situated in the joints of the body and it helps them to function properly.

Doshic Rhythms

All the physiological changes occurring in the body vary at different steps of age, at different stages of digestion, absorption, and metabolism (anabolism as well as catabolism), at different stages of day and night and during certain seasons, and affect the doshas. The changes are rhythmic in nature. During a certain period there is an increase and following the same decrease of a dosha and increase of another one resulting from different external and internal changes in the body. At other times the fall in quantum of a particular dosha is restored. All this rhythmic rise and fall in physiological limits constitutes the doshic rhythm.

It is experienced that sometimes when the rhythmic rise and fall is disturbed or extenuated; and when at the same time the different tissues which normally bear the rhythmic rise and fall of the doshas, are at the lower side of vitality; or in case the rise of the doshas increases the body tissues threshold before the doshic rhythm is restored, the increase doshas can produce or precipitate or aggravate an existing disease.

The doshic rhythms in the human body can broadly be summarised under two main headings : one is Biorhythms and a second one is Metaphysical rhythms (Table - 2-7).

The rhythmic variations of doshas in different seasons (solar rhythm) and their neurohumoral asscssment has been studied by Dr. R.Q. Singh and V.D. Agrawal of Department of Kayachikitsa, Institute of Medical Sciences, Banaras Hindu University, Varanasi (Uttar Pradesh). In the present study, the seasonal variations of the three doshas i.e. Vata, Pitta and Kapha have been studied in terms of the three principal neurohumors viz. acetylcholine, catecholamine and histamine respectively. Udupa et al. (1975) had postulated that the three doshas described in Ayurveda possess considerable biological resemblance with the neurohumors and hence these three neurohumors may be taken as indices to measure the activity of the respective doshas (Udupa 1978). The studies show a relative preponderance of acetylcholine, catecholamine and histamine in blood during summer (Griesma), rainy (Varsa) and winter (Hemanta) seasons respectively. The plasma cortisol levels followed the pattern of catecholamines. These observations thus support the Ayurvedic concept of Dosha Samchaya (accumulation) in specific seasons. Summer,

Table - 2-7 : Table Showing the Broad Classification of Doshic Rhythms

1. Biorhythms	a. Life Rhythm	i) Childhood (balya avastha)—Kapha predominance
		ii) Young adulthood (yuva avastha)—Pitta predomi—nance.
		iii) Old age (Vriddha avastha)—Vata predominance.
	b. Dietary Rhythm	i) Immmediately after intake of food—Kapha increase
		ii) Middle of digestion—Pitta increase.
		iii) End of digestion—Vata increase.
2. Metaphysical Rhythms	a. Solar Rhythm	i) Adana Kala (uttarayana)—late winter, spring & summer—predominant Vata dosha.

		ii)	Visarga kala (Dakshinayana)—rainy, autumn and early winter—Kapha and Pitta predominance.
b.	Circadian Rhythm (24 hour cycle)	i)	Beginning of the day and night—Kapha predominance.
		ii)	Mid of day and night—Pitta predominance
		iii)	End of day and night—Vata predominance.
c.	Seasonal Rhythm		(See under Solar Rhythm above)

Rainy and Winter are therefore classically referred to as Dosha Samchaya Kala (Period of Doshic accumulation or predominance) for Vata, Pitta and Kapha respectively. Therefore, the best measures should be adopted to maintain their equilibrium in the respective Samchaya (accumulated) period of time.

Tridoshas—Cause of Internal Diseases

As has already been mentioned previously, tridoshas are responsible to maintain the body and life while they are normal and balanced. But when they are imbalanced and vitiated due to external and internal causes, produces various diseases (Sushruta Sthana 24th chapter). The derivative meaning of dosha is to vitiate, the body (Dushanat doshah). Charaka has also pointed out that all of the diseases cannot originate apart from Tridoshas (Charaka Sutra 19/5).

In scientific terms, the balanced state of tridoshas has been described as health and it means that all the biologic elements like lipids, proteins, sugar, electrolytes, hormones, enzymes etc. and neurohumors (Acetylcholine, catecholamines and histamine) are present in normal amounts and are of good quality.

The unbalanced state of the three doshas gives rise to disease. For example, tumor and atrophy of an organ are interpreted as localised increase or decrease of kapha respectively. Convulsions and sluggish movements are interpreted as increased or decreased Vata respectively. Hyperthyroidium i.e. Bhasmak disease and low body temperature, Hypothyoidism are interpreted as increase or decrease in Pitta respectively.

Therefore it is clear from the above that Ayurvedic concept of tridoshas helps in understanding the complex metabolic, physiological as well as s pathological processes in the body in the form of normal or abnormal functioning of the three doshas.

The practical utility of this line of thought is that it not only simplifies the understanding and approach to the disease, but also makes it possible for the physician to prescribe rationally on the basis of symptoms even before the disease becomes manifest (i.e. Incubation period). Thus if the patient complains of a burning sensation, the physician gives remedies which would subdue pitta, and advises the patient to avoid hot, pungent, and sour food items and a hot environment.

Ayurvedic physicians have realised that medicine constitute only a part of treatment. Diet, activity, psychological factors, environment etc., also influence and modify doshas and play an important role in curing the disease.

Thus, the same biologic process is interpreted by the two systems of medicine in their own scientific ways. The outlook of modern medicine appears to be more specific, while that of Ayurveda is a general and broad based one. The treatment is likely to be more specific and fast acting in modern medicine, while the broad spectrum treatment of Ayurveda apart from curing the disease, is likely to improve the constitution of the individual and does have the greater advantage of avoiding drug toxicity and drug induced diseases (iatrogenic diseases) as one often come across with the modern drugs and treatment.

Prakriti (Constitution and Temperament)

Medical scientists all over the world are becoming more and more alive to the importance of constitution in the causation and progress of several diseases generally known as constitutional diseases. This recent concept is discussed in greater detail in Ayurveda Samhita under the concept of

Prakriti. Prakriti in Ayurveda generally means 'Doshic Prakriti' formed on the basis of doshas at the time of fertilization of the sperm and ovum (Sukrā and Artava). The knowledge of prakriti is utilised for predicting the proneness, the severity, prognosis and the prevention of disease.

Secondly the study of Prakriti is one of the methods of clinical examination of a patient to diagnose any disease as described in the classical Ayurveda. In a patient it enables the physicians to assess Dehabala (immunological tolerance) and in a normal person an insight into the 'Vyadhyautapadaka Pratibandhakatvam' (resistance to disease and prophylactic capacity). As an example, a case of Amlapitta (a disease due to vitiation of pitta), exhibits symptoms relevant to one of pitta prakriti in a greater form while in a Kapha (sleshma) prakriti, the symptoms are mild. Thus with the knowledge of doshic prakriti in a diseased individual treatment, rehabilitation and prevention of relapse can be rationally planned.

In a vast majority of the individuals, there may be dominance of one or more doshas. Accordingly the constitution of the individual is described as Kapha Prakriti, Pitta Prikriti or Vata Prakriti. Let us consider a simple example of teething in children. It usually causes distress and children suffer from certain disorders. In some, there is cough and cold, and in others fever. Some suffer from vomiting and diarrheoa. These disorders give us an important clue to the inherent weakness of the tissues which is determined by the Prakriti. Thus a Kapha Prakriti child will have cough and cold, a Pitta Prakriti child will have fever, and whereas a Vata Prakriti child will have vomiting and diarrhoea.

The biological molecules (or elements or humors) of Vata, Pitta and Kapha are derived from the five basic elements and their qualities are reflected in these molecules, which in turn constitute the body and are thus evident in the physical characters of the individual and determine his/her personality. Thus Vata constitution individuals are usually slim, tall and weak. The hair and nails are dry and the voice is low and weak. They are full of activity but get exhausted fast. They have a poor appetite, much thirst, a wavering mind, weak sex desire, insomnia and usually a short life span.

Individuals with Pitta constitution have a delicate, hot body, wrinkled skin and soft, scanty hair. Their activities are average in nature. They have a good appetite, limited sex desire, perspire a lot and feel more thirsty. These people have emotional outbursts, a moderate life span. As these individuals have hypermetabolic activity they crave for cold drinks, air-conditioned rooms and sweet food.

The Kapha Prakriti individuals have a soft, oily, cold body. Their activities are slow. They have a poor appetite, good libido and are less thirsty. Usually their life span is long. They have low basal metabolic rate (BMR), so they desire hot, spicy food and warm clothes.

Gurunatham et al. (1969) had studied prakriti and disease proneness in 77 normal healthy persons and reported that on an average, the incidence of diseases is most in Vata dominant and least in Kapha dominant individuals. Singh and Dubey (1969) studied 100 cases of arthritis using a proforma specifically prepared for the purpose. Their observations revealed that the persons suffering from rheumatic arthritis, rhumatoid arthritis, and osteoarthritis, are predominantly of vatic, paittic and kaphaja (sleshmic) prakritis respectively. Similarly the role of Prakriti in constitutional diseases like peptic ulcer, diabetes mellitus, bronchial asthma etc., was also studied with the help of a protocol, whose validity was tested. The data thus collected were utilised to frame rules for predicting the proneness to the respective diseases.

According to Ayurveda the body and mind are very much interwoven at all levels of existence. Therefore, the mind also reflects in the body constitution and characteristics of the individual. Three qualities of the mind are described namely, Satva, Rajas and Tamas. These are the functional units of the brain.

Satva particles are essentially utilised in the process of thinking, reasoning, imagining, conceiving new ideas etc. Thus persons with a Satvik constitution will have mental clarity and purity of thoughts.

Raja activity endows the person with a lot of energy and emotional outbursts.

Tama particles are equally important as man can enjoy sleep and the brain can rest only when tamas dominates. But excess of Tama leads to inertia, passivity and ignorance.

Satvic constitution is considered a healthy constitution. Whereas those of Rajasa and Tamasa (dominance of Raja and Tama particles) are considered otherwise. Thus disturbances of these functional units, namely Rajas and Tamas can inturn vitiate the structural units of our body, i.e. Vata, Pitta and Kapha molecules and can lead to psychosomatic diseases.

According to Ayurveda, health is a balanced state of the three doshas. That means that all the biological elements are present in normal quantity and of good quality. Various factors like diet, environment, stresses and strains can play a significant role in vitiating these elements and their imbalance results in ageing, diseases and death. The various organic manifestations of diseases depend upon several factors like heredity and body constitution, which in turn determine the state of the organ or organ susceptibility. Thus hyperacidity, hypertension or bronchial asthma may be different organic manifestations encountered in individuals subjected to stress.

SAPTA DHATU PRINCIPLE

Sapta dhatus (seven primary tissues) are the constituents of the various structures of the body. Because, they support and maintain the form of the body, they are called 'Dhatus' (derivative meaning of dhatu is to support and nourish the body). Because these sapta dhatus will also be vitiated or affected by tridoshas, they are also termed as 'Dushyas' (to be vitiated by doshas).

It is to be noted that, according to the functions performed in the body, at different states and time, the tridoshas are also labelled as dhatus and malas, as mentioned by Acharya Vaghbhatta - 'because doshas produce dushana (derangement) in the body, so they are termed as dosha; because they maintain the body (Dehadharana) hence called as dhatu; and since they mean the body Malina (dirty doshas) are called Malas.

The Sapta Dhatus are of seven types as noted in the Table-2-8.

Table - 2-8 : Table Showing the Sapta Dhatus

Name of the Dhatu	*Physiological equivalent*
1. Rasa and Rakta	Plasma and blood
2. Mamsa	Muscular tissue
3. Meda	Adipose tissue
4. Asthi	Bone and cartilage tissue
5. Majja	Bone marrow
6. Shukra	Semen and other reproductive elements.

The Dhatus may be again divided into two groups: Some are of Sthayi or Poshya (stable or need to be nourished) and some are of Asthayi or Poshaka (unstable or which nourishes). Sthayi Dhatus support the body by providing it with basic tissues whereas Asthayi dhatus are responsible for supporting, nourishing and maintaining the Sthayi Dhatus.

Acharya Charaka has mentioned in this context that from Ahara Rasa (digested food) are produced and nourished the Sapta Dhatus mentioned above and the Ojas (the essence of all Dhatus) and also such parts of the body as the joints and related structures etc., which bind them (Charaka Sutra 28/5). Thus these Sapta Dhatus are being continuously formed, destroyed and beformed with necessary materials derived from ahara rasa (digested and assimilated food).

It has been postulated that the nutrient materals in the food that we take undegoes transformation under the influence of their own Agni or Ushna (heat) and are there after transported to the Dhatus through their own specific transporting channels (srotamsi) (Charaka Chikitsa 8-39). It has thus been described that the seven Dhatus undergo two kinds of transformations (paka) under the influence of its own Agni (heat).

1. Prasada paka.
2. Kitta paka.

Prasada paka (essence transformations) of ahara rasa nourishes (i) Seven dhatus; (ii) Ojas (the end product of digested diet responsible for the resistance and luster of the individual; essence of all dhatus); (iii) Materials relating to the nourishment of basic structures of five senses; and (iv) also such as the joints and related structures etc. which bind them (Charaka Sutra 28/4).

Kitta paka (Transformation of waste products) nourishes sveda (sweat), Mutra (Urine), Purisha (Stool), Vata, Pitta,

Kapha and malas (excretary materials) of eye, ear, nose, throat, mouth, hair follicles and external genitalia. In this way, all of the essential elements and waste products of the body are nourished. Thus, essential rasas and malas nourishing the body in a balanced way are responsible for dhatu samya (homeostasis) (Charaka Sutra 28/4). Acharya Sushruta also described the above mentioned postulate thus "Dosha Dhatu Mal Moolam He Shariram" (Sushruta Sutra 15/3). It means that doshas, dhatus and malas, are the mool (root or base) of the body on which the body is supported and maintained.

Functions of Sapta Dhatus

These are enumerated in the Table 2-9 and are described by Acharya Sushruta.

Table - 2-9 : Table Shows the Functions of Sapta Dhatus

Dhatu	*Action*	*Function*
Rasa (Plasma)	Nourishes rakta	Makes the individual cheerful
Rakta (Blood)	Nourishes mamsa	Clarifies the complexion.
Mamsa (Muscle)	Nourishes meda	Develops the body
Meda (Fat)	Nourishes Asthi	Responsible for softness, diaphoresis, body strength
Asthi (Bone)	Nourishes majja	Supports the body
Majja (Bone marrow)	Nourishes Shukra and fills up the asthis	Responsible for enjoyment, liking and body strength.
Shukra (Semen)		Gives patience, enjoyment, body strength and liable to be excreted out with the association of fair sex. Responsible for reproduction.

The Excess and Deficient Growth of Dhatus

By taking nutritious food, proper exercise and by taking Rasayana Dravyas, the Dhatus protect the body by the normal physiological functions and is termed as "Upachaya."

When the Dhatus grow out of proportion to their natural state, it is called "Dhatu Vriddhi" (Hypertrophy of Dhatus). This type of growth of Dhatus is not beneficial to health of the individual as already pointed out before under Agni, the hypertrophy of Dhatus also takes' place due to Ama Samchaya produced by Mandagni. When the "Ama" produced by Mandagni obstructed the minute Srotas, the Rasadhatu remains out side the cells resulting in the hypertrophy of the respective Dhatus. This type of Hypertrophy of Dhatus is called "Sama Vruddhi" because of this, many diseases will develop in the individual.

Similarly "Dhatu Kshaya" (Atrophy of Dhatus) also take place because of Tishnagni, resulting in various bodily ailments.

Therefore hypertrophy and Atrophy of Dhatus always indicates pathological state of body and does not protect the body's normal health.

THE CONCEPT OF MALAS

As mentioned already before-doshas, dhatus and malas are the three essential components of the living body which maintain the life and health of the individual. If the three doshas are displaced due to excessive increase or other causes, they are called 'Malas' (impurities) "Aggravated Vata, Pitta, Kapha and any other aspects that remain in the body causing harm to the body are all termed malas (Charaka Ch. Sariravichaya). When these malas move along improper channels or are obstructed in their path, diseases come about. Sushruta has mentioned about the functions of malas and are shown in the Table 2-10.

Table - 2-10 : Table Shows Functions of Malas (Sushruta)

Malas	*Functions*
Purisha (Stool)	Supports and maintains the body and also supports vayu and agni.
Mutra (Urine)	Fills up the urinary bladder and produces humidity in the body.
Sweda (Sweat)	Keep the skin wet and tender.

Doshas originating from the malas produce various types of gases in the alimentary tract as mala form of vata and various excretions from nose, mouth etc. in the form of mala of Pitta and Kapha.

Thus, when doshas are worn out to such an extent that their reversion to the original state is not possible either immediately or during a certain period (i.e. till they are restored to balanced state by curative means), and cannot be utilised by the body, then they are called waste products or malas. For example, Carbon dioxide and other gases are malas of Vata; Stercobilin and Urobilin are malas of Pitta; whereas Urea and Uric acid are malas of Kapha (Mrs. Vaishali N. Dadkar).

THE CONCEPT OF AGNI

In addition to the Tridosha as the basic biologic elements of the living body, Ayurveda has given importance to another element namely, 'Agni,' and considered a very important element for the promotion of health of an individual. The Agni is also called Pitta (Pachakapitta), because its main function is to digest food with the help of Samana Vayu and Kledaka Kapha (see under Tridosha).

Thirteen types of Agnis in the body have been described of which 7 are Dhatvagnis (tissue enzymes), 5 Bhootagnis and 1 Jatharagni (digestive fire in the stomach). (See under classification of Agni).

Briefly speaking, the food we take will be digested by the factors mentioned above producing 6 types of rasa (i.e. sweet, sour, salty, pungent, astringent, and bitter). The food will be acted upon by Bodhaka kapha (produces sense of taste) in the mouth and Kledaka kapha (Moistens food) in the stomach. The digested food will ultimately lead to Maḍhura vipaka (sweet digestive juice) and later on it will be acted upon by pitta. Then the digestive fire (jatharagni) will dry up the waste products and propel them into large intestine.

Figure - 2-1 : Figure Shows the Digestion of Food.

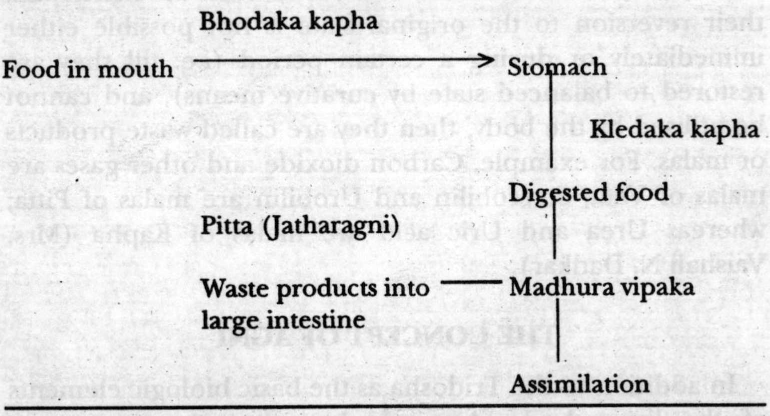

Ahar (diet) is the basis of all living organisms which gives strength, resistance (ojas) or power (tejas) and maintenance of the body throughout life (Sushruta Sutra 1/27) and also continuity of life of a species by producing the reproductive elements, sperm and ovum (shukra and sonita) respectively.

Whatever food is taken, it must be digested and metabolised to maintain the life of the individual and is performed by Agni present in the body of the individual. Thus, the Dehagni (Agni of the body) has been described as the cause of life, complexion, strength, health, nourishment, lustre of the body, Ojas (resistance), Tehja (power) and prana (life energy) as mentioned by Charaka (Charaka Chikitsa 15/3). Describing about the importance of agni, Charaka has mentioned that after stopping of the function of agni, the individual dies; when agni functions properly the individual survives, remaining healthy; and becomes diseased when the same is disturbed and hence Agni is described as Mool (basis) of life (Charaka Chikista 15/4). The food must be digested and metabolised properly by agnis of the body because undigested food is not able to produce the body elements mentioned above.

It is to be kept in mind that these agnis are not present in the body in the form of agni as the name suggests but it is in the form of 'Pitta'—which performs the various functions like digestion, production of heat in the body, vision, complexion, valour, cheerfulness etc. when normal and when abnormal the 'Pitta' causes the functions just contrary to as mentioned above (Charaka Sutra 12/11).

Classification of Agni

Agni in the form of pitta has been divided into 13 types according to function and site of action. There are 5 Bhootagnis, 7 Dhatwagnis and one Pachakagni—as shown in the Table 2-11.

Bhutagnis

As already mentioned that all of dietic materials are composed of Panchabhutas. Therefore all 5 groups of dietetic materials contain their own agnis. As for example Akashiya dravyas contain Akashagni, Vayavya dravyas

Table - 2-11 : Table Shows the 13 Types of Agni

Bhutagnis	*Dhatuwagnis*	*Pachakagni*
Akasha—akashagni	Rasa—rasagni	Pachakagni—also called
Vayu—vayawagni	Rakta—raktagni	Jatharagni, antaragni
Tej—tejagni	Mamsa—mamsagni	(digestive fire in the
Jala—jalagni	Meda—medagni	stomach), Koshtagni.
Prithvi	Asthi—asthyagni	
	Majja—Majjagni	
Tatal : 5	7	1 = 13

contain Vayawagni, Tejas dravyas contain Tejagni etc. All of the different types of Bhutagnis digest their own moieties of substances present in the various food materials. Acharya Charaka has mentioned that five Bhutagnis digest their own part of the substance present in the food materials. After the digestion of food by Bhutagnis, digested materials containing the elements and qualities alike to each bhutas nourish their own specific dhautic elements of the body (Charaka Chikitsa 15/13, 14). These bhutagnis act after the Jataragni present in stomach and duodenum acted upon the food and making them disintegrated. In modern physiological perspective Jataragni action can be equated with the digestion in stomach and small intestines and materials in the liver.

Dhatwagnis

All of the seven dhatus (seven elemental tissues of the body) contain their own agni to metabolize the nutrient materials supplied to them through their own Srotas. Rasadhatu contains Rasagni, Rakta dhatu contains Raktagni and Mamsa dhatu contains Mamsagni and so on so forth. All of the seven agnis contained in seven dhatus metabolise the substances supplied to them to nourish and constitute the tissues alike to them. Acharya Charaka has mentioned this fact as that seven dhatus which are the support of the body contain their own agni, and by their own Agni digest and transform the materials supplied to them to make the substance alike to them for assimilation and nourishment. (Charaka Chikitsa 28/15). The modern idea of assimilation has also been pointed out by Acharya Charaka. In this context Acharya Charaka has mentioned that Dhatwaharah (nutrient substances supplied to dhatus) Dhatavo Prakriti—Manuvartante (are transformed alike to the dhatus concerned) (Charaka Sutra 28/3). Explaining briefly the digestive and metabolic functions of Agni Acharya Charaka has mentioned that various types of dietic materials eaten are digested by their own agni (Bhutagnis), encouraged and enhanced by Antaragni (Jataragni) and further digested and metabolised by dhatuwagnis to associate the body with the nutrition, strength, complexion and happy life along with providing energy to the seven dhatus (Charaka Sutra 28/3).

In the context of agni, it would be worth noting of the ideas of Acharya Sushruta regarding Agni. Sushruta himself raised a question and answered the same. Sushruta has questioned that whether the Agni is different from pitta or pitta itself is Agni. Answering this he mentioned that Agni is not different from pitta due to its Agneya (firely) quality. The enhanced pitta is treated as the alleviation of Agni is done; that is to say, heat of the body is treated by the applications of substances having sheeta (cold) qualities. In the condition of diminution of Antaragni (Jataragni) such substances are used to enhance the Agni which have the qualities like ushna (hot) tikshna (sharp) and having the rasas like Katu (bitter), Amla (sour) and Lavana (salty) which is alike to pitta. Authoritative statements also support the same views. Hence it can be said that Agni is not different from Pitta (Sushruta Sutra 21/9).

Pachakagni (Synonyms: Jatharagni, Antaragni, Koshtagni)

Pachakagni is the pitta present in the Amashaya and Pakvashaya (stomach and duodenum respectively). This digest the ingested food. It is in liquid form and being Sneha (unctuous), Ushna (heat), Tishna (sharp) in quality digests the food easily and therefore known as Pachakagni. Pachakagni also supports other Agnis in the body so that they carry their normal digestion and assimilation of food substances.

As long as the Jatharagni is in its normal state and amount, other Dhatwagnis and Bhutagnis also will be in equilibrium carrying on their functions. If there is deficiency in the activity of Jatharagni, then other Agnis would also become less active. The life span of an individual, his/her strength, colour, Tejas (power), Ojas (resistance) etc. are all dependent on Agni. If Agni is in Samya (homeostatic state) state, then, he will be healthy, otherwise he will be prone to frequent illnesses.

The Normal and Abnormal States of Pachakagni

Pachakagni can be divided into 4 types depending on its nature.

1. *Samagni*: The agni which digests the ingested food without causing any ill-health is called Samagni. If a person has this type of Agni, it helps him lead a normal life.
2. *Mandagni*: When the Agni cannot digest even light food and takes relatively long time to digest and the subject complains of heaviness of food, distension of stomach etc., it indicates Mandagni. This type of Mandagni is naturally found in Kaphaja Prakritic individual and those who consume Kapha producing food substances.

3. *Tishnagni* : This Agni is that type which digests heavy food in a short time. The symptoms complained of by those individuals having Tishnagni are: Burning sensation in epigastric region (stomach) and all over the body, sour eructations, giddiness, thirst etc. This type of Agni is found chiefly in Paittic Prakritic individuals and those who consume Pitta producing substances.
4. *Vishamagni*: This type of Agni causes irregular digestion producing flatulence, Abdominal colic, constipation etc. This type is found in Vatic Prakritic individuals and those who consume Vata producing substances.

Out of the four different Agnis, only Samagni is the best. The remaining three agnis produce illness, and the majority of illness are due to Mandagni. That is why Vishamagni and Tishnagni are considered under Mandagni and treated as such by Ancient Ayurvedic Physicians.

The Abnormalities of Agni and Production of Amarasa

As described above, the three types of Koshtagnis i.e. Mandagni, Tishnagni and Vishamagni produces illness due to their unequal, untimely, digestion of food. The resulting indigested food remains as 'Ama.' The Rasa dhatu produced out of such indigested food is also abnormal and is known as 'Amayukta Rasa Dhatu.'

The Table 2-12 shows the comparison between properly digested Rasa and improperly digested 'Amarasa.'

THE CONCEPT OF SROTAS

The term Srotas mean a channel through which the nutrient materials pass the various tissues for nourishment. The derivative meaning of the root verb Sru denotes the exudate or to ooze. Charaka has defined the Srotas as

'Sravanat Srotamsi' meaning thereby the structutre through which Sravanam (oozing, filtering or permeation) takes place.

Table - 2-12 : Characteristics of Properly Formed Chyle (Samya Rasa Dhatu) and Improperly Formed Chyle (Sama Rasa Dhatu)

	Properly formed Chyle	*Improperly formed Chyle*
	Prakrit (Samya) Rasa Dhatu Character	Sama Rasa Dhatu Character
1.	Achcha (without Kashmala)	Avila (mixture of Kashmala)
2.	Tanu (water liquid)	Styana (thick liquid)
3.	Snigdha (Slimy)	Bahupichchila (excessively sticky)
4.	Odourless	Foul smelling
5.	Can penetrate into macro-, micro-pores	Can not penetrate into macro-, micro pores

Source : Srikanta Murthy: Ayurved Vikrit Vigyan, translated into Telugu by Kalyan Sharma G., Dattatreya & Co., Rajamundry (AP), 1980.

Srotamsi of the body are of various kinds, may be Sthula (gross) or Sukshma (Subtle). The Srotamsi comprises all channels, spaces (big and small), perceptible and imperceptible that compose the internal transport system of the body. Charaka has described Dhamani (Artery) as the first transporting channel because with each beat of heart, pulsation (Dhamant) occurs and therefore called as Dhamanis. In the order Srotamsi come second for which Charaka has mentioned that because of Sravanam (oozing, filtering or permeation), they are called Srotas

(Sravanat Srotamsi) (Charaka Sutra 30/12). In the perspective of modern anatomy and physiology it can be well understood that in the circulatory cycle, arteries are the first structures through which blood goes to the different parts of the body; further these arteries are branched and rebranched as finer tributaries and arteries. The arteries are further branched into fine capillaries through which the nutrient materials to the tissues are supplied by oozing and permeation. Thus the structures of second order mentioned by Charaka 'Srotamsi' are capillaries. The structures as Sira (veins) taking part in circulation are stated as third in the order. After Srotamsi come Siras for which Charaka has mentioned that because of Sarana (slow going), these are termed as Sira (Sarnat Sirah (Charaka Sutra 30/12).

After the nutrient materials are supplied to the tissues by arteries, again, the blood is collected in venules, smaller veins, larger veins and come back to the heart to be oxygenated in the lungs and returned to heart to be again pumped out into circulation. Thus the circulatory cycle becomes complete. The manner in which Charaka has explained about the Srotamsi, it is clear that the Srotamsi are the channels transporting the resultant nutrient materials of Dhatus (Charaka Vimana 5/3). In this context Charaka has used the word Abhivahi which denotes the meaning of both way transporting that is to say, Srotamsi transport the nutrient materials to the tissues and return back the reduced material to the venules and veins thus completing the circulation. Sushruta has also used the term Abhivahi for the Srotamsi.

Classification of Srotamsi

All of the different tissues of the body get nutrition through their own Srotamsi. Charaka has classified Srotamsi into 13 important varieties. Seven Srotamsi are of seven dhatus, three Srotamsi—Anna vaha, Prana vaha and Udaka vaha and other three are Mutravaha, Swedavaha and Purishavaha. Vata, Pitta and Kapha are stated to traverse the entire body and move through different kinds of Srotamsi. Manasika (Mental) doshas like Rajas, Tamas and Satwa which are beyond sense perception have the entire body as their vehicle, and field of operation.

These Srotamsi also transport the factors causing Prakopa (excitation) and Shaman (alleviation) of doshas. The Srotamsi of different tissues or structures take the form of the specific tissues or structures to which they supply the nutrient material. They are in the circular form, may be gross or subtle. They may be big in size, like the branching of the stem (Charaka Vimana 5/25).

Figure - 2-2 : Figure Shows Circulation of Blood According to Charaka

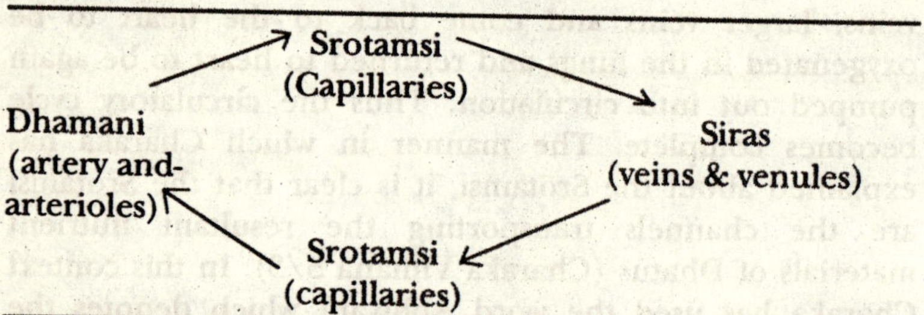

Table - 2-13 : Table Shows the Classification of Srotamsi (Charaka)

Srotamsi	*Location*	*Number*
Sapta dhatus	Specific tissues	7
Annavaha	Oesophagus, Stomach	1
Pranavaha	Heart, stomach, intestine	1
Udakavaha	Pancreas	1
Mutravaha	Urinary Bladder, Urethra	1
Swedavaha	Skin, marrow	1
Purishavaha	Intestine, Anus	1
Total		13

The impairment of Agni (i.e. digestion and metabolism) lead to Srotovaigunya (impairment of functional integrity of Srotas) leading to its inability to perform its normal functions. Srotodusti is stated to produce Srotorodha (obstruction of the Srotas) resulting in the obstruction to the normal flow of doshas and poshaka dhatus (nutrient material) and stasis of malas (waste products). The doshas thus retained are stated to interact with dushyas (sapta dhatus) of the affected region. This phenomenon has been described as "Dosha Dushya Sammurchhana." The site where such an interaction takes place is stated to be the region where the process of disease is primarily initiated. Thus the Srotas has got an important role in the production of disease. So long as there is no impairment in the function of Srotas, there will be no disease. In view of this fact Sushruta has mentioned that the provoked doshas while circulating in the body, wherever they are occluded produce Khavaigunya (Impairment of Srotas) and the disease is produced at the same site (Sushruta Sutra 24/17).

OJAS—AYURVEDIC CONCEPT OF ENERGY IN HUMAN BODY*

V. Narayana Swamy

Definition

The Sanskrit term Ojas is used mainly to indicate in a person, vigour, vitality etc. In Vedic literature, Ojas is equated to pranasakthi, meaning life energy and cause of strength (Ojah bala hetu bhutaha). In Ayurveda it is described as a material circulating in the tissues and a part of it is remaining constantly in the heart. The presence of this during life gives energy to a person, reduction of which

* Reproduced with permission from: Narayana Swami V., Ojas-Ayurvedic Concept of Energy in Human body, Aryavaidyan, 1 : 1: 21-25: 1987.

leads to various diseases and the total absence of which leads to death. (Ennase niyatam nasaha—Yasmin tistati tistati) (Ash. Hari. Sutr. 11-37).

Ojas or Human Energy

Having considered briefly the working of the body, we will come to the subject of human energy. Ayurveda considers, the working of the entire body with vigour and vitality, is due to what is called ojas. Ojas is a material (dravya) in the body which has got certain characteristics (guna)and certain functions (karma). This substance is the quintessence of tissue metabolism (sapthadhatus). It is said that as honey is gathered from various flowers by the bees, ojas is gathered from the seven tissues mentioned earlier. Another simile is given, as ghee pervades all through the milk, ojas pervades all through the tissues. It is oily, reddish yellow and cold (somya). (Cha. Sutra XVII-75).

It is transmitted through the semen to the mother's womb and joins the ovary during fertilisation. It protects and nourishes the embryo, by its sliminess (kalala). Later in the sixteenth week it enters the heart of the foetus and circulates. It is said that in the eighth month of pegnancy, ojas alternates its existence from the mother to the foetus and so if delivery takes place during that period it is dangerous to the mother or the foetus depending on the presence of ojas in the mother or foetus. If the ojas is with the mother the foetus dies and if the ojas is with the foetus the mother dies (Sush. Sarira IV-30 and also see Cha. Sutra XXV 9-12).

Varieties of Ojas

Two varities of ojas are described, one is called slaishnika ojas which is mucilaginous in nature and is the one that circulates throughout the body. The quantity of it is abdhanjali, one's own cupped palm full. The larger the man, greater the quantity and smaller the man lesser the quantity. This is called apara ojas and is attached to the vessels from the heart. In diabetes it is the apara ojas which is lost and not para ojas which is reduced. This ojas which is the substratum of life is eight drops only in quantity and is located in the heart. The loss of this para ojas portends death (Cha. Sutra XXX-7).

Causes for Its loss

Ojas becomes less in the body both by mental and physical causes. The prominent mental causes are anger, fear, anxiety, sorrow, worry etc. The physical causes are loss of nourishment, excessive physical activity which tires a person, indulgence in uncongenial, dry and pungent foods (Ash. Hri. XI-39).

The loss is explained in three stages depending on the quantity and quality of the loss. The first stage is visramsana, slipping from its place or leakage from its circulation. In this condition the symptoms are loosening of joints and impairment of the functions of the body (Sush. Sutra XV-24). The second stage is vyapat, which indicates the changes that has taken place in the quality of the ojas. The signs and symptoms of this condition are heaviness of the body and limb oedema, discolouration of the skin and sleeplessness (Ibid.).

The third stage is total loss which is indicated by symptoms of fear, feeling of insecurity, constant thoughts, loss of strength, reduced functioning of sensory organs, loss of colour and dry skin (Ash. Hrudaya Sutra XI-40).

Ojas versus Bala or Strength

Ayurveda classifies strength of the body in three categories. Sahaja bala—natural and innate strength of the person. This is a genetic factor and depends on the race and climatic condition of a person. The second is kalaja or seasonal and is also according to the age. The man is relatively strong in cold season and his strength is poor in summer and moderate in other seasons. The third is yuktikritha and that is gaining and maintaining strength by exercise, proper diet and medicines (Cha. Sutra XI-36). In this category we also include mental attitude—a feeling of relaxation and avoiding stress, thoughts, and emotions that consume more energy.

The Role of Ojas and Bala in Developing Immunity Against the Diseases (Vyadhi Kshamatva)

Ojas and bala (general strength of the body) contribute a great deal towards developing resistance against diseases (Vyadhi Kshamatva). All persons do not have the same capacity to prevent diseases (Cha. Sutra 28-7). There are different factors starting from heredity to the way in which one lives and the routine he adopts. In developing the resistance or immunity against diseases two terms are used, one is, 'Vyadhibala viroditva' developing and agents to combat the strength of the disease; that means, the virulence of the disease is brought down. The other thing is, 'vyadhi utpada prathi-bandhatva,' the capacity to inhibit or contain the factors that produce the disease. The capacity to resist the disease depends on factors mentioned earlier namely, genetic factor, seasonal factor and on his attitude to live normally.

Ojas plays a pronounced role in the maintenance of the strength in a person and if found less, care should be taken to replenish the lost ojas. This is done by diet and medicines which are called Jeevaneeya gana or life-giving group of diet and drugs. (Ash. Hri. XI-40).

Diet

In this category of life giving diet, milk and ghee come first. Ayurvedic texts describe these as Jeevaneeya, that which prolongs life, jeevaneeyam ksheeram uttamam rasayanam (Cha. Sutra 28-214). Ghee also is described as one which gives life energy : (Vyasas-Sthapanam param-Ash. Hri. Sutra V-38). The question of cholesterol in blood is nowadays worrying the person and even many vegetarians exclude these from diet. From the stand point of Ayurveda, these are essentials and among the fats ghee is said to be the best (Snehnam Uttamam). In non-vegetarian diet mutton soup is said to increase the ojas.

Drugs

There are certain drugs which increase the ojas and they are also classified as jeevaneeya gana oushadha—group of drugs which sustain life. Some of them are:

1. Asparagus racemosus.
2. Withania somnifera.
3. Hemidesmus indicus L.
4. Phaseolus trilobus Ait.
5. Ipnomea paniculata.
6. Tinospora cordifolia L.
7. Curculigo orchioides.

Anyone of these drugs two or more can be boiled in water or milk and filtered and taken to increases the ojas. Milk is better than water.

Conclusion

Ojas is the quintessence derived from the metabolism of the tissues and it is essential for a virile life. It is reduced by emotional disturbances, starvation and over work. The man loses his strength and immunity against the diseases by its reduction and loss. The drugs and diet which are classified as jeevaneeya gana restores the ojas in the body.

NOTES AND REFERENCES

1. Satyavati G.V., Some Traditional Medical Systems and Practises of Global Importance, Ind. J. Med. Res., 76 (Suppl.), December, 1982.

2. Dwivedi, L.D. and Guru L.V., Introduction to Ayurveda, Krishnadas Ayurveda Series 20, Krishnadas Academy, Varanasi, 1988.

3. Athavale VB., Tridosha Theory and Modern Science, Probe: XXVII :4: 1988.

4. Notes on Ayurveda, Ayurvedic System of Medicine, Rangarajan Siddha Tutorial College, Madurai, Tamil Nadu.

5. Devaraj T.L., Speaking of: Ayurvedic Remedies for Common Diseases, Sterling Health and Cure Series, New Delhi, 1985.

6. Narayana Swamy V., Ojas—Ayurvedic Concept of Energy in Human Body, Aryavaidyan: 1 : 1, 1987.

7. Vinaya Kumar A., Understanding the Principle of Tridosha in Ayurveda, Ayurveda Samachar: 14 : 6, 1991.

8. (Mrs.) Vaishali N. Dadkar, Basic Principles of Ayurveda and Their Implications in Clinical Medicine, Probe: XXIV: 2, 1985.

CHAPTER 3

Health and Disease

HEALTH

The definition of Health or 'Swasthya' in Ayurveda is a highly comprehensive one. As defined by Sushruta the renowned surgeon of Varanasi, Uttar Pradesh (Circa 1000 B.C.:

"The person who has sama doshas (balanced doshas), Samagni (proper digestion and transformations occurring in the body), the function of sapta dhatus (tissues of his body) and Malas (excretory products) are normal and balanced and whose indriyas (cognative) and connative senses together with mind functioning properly and who is happy is called as Swastha (healthy)" (Sushruta Sutra Sthana 15/45).

Thus, the main aim of health as defined in Auryveda is to maintain the health of the individual because only healthy person can be considered to achieve the goals of his or her life i.e. the four purusharthas (main achievements)—Dharma (religion), Artha (wealth), Kama (fulfilment of worldly pleasures), and Moksha (salvation). Rogas (diseases) are the looters of health and health is the great achievement of life (Charaka Sutra 1/5). It was therefore considered essential to maintain life not only in a disease-free condition but also in a perfect positive health of body, mind and spirit.

To maintain the helath, it is essential to maintain the balance of doshas because it is responsible for health, and imbalance of doshas (dosha vaishamya) are the cause of a disease. Hence to remain healthy, dosha samya (Homeostasis) (internal equilibrium of the body) is very necessary. Here, a pertinent question may be raised that how the dhatu samya can be maintained, when there are great variations in daily regimen and environments of the individuals (which cause the imbalance of doshas. To overcome this problem, ancient Ayurvedists advocated individuals to observe certain routine activities which are suitable and advantageous for them according to Desha (locality), kala (time), Paristhithi (situation). For observing such activities, there is a description of (a) Ritu charya (dietary regimen to be adopted according to season), (b) Dina charya (adoption of regimen and daily routines in a proper manner), and (c) Sadvritta (Ethics). In addition to all these, certain recommendations for the proper intake of food, sleep and proper behaviour, together with all the other essential things needed to maintain good life have been elaborately described in all of the classical texts of Ayurveda. All these topics dealing with the maintenance of health are included in Swasthya vritha (i.e. observing such essential regimens and routine works throughout the life).

In the daily routine (Dinacharya), importance is given to the use of medicated gargles, oil massages and regulated physical exercises. Further the 'daily regimen' advocates not to suppress certain natural physical urges like micturition, defecation as also hunger, sleep, tears etc. On the other hand, suppression in literal sense is advocated of harmful psychic urges like greed, fear, anger, jealousy, malice and excessive attachment to any thing. Great emphasis has been laid on personal hygiene including cleaning of various parts of the body individually, apart from bathing the whole body. Equal importance is given also to psychic health or what Charaka calls, sadvritta, implying mental discipline and a strict adherence to moral values and principles.

Personal hygiene as propounded by Ayurveda is thus physical, social and universal in its concept as well as application. Ayurveda thus expounds a whole way of life embodying not only the physical and psychological effects but also the philosophical, ethical and moral aspects, on one hand, and the individual and universal health on the other. This holistic and universal concept of health must be considered as a contribution of Ayurveda.

In addition to the hygienic measures and regimens advocated for maintenance of helath. certain drugs which promote health (Swasthya youjaskarma), other than those which cure diseases (Artasya Rogante), have been advised by Charaka (Charaka Chikitsa 1/1-4). This is known as Rasayana (Geriatrics). This thereby has been advised for those desirous of having a long life span, good memory, intelligence and a constant youth age. Among 8 parts of Ayurveda, Rasayana has been dealt with as a separate and independent branch which elaborately prescribes about the drugs and ways and means (Achara Rasayana) to promote the health of the individuals.

DISEASE

Definition of Disease

The definition of disease is implied in the very structure of the disease, because so many different kind of disturbances can make a person feel not at ease and lead him to seek the aid of a physician.

Modern Medicine in practice is broadening this concept to any state, organic or psychic, real or imaginary, that disturbs person's sense of well being. In this sense disease may threaten life or simply interfere with its enjoyment; it may prevent the sick person from functioning as a normal human being or simply from reaching the self selected goals (Etymological meaning of the word Disease is dis and eased i.e. not feeling of easiness (D.P. Sahu, 1981) of Purushartha.

According to Ayurveda, diseases are as a result of primary disturbances of the doshas or dhatus.

Thus note:

(i) The doshas Vata, Pitta and Kapha and any other factors that remain in the body causing harm to the body are all termed Malas (Impurities) (Charaka Ch. Sariravichaya).

(ii) When these impurities move along improper channels or are obstructed of this channels, then diseases originate (Sushruta Ch. Vyadhi Samuddesiya).

(iii) When Doshas increase in their own channels, it is accumulation; provocation is when they spread over to other channels. The occurrence of disease is when symptoms corresponding to the disturbance is seen (Vaghbhatta Ch. Doshabhadiya).

(iv) Samprapti (Pathogenesis) is defined by Acharya Vagabhatta as "The manner is which doshas are vitiated and traversing through the body produce the disease (Astanga Hridaya Nidana I). The other synonyms of samprapti are Jati (origin of disease) and Agati (establishment of a disease).

The Disease process is described in various stages, namely:

1. Samchaya (Stage of accumulation of abnormal dosha)
2. Prakopa (Stage of exacerbation)
3. Prasara (Stage of spread allover the body) and

4. Sthanashraya (Stage of localisation at weak sites, thus locally accumulated doshas give rise to localised diseases)
5. Purvarupa stage (Premonitory or prodromal signs and symptoms)
6. Rupa stage (Disease is clearly differentiated with characteristic signs and symptoms).

(For detailed description of the evolution of disease and clinical manifestations—see chapter on Clinical Manifestation of Disease).

In Ayurveda, various manifestations at the different stages of disease are described so that early diagnosis and treatment become possible. This is important in the light of the fact that in modern medicine the initial stages (up-to sthanasraya) fall in the incubation period and very little attention is paid to them (except in epidemiological studies).

The Origin of Diseases as Described in Ayurveda

The impairment of Agni (digestion and metabolism) lead to Srotovaigunya (impairment of functional integrity of srotas or channels) leading to its inability to perform its normal functions. Srotodusti (diseased srotas) is stated to occur leading to srotorodha (obstruction of srotas) resulting in the obstruction to the normal flow of doshas and poshakadhatus (nutrient material) and stages of mala (waste products). The doshas thus retained are stated to interact with dushyas (Sapta dhatus) of the affected region. This phenomenon has been described as "Dosha Dushya Sammurchanna." The site where such an interaction takes place is noted to be the region where the disease process is primarily initiated. Thus, the srotas have been given an important role in the production of disease in Ayurvedic

Medicine. So long as there is no impairment in the function of srotas there will be no disease. In view of this fact, Acharya Sushruta has mentioned that the provoked doshas while circulating in the body and wherever they are occluded produce Khavaigunya (Impairment of srotas) and the disease is produced at the same site (Sushruta Sutra 24/17).

DIETETICS IN AYURVEDA

The basis of health and life is Ahara (diet). Sushruta says that the basis of life, strength, complexion of body together with the resistance power is Ahara (diet) (Sushruta Sutra 1/28). Charaka has described about Ahara in 4th chapter named as Annapana Chatuska in his classical text.

Ayurvedic texts describe 4 kinds of Ahara dravyas with various species of grains used along with their qualities and functions.

These are:

Ashita (eaten by biting with teeth as bread)

Peeta (taken as drink as milk and water)

Leedha (which is taken by licking e.g. condiment, pickles etc.)

Khadita (eaten by mastication as fried grain)

Details about the method of taking diet have been also described—Charaka says that the individual shall take such diet which is liked by him/her in all respects as colour, smell, taste and touch etc. If the Ahara is not taken according to the methods described, it is called Atiahara which causes untoward effect in the body (Charaka Sutra 27/3).

Various Ahara dravyas have specific qualities and actions.

e.g. Water—moisture in the dietic materials.

Salt—Causes looseness of diet

Kshara—(Alkalies)—Causes digestion

Madhu (Honey)—Causes unification of skin and muscles (elemental tissues) as result of catabolic activity of the body.

Sarpi (Butter)—Causes unctuousness

Milk—Useful for all elemental tissues of the body

Meat—Causes development of the body

Rasa—Causes replenishment of tissues.

All of the Ahara dravyas have been classified into 12 categories and their qualities and functions have been elaborately described by Charaka.

Then Ahara dravyas are taken according to the need and availability. When we compare with the modern nutritional standards advocated, it appears reasonable to conclude that ancient physicians were aware of the proper diet required having all of the required substances to maintain the health of the individual. The qualities and amount of each nutrient required for a particular individual however has not been described in ancient texts, but broad outlines were given. For example, Charaka has mentioned that an individual should take such quantity of diet in accordance with the Agni (digestive power), which is properly digested without producing any untoward effect on the body, that quantity is said to be proper for the individual concerned (Charaka Sutra 5/4). Charaka has also described 8 methods of eating known as "Asta Ahara Vidhi Vishesayatana" which is necessary to be followed to maintain health.

These are:

1. Prakriti—Depending on nature of food
2. Karana—Processing of food

3. Samyoga—Combination of dietic materials which are mutually compatible
4. Rashi—Quantity needed
5. Desha—Place where the foods are available as consumed by local community
6. Kala—Based on time (seasonal and diurnal variations)
7. Upayoga samstha—Depending on digestive capacity
8. Upayokta—Diet should be suitable and easily digestible to the individual concerned

Charaka has also described the Ahara vidhi vidhanas (Methods of taking meal). These are:

1. Ushnamashniyat—(Warm meal should be taken)
2. Snigdha masniyat—(Unctuous meal should be taken)
3. Matra vadashniyat—(Proper quantity of meal should be taken)
4. Jirna Ashniyat—(Meal should be taken after the digestion of the previous meal)
5. Virya birudhamasniyat—(Meal should not be incompatible)
6. Ishta deshe Isht sarvopakare namasniyat - (Meal should be taken at favourable place with all needed equipment).
7. Natidrutamashniyat—(Meal should not be taken hurriedly).
8. Natibilambita mashniyat—(Meal should not be taken for a long time).
9. Ajal phanahasan Tanmana Bhoonajeeta—(Meal should be taken without speaking and laughing and being concentrated at the meal).

10. Atmanamabhismikshya Bhoonjeete Samyaka—Meal should be taken having an alround consideration of oneself what is suitable and what is not suitable should be considered and whatever is satmya (suitable) should be taken (Charaka Vimana 25, 1-9).

All these advises mentioned by Acharya Charaka should be followed with regard to diet in order to have a long, happy, and healthy life.

NOTES AND REFERENCES

1. Dwivedi L.D., Guru L.V., Introduction to Ayurveda, Krishnadas Ayurveda Series 20, Krishnadas Academy, Varanasi, 1988.
2. Satyavati G.V., Some Traditional Medical Systems and Practises of Global Importance, Ind. J. Med. Res., 76 (Suppl.) December 1982.
3. Sahu D.P., Basic, Concept of Disease with Special Reference to Ayurveda and Yoga, J. Res. Ayur. Siddha, 11: 4: 1981.

CHAPTER 4

Causation of Disease

According to Ayurveda, though there are many causes to produce various diseases in the body, whether exogenous or endogenous, still the diseases occur under the influence of tridoshas only. Even Agantuja diseases caused by exogenous causes (e.g. trauma) soon after they have been established in the body, are embraced by doshas. The following statements stress the above Ayurvedic concept:

1. Tridoshas maintain the body health and life whilc they are normal and if the doshas are vitiated by whatever cause, they are only responsible to produce various diseases in the body. (Sushruta Sutra 15/13).

2. Vagbhatta: The increase or decrease of one or more of the tridoshas is the main cause of diseases as it more or less upsets the biological activities of the Dhatus.

"Dosha eve hi Sarvesham rogatnameka karana." Doshas are the sole cause of all diseases.

3. When malas (impurities) move along improper channels or are obstructed in their path, diseases result (Charaka Sharir Vichayadhayay).

4. "Wherever excited doshas moving about in the body are obstructed due to abnormality of their channels,

there diseases originate" (Sushruta—Ch. Vyadhi Smuddesiya).

5. When doshas increase in their own channels, it is accumulation. Provocation is when they spread to other channels. The occurrence of disease is when symptoms corresponding to the disturbance is seen (Vaghbhata—Ch. Doshabhediya).

Aetiology (Nidana) of Diseases

The term Nidana is used in two senses. First sense being, the diagnosis of the disease and the second sense being, the etiology of the disease. Therefore, the meaning of Nidana may be understood according to the context.

Acharya Vijai Rakshita, Commentator of Madhava Nidana (author—Vaghbhatta) defined Nidana as the cause which is able to produce disease with its manifestation.

About the importance of Nidana, Vijai Rakshita commented that if Nidana is neglected a physician cannot treat the patient because so long as the cause of the disease is not prevented, the disease cannot be alleviated. Therefore, the principle of treatment is to check the cause of the disease.

To understand Nidana which greatly helps for the diagnosis and prognosis of disease, the aetiology of diseases has been classified into many categories on the basis of various factors and characters of nidana. See table 4-1.

Charaka has mentioned that all of the diseases whether Shariraka (Somatic) or Mansika (Mental) originate due to the three main collective aetiology (Trividha hetu sangraha) (Charaka Sutra 1/54). They are—Asatmyendriyartha Samyoga, Prangyan Paradha and Parinama.

Table 4-1 : Table Shows the Classification of Aetiology (Nidana) of Diseases

Category		*Causation*
I.	1.	Vyabhichari (mixed causes).
	2.	Sannikrishta (immediate causes).
	3.	Viprakrishta (distant causes).
	4.	Pradhanika (important cause as person).
II.	1.	Asatmyendriyartha Samyoga—excessive, erroneous or non-contact of cognative senses (five senses) with their corresponding objects.
	2.	Prangyan paradha—errors of buddhi (intelligence) which causes provocation of all doshas.
	3.	Parinama—change during a period of time.
III.	1.	Dosha hetu (dosha as the cause).
	2.	Vyadhi hetu (disease as the cause).
	3.	Ubhaya hetu (both causes).
IV.	1.	Vyanjaka (stimulator) e.g. in winter season,
	2.	Utpadaka (Producer) Madhura rasa (sweet food) causes Kapha (phlegm production).
V.	1.	Bahya (external causes)—as diet regimen and seasonal variation together with diurnal variations.
	2.	Abhyantar (internal causes) - doshas (tridoshas) and dushyas (saptadhatus).
VI.	1.	Prakrita (normal) as excitation of doshas in their usual period.
	2.	Vaikrita (abnormal) as excitation of doshas in an unusual period.

VII.	1.	Anuvandhya (primary cause) e.g. anxiety, fears etc.
	2.	Anuvandha (secondary cause) e.g. high blood pressure, angina pectoris.
VIII.	1.	Prakrititah (disease according to constitution).
	2.	Vikrititah (disease not according to prakriti).

Examples:

1. Sannikrishta (Immediate causes):

   The immediate causes for diseases origin are:

   e.g. 1. The Kapha Vyadhi occurring in the mid-afternoon is due to the aggravated kapha dosha in the morning.

   2. The intake food having Ruksha (rough) quality the previous day, is the immediate cause of fever.

In general, the dosha-dhatu-malas are the immediate causes for majority of acute illness.

2. Viprakrishta (Distant Causes):

   These are the remote causes for origin of diseases.

   e.g. 1. The kapha excessiveness produced during Hemanta Ritu (season) is the Viprakrishta cause of Kaphaja disease occurring during vasanta Ritu.

   2. In the same way, improper dietary habits are the remote cause of many illness.

3. Pradhanika (Main cause):

Without other provocating factors, the cause by the strength of itself, can produce illness in the individual.

e.g. Intake of poisonous substances.

4. Vyabhicharika (Mixed causes):

These are also called Gauna. Two or more causes collectively cause illness.

e.g. The growth of parasitic infection is mostly due to lack of exercise, improperly cooked food, etc.

5. Utpadaka (Stimulator):

This is similar to Pradhanika. The ingestion of Madhura rasa containing Dravyas, during Hemanta Ritu, is resulting in aggravated kapha dosha.

6. Vyanjaka (Producer):

Not so important promoting factor or precipitating factor.

e.g. The Kapha samchaya (accumulation) during Hemanta Ritu gets liquified due to sunrays exposure during Vasanta Ritu causing Kaphaja ailments.

7. Prakrita (Normal):

Factors appearing in the normal period.

e.g. Aggravation of kapha in Vasanta ritu.

8. Vaikrita (Abnormal):

Factors appearing contrary to normal period.

e.g. In Varsha Ritu the predominant dosha is Vata, but if kapha dosha gets vitiated it is vaikrita.

9. Anubandhya:

The main factor followed by many Gauna (mixed) causes.

e.g. Poison.

10. Anubanda:

    Cause which suppress the main cause.

    e.g. Mixing of cold foods with poison.

11. Bahya (External causes) (Agantuja):

    e.g. Food, water, air, krimi (microbes, parasites), sharp instruments, change in seasons etc.

12. Abhyantara (Normal causes) (Internal doshas).

    e.g. Tridoshas, Dushyas.

13. Dosha prakopa causes (Provocative factors of doshas):

    e.g. Madhura, four rasas.

14. Vyadhi Utpadaka causes:

    Factors which causes only diseases.

    e.g. Mridbakshana is the cause of Pandu Roga (Anaemia)

15. Ubhaya hetu:

    Causing simultaneous changes both in Tridoshas and disease.

    e.g. Improper dieting habits.

16. Aashyapakarsha (Rupa) causes:

    The factors which cause movement of Tridoshas from their equilibrium state to distant places and cause disease.

    e.g. Vata dosha. Vata dosha brings out the immobile Pitta dosha from its normal location and cause paittic symptoms such as Thirst, Vomiting, Vertigo etc.

17. Nidanardhakar Roga Causes:

    In many instances at first a particular illness arises only to be followed by another one. At this time the primary disease becomes the cause for the secondary illness and is called Nidanardhakar Roga.

e.g. Day time sleep produce cold and Rhinitis followed by cough, and on longstanding, leads to Tuberculosis. In the same way, Jwara (fever) causes Rakta pitta, Raktapitta causes fever and by contamination of the two produces debility. Another example is the formation of Udara Gulma (Abdomen lumps) due to Haemorrhoids (Moola-shanka).

Thus the Atiyoga (excessive contact) Ayoga (non-contact) and Mithya yoga (erroneous contact) of Asatmyendriyartha Samyoga, Pragyan Paradha Parinama have been said to be the chief cause of diseases. But in this context as it has already been pointed out before, it should be borne in mind that even these collective categories of etiology produces diseases through affection of Tridoshas only, because, it is the Tridoshas whose imbalance through whatever cause give rise to diseases.

Now after knowing this fact that tridoshas are the root of all diseases it becomes necessary to know how these Tridoshas are vitiated and responsible to produce diseases. Explaining this fact Sushruta mentions that specific cause provoking specific dosha produce specific disease like vatika, paittic and kaphaja etc. (Sushruta Sutra 24/12). Further, the same vitiated doshas involve any one of the elemental tissues like Rasadhatu, Raktadhatu, Mamsadhatu etc. and they produce diseases like—Rasaja (produced from vitiation of Rasa), Raktaja (Produced from the vitiation of Rakta) and so on. In this context Charaka has opined that all of the Nija Vikaras (endogenous diseases) originate from tridoshas as the bird flying in the sky even throughout the day cannot supercede its own shadow, in the same way, none of the nija vikaras are able to be produced from without vitiated doshas (Charaka Sutra 19/5).

(i) Though all of the ancient scholars of Ayurveda have mentioned the specific aetiology for some disease known during their periods of time, but some of the common causes for provocation of each dosha have also been described in ancient texts (see table 4-2).

(ii) In addition to tridoshas, Agantuja karanas (exogenous causes) also are responsible to produce disease. Among exogenous causes, different types of trauma, intense cold, and heat and injury caused by instruments, weapons or animals are included. It is to be noted that soon after the exogenous causes affect the body to produce the disease, that very agantuja disease will be embraced by doshas. Therefore again, the importance of doshas giving rise to disease even in agantuja cases has been stressed.

(iii) Ama dosha as cause of the disease:

Another important cause responsible for the genesis of various disease is Ama dosha (undigested dietetic rasa). Explaining the term Ama, Acharya Vagbhatta has mentioned that due to inhibition in strength of Agni (jatharagni) the first dhatu rasa has not digested and metabolised in Adho amashaya (small intestine) causing thereby production of Ama rasa. The same Ama rasa or dosha circulating in the body through blood stream causes srotorodha (occlusion of different transporting channels) producing various diseases. Due to srotorodha, movement of vata dosha is affected which may produce vatic diseases like hemiplegia, paraplegia etc., due to the same vayu. If the same vayu disturbs the pitta dosha, paittic diseases may be produced and if the kapha dosha is disturbed, kaphaja diseases may be produced. Thus the Ama dosha may cause various diseases according to the different doshas involved and the different sites where the ama dosha is located. In this context Sushruta has mentioned that—wherever the

Table 4-2 : Shows Common Causes for Provocation of Tridoshas

Vata (Charaka Nidana 1/19)	*Pitta* (Charaka Nidana 1/22)	*Kapha* (Charaka Nidana 1/25)
- Excessive use of Ruksha (rough), Laghu (light) and Cold substances	- Excessive use of hot, sour, salty, alkali like and bitter substances	- Excessive use of fat, heavy, sweet, slimy, cold and sour, salty substances.
- Excessive indulgence in (atiyoga) Purgation Douches	- Taking meal in dyspepsia.	
	- Excessive contact with sunlight, fire.	- Day sleeping - Excessive joy and keeping himself aloof from exercise.
- Excessive exercise		
- Retention of natural urges like micturition, defecation, ejaculation of semen etc.	- Excessive tiredness - Excessive anger - Irregular diet	
Starvation, trauma, sexual indulgence, sorrow, excessive blood letting, excessive awakening etc.		

ama dosha gets located, the symptoms of pain be produced at the site, though the symptoms of vitiated doshas (due to ama dosha) are produced at the same site. (Sushruta Samhita, Uttara Tantra 56th Chapter).

(iv) Effect of micro-organisms as cause of diseases in human body:

In ayurveda, the concept of 'environment' is complex and all embracing which includes physical, biological and psycho-social environments which was given due importance as the causation of disease.

The words Krimi (which nourishes on raw flesh), Rakshasa (which drinks blood), Yatudhana (which causes pain), Pisacha (which raw flesh), Apsara (that swims in water), Gandharva (that makes noises) etc.,—have been used to denote micro-organisms in Atharvana Veda. Nearly a hundred types of organisms have been described (Sahu 1981). Some are said to be drista (macroscopic) and the others are Adrista (microscopic). They flourish in mountains, forests, plants, animals and water. They fly through the atmosphere and the sky and reach the earth. They enter into the food, water, milk etc., and invade the body through the food, reach the blood, ruin the flesh, restrict the growth and cause disease.

It has also been stated in Ayurveda that the organisms should be destroyed to mitigate the ill-effects caused by them. 'Ball, 'Homa,' 'Manidharana' and 'Jambhavi' were used to destroy these micro organisms. Sunrays, fire, 'Guggulu,' 'Peelu,' 'Dhataki,' 'Jatamamsi,' 'Aswatha,' 'Vata,' 'Ajashringi' etc., also destroy them (Sahu, 1981).

The classification of diseases into Adibhautica clearly conveys the role of germs in disease causation. In this way the meaning of 'Bhutabhi shangam' conveys the ways the germs enter the body to cause different diseases.

It is true that the ancient physicians are aware of the definite role of germs in disease causation. They however thought that the germs play only secondary role in disease causation. They appear to take part only in vitiating the dosha-dhatus and malas. But they themselves do not cause disease. As long as the dosha-dhatu-malas are in homeostasis, disease will not occur. But when the germs out number and due to the other provocative factors, disequilibrium of doshas occur, cause diseases. This has been compared to the non-germination of seed in infertile soil. In this way when body is healthy, no germ can cause disease.

Probably because of this, the ancient physician ignored the germs destructiveness and gave more importance to the development of resistance of the individual.

Even though the above concept of the role of the germs in disease causation is not true completely, the rapid growth of microbial resistance to various drugs due to rapid adaption of the microbes shows that the germs may play a secondary role in disease causation at least to some extent and the immunity of the individual is more important than the microbes them selves in disease causation.

Thus to sum up the genesis of rogas, it can be concluded that though there are many causes to produce various diseases in the body but whatever may be the cause, whether exogenous or endogenous, soon after they get established in the body, they are embraced by doshas. Hence, the statement of Sushruta stands to be true that—tridoshas are the maintainer of body health and life while they are normal, and if the doshas are vitiated by whatever causes, they are only responsible to produce various diseases in the body (Sushruta 15/3) (Dwivedi and Guru, 1985).

NOTES AND REFERENCES

1. Dwivedi L.D., Guru L.V., Introduction to Ayurveda, Krishnadas Ayurveda Series, 20, Krishnadas Academy, Varanasi, 1988.
2. Varier N.V.K., From the Pages of Vaghbhatta, Aryavaidyan: 1: 4: 1988.
3. Srikanta Murthy K.R., Ayurveda Vikrit Vigyan, translated in Telugu by Sharma K.L., Dattatreya & Co., Rajamundry, 1980.
4. Sahu D.P., Basic Concept of Disease with Special Reference of Ayurveda and Yoga, J. Res. Ayur., Siddha: 1: 4: 1981.

CHAPTER 5

Clinical Manifestations of Disease

Disease is not a static entity but is a dynamic process involving a dramatic or insidious onset, a short or prolonged course and ending in recovery, disability or death. Any illness appears to have basically two phases in its evolution. One is the Pre-pathogenesis phase characterised by the period preceding the onset of disease in man. Under optimal conditions, the interaction between the causative agent, host (man) and the environment results in disease that may range from a single isolated case (e.g. Tonsillitis) to epidemics (e.g. malaria). The second is the Pathogenesis phase characterised by the entry of the disease agent in the human host. A certain period of time (known as incubation period) usually elapses between the entry of the causative agent and onset of clinical manifestations (symptoms and signs) of illness in the individual. The patient during the incubation period may remain apparently healthy and ambulant but nevertheless is not free from identifiable or non-identifiable tissue and physiological changes which occur during the incubation period. These changes are thus subclinical i.e. it is difficult to recognise these by the usual methods of diagnosis. After a period of incubation, when the health equilibrium is disturbed, the clinically evident signs and symptoms of that specific illness begin to appear indicating that the patient is sick. The clinical features may not be clear-cut during the first few days of illness (e.g. Typhoid fever) (early pathogenic period) but as the disease advances these signs and symptoms usually become clear-cut to enable a clinical diagnosis to be made with ease. The end results of the disease process may be complete recovery, chronicity, disability or death. All these course of events have been termed as the natural history of disease. Therefore, at one end of the spectrum of disease are inapparent infections or subclinical cases which are not ordinarily identified and at the other end are fatal illnesses. In the middle end of the spectrum the illnesses range in severity from mild to severe.

Certain diseases having infective origin especially communicable diseases usually pass through six stages during the course of the illness. These are briefly described below:

(1) **Incubation Period:** It is the time interval between the entry of the disease agent in the body and appearance of clinical symptoms and signs.

(2) **Prodromal period:** This is a short period ranging from 1 to 4 days and is characterised by rather vague symptoms and signs such as headache, fever, bodyache, restlessness, constipation etc. Clinical diagnosis is usually not possible during this stage because of vagueness of clinical findings. The patient is nevertheless infectious to others.

(3) **Fastigium:** The patient is ill and takes to bed; the clinical features become clear-cut and there is no difficulty usually in diagnosing the condition on clinical grounds.

(4) **Defervescence:** The body defences begin to take an upper hand over the infectious pathogen; the patient begins to feel better.

(5) **Convalescence:** The patient recovers but may still harbour in disease agent (convalescent carrier).

(6) **Carrier:** The individual recovers from illness and in some cases may continue to harbour the disease agent for varying periods (Chronic carrier) (e.g. Amoebiasis, Typhoid fever).

Cardinal Manifestations of Disease

When the health of an individual is disturbed or deranged due to any cause, it manifests itself in the form of symptoms and signs, which constitutes disease or illness.

Symptom: Is defined as that perceived or felt by the patient in the form of altered or disagreeable sensations or functions of the body and mind. Symptoms are the external manifestations of the internally deranged Dynamic Force. It is the subjective evidence of disease.

Example of altered sensations: Burning in stomach, burning headache, numbness in any part of the body etc.

Example of altered functions: Loss of appetite, sleeplessness, difficulty in breathing, constipation, paralysis, deafness etc.

Sign: Is defined as that perceived or observed or detected by the examining person or physician. It is an objective evidence of disease.

Examples: Yellowness of eyes is a sign of jaundice, breathlessness or dyspnea on exertion is a sign of heart disease. Pallor of conjunctiva is a sign of anaemia etc.

Syndrome: Is defined as a combination of symptoms and signs which occur in disease. For example, redness, swelling, pain, tenderness (pain on pressure), limitation of function or movement of the affected area constitute the syndrome of inflammation. Fever, vomiting and tenderness at Mc. Burney's point is a syndrome of Appendicitis. Coldness of the body, cold perspiration, fainting and low blood pressure is a syndrome of shock etc.

Subjective symptoms are of great diagnostic value when properly elucidated, interpreted, and analysed and may, at times suggest the right diagnosis even before physical examination is carried out.

A study of symptoms is an integral and preliminary part of any clinical examination. The science of symptoms is called symptomatology. A group of symptoms, characteristic of a disease process, is referred to as a symptom complex. By pathognomonic symptom is meant a symptom characteristic enough to clinch the right diagnosis.

It is important to realise that a symptom although strongly suggestive of disease of one system, may also be encountered in diseases affecting one or more of the other systems. For example, dyspnea (breathlessness), although suggestive of heart disease, may also be noted in respiratory and renal diseases. Similarly, fits or convulsions although usually neurological in origin, may be due to heart disease (Stokes-Adams attack) or renal failure.

Therefore, the natural history of disease or the course of disease process in man comprises basically two phases:

(1) **Pre-pathogenesis phase:** This refers to the period Preliminary to the Onset of Actual Disease in man. Man is not yet involved but he is in the midst of disease. Potentially we are in the prepathogenesis period of many diseases, e.g. Typhoid fever, Poliomyelitis, Tetanus etc., but only when the three factors, namely, the causative agent (living and non-living), the host (man) and the environment (physical, biologic and social) interact, the disease process is initiated in man. This is also known as the 'Epidemiological Triad.' Under optimal conditions, the interaction between the agent, host and

environment results in disease that ranges from a single isolated case to epidemics.

(2) **Pathogenesis phase:** This period begins with the entry of the disease agent in the human host. A certain period of time usually elapses between the entry of the disease agent and onset of clinical signs and symptoms; this is called the 'incubation period,' which varies from one disease to another. The patient during the incubation period may remain apparently healthy and ambulant but nevertheless is not free from tissue and physiological changes which occur during the incubation period. These changes are subclinical i.e. it is difficult to recognise them by the usual methods of diagnosis. Medical science has not yet advanced to the extent that disease can be diagnosed in the incubation period. After a period of incubation, when the health equilibrium is disturbed, the signs and symptoms of disease begin to appear indicating that the patient is sick. The signs and symptoms may not be clear-cut during the first few days of illness (early pathogenesis period) but as the disease advances these signs and symptoms usually become clear-cut to enable a clinical diagnosis to be made with ease. The end results of the disease process may be complete recovery, chronicity, disability of death.

KRIYA KALA

Due to many causes (both external and internal), the Tridoshas get vitiated first and also vitiate the Dhatus, resulting in illness. Therefore, from the time of origin of the imbalance of the Tridoshas, a sequence of pathological changes occur in the body beginning at microscopic level (biochemical) to macroscopic level (organic and tissue changes). All this combined together is termed as the disease process. This disease process is also known as 'Kriya

Kala.' It has been defined as the knowledge pertaining to the pathological changes that occur in the Dosha, Dushya (Dhatus), Agni, Srotas and other elements of the body.

The Different Kriyakalas

The biotransformations occurring in the body to maintain homeostasis (Dosha satmya) are very subtle. The main factors involved for the changes to maintain homeostasis are mostly related to the seasons and dietic habits of the individuals. The pathological changes that are due to the effect of seasons on doshas, resulting in their imbalance is termed as 'Ritu Kriyakala and those due to changed dietary habits are termed as 'Vyadhi Kriyakala.' Each dosha passes through stages namely—Samchaya, Prakopa and Prashamana in every season. Through the Ritu charya, Dinacharya and dietary regulation, subclinical manifestations resulting from Dosha vishamya (vitiated doshas) can be controlled.

Due to excessive intake of food and exertion, the effects of the vitiated doshas tend to be strong and the clinical manifestations resulting from them cause acute illness.

The Kriyakala has been divided into 6 types for the purpose of delineation of the spectrum of the illness. These are :

A. Samchaya
B. Prakopa
C. Prasara
D. Sthana Samsraya
E. Vyakti
F. Bheda.

A. The First Kriyakala—(Samchaya)

Samchaya means accumulation occurring at the predominant site or location of the doshas.

e.g. Vata vrudhi (Predominence); Pakvasaya (Intestine) Pitta vruddi: Adho Amasaya (lower part of stomach) Kapha vrudhi.

If the vruddi is less vigorous the following manifestations are seen.

1. Vata Samchaya character:

   a. Sthabda koshtatha: Heaviness of stomach, with sensation of immobility.

   b. Poorna koshtatha: Always feel fullness of stomach.

2. Pitta samchaya character:

   Yellowish discoloration of skin, slight rise in body temperature.

3. Kapha samchaya character:

   Heavyness of lower parts of body, laziness, disinterest in work.

When the above said manifestations are perceived by the body, it tries to regulate itself by showing aversion to foods which are thought to have provoked the dosha and taking those foods which may ameliorate the condition. Therefore, it is seen as a natural host defence mechanism against disease entry into the body.

At this stageof Samachaya if proper precautions are taken with regard to food intake and exercise, the disease can be cured at the subclinical stage only. On the otherhand, if the person neglects the Samchaya symptoms and continues to consume the provocative factors, it results in the more vitiation of doshas and this leads to the stage of Prakopa.

B. The Second Kriyakala—(Prakopa)

The accumulated doshas if uncontrolled will spread to other sites resulting more manifestations.

1. Vataprakopa character:
   - (a) Koshta thodamu: Uneasy feeling in epigastric region, pain.
   - (b) Samcharana: Heavy feeling in the upper part of the abdomen.
2. Pittaprakopa character:
   - (a) Amlika—Sour vomiting
   - (b) Pipasa—Thirst, Burning in throat
   - (c) Paridahamu—Burning pains in stomach, throat and esophagus.
3. Kaphaprakopa character:
   - (a) Aversion to food
   - (b) Burning in chest, pain and breathlessness.

Even though the above said clinical features cause ill-health and are severe compared to Samchaya they are not as severe to cause any loss of work etc. When proper treatment is instituted during this period, the abnormal doshas can be brought to normal and to their original sites. But in practice, few patients consult the physician during this stage..

C. The Third Kriyakala—(Prasara)

Prasara is the stage where the vitiated doshas affect other sites of the body in more severe form causing pathological changes there also.

It is to be noted that out of the three doshas, only Vata dosha has the capability to spread to other regions of the body. Pitta and kapha do not have the inherent capacity to spread by themselves, but need the help of vata to move to the places. During this prasara stage, the vitiated pitta and kapha are carried to other sites with the help of vata. The way the vitiated tridoshas travel to other places has been compared to the behaviour of flood waters which over power the gates of the dam and flow downwards with great furiosity. In this way, the displaced doshas manifest themselves. These are described as follows:

1. The features of vata prasara:
   - (a) Spreading to an abnormal site (Vimarga Gamana)
   - (b) Rumbling sensation in Intestine (Aatopa)
2. The features of Pitta prasara:
   - (a) Voshama—Burning sensation of pain, Thirst.
   - (b) Choshama—Burning in stomach and chest
   - (c) Paridhaha—Burning in every part of the body.
3. The features of kapha prasara :
   - (a) Anorexia, Dyspepsia, Angasada and Chardi.

The above said clinical manifestations are seen in majority of patients. In addition other clinical manifestations may be observed depending on the displaced sites of the vitiated doshas.

Compared to Samchaya and Prakopa, Prasara stage of illness is more in severity. The resulting illness leads to prostration and inability to do work.

The Progression of the Clinical Manifestations

The vitiated doshas in earlier stages of illness (Samchaya, Prakopa, Prasara) move from Mahakoshta (Alimentary tract) to all parts of the body through Rasa Dhatus, expressing their manifestations. That is why the features of the first 3 stages of Kriyakala are termed as Paridhavamana (rotating dosha characters).

The vitiated doshas in the first 3 stages of Kriyakala are not so powerful to alter the Saptadhatus. As long as the Saptadhatus have their own strength not affected, they cannot be altered by vitiated doshas. Therefore if patients consult an experienced physician when their illness is in early stages only, then the dhatus can be protected from further damage and organic/tissue changes can be prevented. It also results in increased immunity (resistance) of the body.

Paridhavamana (the rotating) dosha characters:

I. Vata Vruddii (Aggravated)

a. Vata Vyadhi—Karsyavata (weakness of body), discolouration of body skin to karshna (red colour mixed with black), Aruna (light red), Shyama (black) etc. or the disappearance of the original colour of the skin and its replacement by the above said colours.

1. Pathological changes in character: Karyavata (slimness of the body), Kharatva (stiffness), Parushatva (hardening), Sushiratva (emptyness), Ruksha (dryness), Rankshya (lack of softness).

2. Pathological changes in activity:

Soola (pain)
Ruk (Severe pain), Bheda (cutting pain)
Thoda (pain resembling pressure)
Vyadha (Pain, uneasiness)
Aarti (spasmodic pain)
Bhanga (breaking pain)
Soandana (pain as if applying pressure and releasing it)
Dausana (knawing pain)
Vimodhana (Pain as if chilling)
Vudreshtana (squeezing type of pain)
Tadana (pain as if beaten with stick)
Peedana (unbearable pain)
Chedana (splitting type of pain)

Veshtana (pain as if tied with thread)
Supti (hypo or anaesthesia)
Anga harsha, romaharsa

3. Altered movement

Sransa—loosening of joints
Tyaga—forgetfulness
Bhramsa—destruction
Sthamba—stoppage
Bhanga—breaking, dryness
Cheshta—movement of body
Chala—movement of some part of body
Sankocha—constriction
Kampa—tremors
Sputani—fractures
Kshobha—pain
Vikshepa—always uneasy feeling in limbs
Vislesha—weakness of all limbs
Vudghatana—contact of one part of body with the other.
Namana—bending down
Vunnamana—getting up (swelling)
Humdana—bending side
Pangutiva—lameness
Kubjatva—kyphoscoliosis
Paripathan—unable to stand
Parva sthamba—debility
Parva sankocha—destruction of joints
Parva kheda—pain in joints
Asthikheda—bone pains
Kantho dhavamsa - pain in throat (pain during swelling)
Vakaparushya—hoarseness
Karnanada—buzzing ears
Dhristi vramoha—unable to see objects clearly
Aasya-vyrasya—bitter taste
Jrumbha—excess yawning

Aadhmana—flatulence and distension of upper abdomen
Sanga—inability to pass urine and stools
Trusha—thirst
Vushna kamitva—desire for hot foods
Garbha Vikara—deformed foetus,
Prolonged pregnancy, loss of semen, sleeplessness, excessive love, fear, tears, sympathy, irrelevant talk, unstable mind etc.

(b) Deficient Vata characters:

Manda chestatha—slowness of work

Adpavakatvam—less talk
Apraharsha—unhappiness
Muda sanjatha—idiocy
Angasanda—weakness of body
Prasekam—bleeding from mouth and nose.

II. Pitta:

(a) Pitta aggravation characters:

1. Change in colour—e.g. yellow discolouration in eyes, urine, stool, nose, skin in addition appearance of blue, red, yellow colour.

2. Altered activity - Excess heat, burning

Kandu—itching, urticaria
Kodha—eruptions
Kleda—excess fluid
Srava—excess discharges
Paka—ulcerations
Trusha—thirst
Poothigandhi—foul smell
Brahma—giddiness
Moorcha—faintness
Santhapa—excess sleep

Aasyavrasya—feeling of bitter, sour, and salty taste
Seethakamitva—desire for cold substances.

3. Mental changes :

Tamah pravesa—lack of knowledge about environment,
Aarathi—unhappiness
Mada—weakness of senses, sluggishness

b. Pitta weakness:

Mandagni—deficient agni
Arochaka—dystaste
Aviaka—dyspepsia
Mandoshnatha—deficient heat
Nishprabhata—lustreless eyes, face and skin
Angaparnshya—lacking softness of body parts
Sthamba—immovability. tumours, heaviness, whiteness of eyes and nails, coldness of body etc.

III. Kapha:

(a) Aggravated kapha characters:

1. Varna alteration—whitish discoloration.

2. Alteration in activity

Sythya—coldness
Kandu—itching
Atisneha— excess sliminess
Kleda—swelling, edema
Vutseda—swelling
Sthirya—loss of movement, heaviness, hardness, excessive discharge from nose and mouth etc.
Apakti—dyspepsia
Vyrasya—sweet and salty tastes

Sandhivisesha—weakness of joints
Tandra—Yawning, excessive sleep
Mental disorders—lack of interest, unsatiety.

(b) Deficiency of kapha and its characters :

Ruksha—emptiness of stomach
Parisosha—dryness
Antardaha—burning sensation inside the body
Thirst—desire for water
Dhumayana—sensation of vapours coming from body
Sandhi sydhilya—Angamardha (body pains) - suffering due to excessive Ruksha
Vepana—mild trembling of upper and lower limbs, giddiness, weakness etc.

D. The Fourth Kriyakala—(Sthana Samsraya)

Sthana Samsraya may be defined as the accumulation of Doshas at one site. The aggravated doshas move all over the body with the help of Rasadhatu. In this way, the vitiated doshas move in the three stages of Kriyakala i.e. Samchaya, Prakopa and Prasara. But it is to be noted that due to altered dietary habits or weakness of ojas and many other causes which obstruct the srotas. in addition to doshas, Dhatus are also affected. Because of this reason, Koshtagni (Pachakagni) also gets vitiated and produces Amarasa. This Amarasa then gets mixed up with the Dhatus and then spreads all over the body, but accumulation takes place only extracellularly. The provocative factors also get accumulated in these dhatus. This is called Sthana Samsraya. Therefore, for the Sthana Samsrayavastha to get manifested, the three pathological changes are essential viz., excessive secretion of Amarasa, obstructed srotas (srota dhrusti), deficient ojas. The places where this three pathological changes were induced, those places or anatomical sites of the body show the manifestations of illness. In this way, the Amasaya derived doshas flow through srotas and reach the sapta dhatus (which constitute the body structure). This flow of doshas to Dhatu is described as 'Sakhabhi gamanam.' Thus the displaced doshas produce clinical manifestations which are termed as 'Purva Rupa.' That is the group of subclinical symptoms manifested before the full blown disease picture (Rupa). This whole disease process has been described as Sthana Samsraya.

The Purva Rupa stages is of two types:

(a) Samanya Purva Rupa:

The resulting manifestation due to Dosha—Dushya Samurchana are non-specific and mild in character. Majority of the illness are of this kind only. Therefore, it is difficult to diagnose them easily and the vitiated doshas cannot be identified. But the nature of the disease may be predicted.

(b) Visishta Purvarupa:

The mild expression of the specific symptoms and signs of forthcoming disease itself constitute visible purvarupa.

If the physician can percieve the illness in this stage the physician may be in a position to prevent its further progression and treat accordingly. If the disease occurs, then also permanent cure can be effected. The pathological changes occurring in the organs can be brought back to normal and the patient's health is restored.

E. The Fifth Kriyakala—(Vyakti)

When the disease is not treated in the 4th stage (Sthana samsraya) itself, it then progresses to the fifth stage known as 'Vyakti' where the full blown clinical features of illness are observed. This stage of illness is also known as 'Rupa.' The symptoms for Rupa as described in ancient texts are: Sansthana, Vyanjana, Vinda, Lakshana, Chihna and Aakriti.

In this stage, it is not difficult to diagnose the specific illness because the clinical manifestations are completely expressed. We can also elicit the underlying provocative factor for the specific disease.

The clinical manifestations can be divided into two types:

1. Common Symptoms: These are common for many illness and therefore non specific.
2. Particular symptoms: Depending upon the Dosha-Dhatu-Srota affection specific manifestations are seen.

The main provocative factors are labelled as Agantuja (external) and Sthana (local).

Agantuja causes—Due to altered dietary habits, the aggravated doshas, getting mixed with the rasa dhatus and spreading throughout the body carry various clinical features constitute Agantuja Dosha. The predominant dosha which causes the specific illness during the Sthana samsraya is known as 'Sthanka dosha.' This also is termed as principal factor.

Therefore during the Rupa stage of illness, the common symptoms produced are due to Agantuja dosha and specific symptoms are due to 'Sthana dosha.' When we compare manifestations due to Agantuja and Sthanka, it appears that those due to Agantuja are more severe and in number, than that of Sthanka causes.

This is the reason why, Agantuja causes have taken predominance over Sthanka causes—i.e. as the main aetiology of diseases in classical Ayurvedic texts. For example Vata jwara (fever). Here Vata dosha is Agantuja. In Vata fever, the main symptom is rise in temperature and its principal cause is pitta dosha. But the role of pitta is not discussed here. This is deliberately pointed out by the ancient Ayurvedists in the belief that the physician will be able to diagnose and perceive the Agantuja cause more easily.

Note that the two doshas (provocative factors), Agantuja and Sthanka need not always be present separately in any disease process. They can be combined together. For example in diseases due to excessive intake of paittic producing substances, the paittic dosha itself constitutes the Agantuja and Sthanka.

During treatment also, the physician should concentrate more on the Agantuja cause and its elimination. In majority of cases, once Agantuja factors are removed by treatment, Sthanka factors also get subsided. However, in certain diseases, treatment may be needed for both factors involved in disease causation.

Whatever may be said, one should remember that treatment should be directed at the predominantly affected dosha and the predominant clinical manifestations of illness to get complete cure of the diseased individual.

F. The Sixth Kriyakala—(Bheda)

If still uncontrolled in the fifth stage of Vyakti Kriyakala, then the illness passes on to the sixth stage Bheda. The grossly vitiated dosha-dhatu-srotas then become difficult to treat. The pathological changes induced are not amenable to treatment alone even if the patient is of long lived character and sees a good physician and also the God blessings; then also he may have palliation of symptoms only but has to live as a patient for the rest of the life. If the subject is having short span of life, without adequate treatment, and no sympathy from god, then that patient will definetly die.

Therefore, the stage of Bheda in Kriyakala denotes that its manifestations are completely different from the preceding 5 stages of Kriyakala. In addition, another two groups of symptoms are also included under Bheda. These are:

1. Upadrava (unforeseen manifestation)
2. Prodromal symptoms of death.

Upadrava: The symptom complex evident at the end stage of a severe illness or the symptoms seen during convales cence stage of illness, constitute 'Upadrava.' (Upa= nearby; Dravati=tendency to move). These Upadrava symptom complex can arise not only due to the severe illness from which patient is suffering, but also from dietary habits, physician treatment and old age. In general, the symptoms seen simply belong to those of the predominant vitiated dosha which is the cause of the primary illness. Therefore, it is evident that Upadrava manifestations also subside once the basic vitiated dosha is treated. Also, if the Upadrava symptoms are severe enough than the vitiated dosha, then treatment should be directed towards Upadrava symptoms first, than the dosha itself. This is because the disease with Upadrava appears to be difficult to eradicate by treatment.

It is also to be noted that any disease which reaches the stage of Bheda, need not have Upadrava characters. If the ojas is strong enough and good treatment is given at appropriate time, then Upadrava symptoms usually does not arise.

That's why, during the time of treatment, Ayurvedic medicine stresses the importance of knowing the subject's degree of immunity (resistance to disease) before any treatment can be initiated.

The clinical features of death

If the treatment fails, and the disease pervades the whole body, many symptoms are observed which are peculiar and point towards death. The manifestations are seen in various parts of the body including the senses.

Rishta Bhasa

These are symptoms which resemble those of symptoms of terminal illness but not a terminal illness. Inexperienced physicians may get confused with these symptoms and leaves the case as in the end stage. Therefore, one should always be aware of those apparent symptoms of death and should differentiate from those of death. This has been strongly stressed to in Charaka Samhita.

Udarka

This has been termed as the manifestations resulting from non-treatment or inadequate treatment of the clinical symptoms during the Kriyakala. In three stages of Samchaya, Prakopa and Prasara—prevention of illness, decrease of the strength of the disease process and restoration of health occur; in the fourth stage (Sthana Samsraya)—curability of diseases; in the fifth stage (Vyakti) - curing of the disease; and the incurability and the opportunistic ailments; all these constitute Udarka (end stage of illness).

Therefore an able physician should see that the Udarka and Rista manifestations do not over ride the patient while treatment is being provided.

DOSHA PAKA—DHATU PAKA

Paka has been defined as the complete digestion and assimilation of the substance in question. The vitiated doshas move along various parts of the body with the help of Amarasa. However, this is not a permanent feature. With bodily strength (immunity), slow elimination of the doshas. restricting diet intake and with effective therapy, the strength of the Koshtagni (Jatharagni) increases. With the help of Jatharagni, the vitiated doshas and their associated Amdoshas will also get digested. The digested vitiated factors result in restoration of the tridoshas to their normal place and activity. Therefore, diseases resulting from the vitiated doshas will also get cured. This stage is described as 'Dosha paka Sthithi'. This is good for health.

The Features of Dosha Paka (the Features of Recovering Doshas)

Vata: (Features results from complete elimination of Amarasa) Visada, Ruksha, unobstructiveness, mild pain, Snehana, slow response etc.

Pitta: Reddishness, yellow colour, excess heat, bitter taste, mobility, Nigandha (the original character), taste, digestion of food etc.

Kapha: Phenila (froth formation), Pinditha (hardening), Pandu colour (whitish), Agandha (loss of smell); Nissara (tiredness), cleanliness of mouth.

If the above features of tridoshas are observed in the patient, one can come to conclusion that the doshas are getting restored to their original stage.

It is to be remembered that the digestion or necrosis (death) of the Sapta dhatus is detrimental to the body. When Koshtagni (and other agnis) is increased and starts destroying the Amdravyas, the Dhatus (tissues) also get destroyed along with the process. This results in pus formation and necrotic tissues leading to ulceration. Because of degradation of dhatus the ojas also gets destroyed, and the body also gets morbid leading to death of the individual. Therefore, excessive necrosis of dhatus (tissues) is always harmful to body and points to death.

The digestion of dhatus does not occur simultaneously in all tissues at the same time e.g. in Vidhradhi (*Abscess*), Gulma (Swelling) and other external ailments. Therefore one should be aware of the manifestations of Dhatu paka in order to restore the Dhatus. The physician should see that only vitiated dosha digestion and not that of the Dhatus should be the aim while treatment of the patient is contemplated.

Features of Dhatu Paka (Tissue Destruction)

Hruth sthamba (cardiac pain)
Vishakamba (constipation)
Heaviness of body parts
Distaste
Sleeplessness
Weakness

Pain between umbilicus and chest region (epigastric)

All the above symptoms indicated the early manifestation of Dhatu paka.

Others include:
Loss in inherent characters of the Dhatus
Kshaya (destruction)
Pus formation
Discharges
Excessive debility or senescence
Increased susceptibility to illness

On the other hand, deliberate induction of dhatu paka (tissue necrosis) is needed in certain disorders like Vidhradhi, Grandhi, Arbhunda (Tumors) etc. In these disorders, Bahya swedana, Lepana and selected food intake are carried out to bring a smooth transition for surgical correction of the disease.

CURABILITY OF DISEASES

The decision as to whether a particular disease can be cured or not is based mostly on the Vyakti and Bheda of Kriyakala, the Dosha dushya disequilibrium, the cause of illness etc. Usually, diseases can be divided into two—Curable and Incurable. The disease which can be treated completely without any remnants are said to be curable. The disease which are of long standing and can not be treated completely leading to death are said to be Incurable.

I. Curable diseases have been classified into Two:

(a) Early curable (Susadhya) and (b) not easily curable (Krucchha sadhya).

II Incurable diseases have been classified into two types - (A) Yapya (longstanding illness leading to death in future) (B) Pratyakhyaya or Anupakrama—death is sure with the illness.

I. Curable Diseases

(a) Susadhya (easily amenable) persons of adult age group who respond to any type of treatment-ailments arising from minor factors with no evidence of Upadrava, and with Samana (Equilibrium state) Dosha-Dhatu-Desa (country) and seasonal characters, with single disease, with single vitiated dosha and acute disease are all curable.

(b) Krucchha sadhya (Not easily amenable to cure): These diseases are those which have Nidana, Purvarupa, Rupa characters; unequal dosha, seasonal character; dosha, dhatu-prakriti; with excessive Upadrava, and with two diseased states; with two vitiated doshas, and those who respond to surgery, cauterization methods; in those, who are pregnant women, old age, children are curable with difficulty.

II. Incurable Diseases

(A) ***Yapya***: These are the diseases which are of long duration with Dhatu, Marma, Bone, joint affections with Dwandaja (two doshas) and responding to proper pathya (dietary restriction), Medicines etc.

(B) ***Pratya Khayaya:*** These are the diseases which arise from Tridoshas, having clinical manifestations of severe degree with Arishta character; those with extreme debility and old age patients—illnesses are called Pratyakhyaya dosha.

Death

It is defined as that diseased state of the body which does not respond to the best treatment available at that time. Life is defined as the amalgamation of Sarira (body), the senses, satwa and soul and is known as Life span. Its viyoga (contrary to) is known as Death. The body has been said to die in two ways:

1. Aranthara Death

Even though life is present in the body, some parts of the body (from cellular to tissue level) are always in constant regeneration and death. These are not evident to the individual and go on subconsciously.

The meaning of sarira is 'seeryate'—i.e. with constant destruction. Therefore the constant transformation occur at the cellular level and this death constitutes Aranthara Death.

a. Prakriti: Inhealthy state, the constant biological processes going on in the body leading to aging.

b. Vikriti: Due to vitiated Tridoshas, poisonous bites of animals, plants, the tissue gets destroyed easily. This can be prevented. Some drugs can also be used to prevent or cure the condition. If timely treatment is not administered there will be rapid destruction of the tissues leading to death of the subject.

In the end stage of an illness, the tissue destruction takes place in two ways:

(i) With the combination of pitta and vata doshas, the Apaya bhuta in the Dhatus gets emptied or used up leading to tissue destruction. In this way, whole body gets destroyed and the vital organs lose their performance.

(ii) When there is mixing of pitta and kapha dosha, the Dhatus get necrosed and pus mixed with blood gets discharged outside. In the body, from specific outlets, Grandhi, Vidhradhi, Pidika ulcers arise along with whitish foul discharge. This is called puya or pus. In some diseases the discharge is watery, slimy; in others it is evident as pus mixed with blood.

All these indicate the destruction of tissues and vitiate the whole body with Malas (impurities). Charaka comments that these malas are like swords and the subjects should be protected from these malas.

2. Maha Marana (Death)

When all the dhatus are affected and Avantara death going on in the body either naturally or pathologically, the soul gets separated from the physical body. Along with it the cognative senses and mind also gets separated. In this way Maha marana (Actual death) has been defined as the separation or leaving of the soul (spirit) (Atma) from physical body (Sareera). When Atma leaves the body, immediately, the sarira (physical body) becomes lifeless, immobile, does not respond to stimulation and become dead wood. This panchabhautic wood should then be burned with fire.

Maha marana can be divided into two types:

(i) Kalamarana—The individual's past deeds, virtues, life span etc.—once all these are completed then by nature the body dies. This is invariable.

(ii) Akalamaranam (Untimely death)—Death resulting from disease, accidents, natural events etc., even though, there is life span in the individual—is known as Akalamaranam (untimely death). This can be prevented to some extent.

NOTES AND REFERENCES

1. Vinaya Kumar A., Infectious Diseases: Diagnosis and Management in Clinical Practice 1994 ed. CBS Publishers, Delhi.

2. Vakil R.J., Golwalla S.P., Text Book of Clinical Diagnosis, Asian Publishing House, Bombay, 1969.

3. Sri Kanta Murthy K.R., Ayuveda Vigyan, Viyar translated into Telugu by Sharma K.L., Dattatreya & Co., Rajamundry, 1980.

4. Keim Gertrud, Doshic Rhythm and Their importance in prevention of Illness and Promotion of Health Jl. Educ. Ind. Med. 1: 1982.

5. Pande T.N., Principles of Treatment in Ayurveda, Personal Communication.

6. Sharma K.D., Principles of Diagnosis in Ayurveda, Personal Communication.

7. Narayana D.L., Roga Nirnayam (Telugu), Indian Medicine Sales House, Vijayawada, 1980.

CHAPTER 6

Case–Taking and Examination of the Patient and the Disease

History taking and examination of the patient is done in many ways in different schools of medicine. However, the aim of any system of examination of the patient is to diagnose the illness correctly.

Some of the observations of Ayurvedists in case taking are noted below :

1. Trividhi khalu roga—Visheshajnam bhavathi. Thadhyatha Apthopa deshah Prathyakshah Anumanam chethi - Charaka.

   Charaka has advised three ways of examining the patient.

   They are:

   Apthopadesh—Interrogation of the patient
   Pratyaksha—Direct observation
   Anumana—Inference

2. "Darshan Sparshan Prashnah Parikshetat Rogeenum Rogam Nidana Prakrupa—Lakshanopashayaptibhih."

   Vaghbhata

The procedure advocated by Vaghbhatta is in close proximity to the modern medical history taking and examination of the patient. He has advocated eight methods (Ashtavidhi) of examination of the patient.

They are:

Darshan—Observation
Sparshan—Touch
Prashn—Questioning
Causation of illness—Enquiry
Purva Rupa—Prodromal stage
Rupa—Manifested stage
Upashaya—Therapeutic diagnosis
Samprapti—Pathogenesis

After the eight methods of examination of the subject a systemic examination of the body of the individual is to be carried out. Different approaches are followed by various physicians. However, the general consensus of approach adopted is given below:

1. Main complaints
2. Family history
3. Past history
4. Present history
5. Systemic examination
    - Digestive system (Pachan sansthan)
    - Circulatory system (Raktvah sansthan)
    - Respiratory system (Swas-praswas sansthan)
    - Urinary system (Muthravah sansthan)
    - Nervous system (Nadi sansthan)
6. Chemical examination
7. Symptomotology (Lakshan)

8. Diagnosis (Rognishchith)
9. Treatment (Chikitsah)

***Note*:** Most of the procedures for the systemic examination of the patient are similar to those followed by modern physician. Therefore they are not further described here. The reader may refer to the books on clinical methods of diagnosis in modern medicine for further study. Classical methods of examination are described under Sroto-Partiksha (see later).

In general, therefore, at the time of examination of the patient, the following eight parameters should be stressed in addition to systemic examination.

1. Nadi—pulse
2. Muthra—Urine
3. Mala—stool
4. Jinha—tongue
5. Shabdah—voice
6. Sparsha—touch
7. Netrah—eye
8. Aakriti—face

1. NADI-PARIKSHAH

"Sthirachittah Prasannatma Mansa Ch Visharadah. Sprushedam Gulibhiranadeem Janiyada Dakshinakare."

At the time of examination of the pulse, the clinician should have peace of mind and keep rapt attention, and then examine the pulse of the right hand of the patient with the three fingers (Index, middle and ring fingers).

"Tyaktrah Muthra preshasyay Sukhaseenasyay rogeenah. Antharjanu karasyapi Samhak Nadin Parikshayet."

When the patient has seated comfortably after emptying the bladder and evacuated the bowels, the patient's left hand pulse should be examined.

By examining the pulse, one can ascertain the state of the tridoshas—vata, pitta and kapha, dwanjaja and tridoshaja and also the curability and non-curability of the disease.

The pulse rate in different age groups is shown in table 6 1, 2. The character of pulse in different states of the Tridoshas is shown in table 6.3. The ratio of pulse to respiratory rate is 4:1.

Table 6.1 : Pulse Rate in Different Age Groups (Normal Range)

Age	*Beats per Minute*
In the foctus in utero	150 to 140
In new-born infant	140 to 130
During first year	130 to 115
During second year	115 to 105
During third year	105 to 95
From 3 to 7 years	100 to 90
From 7 to 14 years	90 to 85
From 14 to 21 years	85 to 75
From 21 to 65 years	75 to 65
In old age	85 to 75

Table 6.2 : Changes in Pulse Rate and Rhyhm in Various Physiological and Pathological Conditions

Pulse rate Increased	*Pulse rate Decreased*
Physiological	
children	familial or hereditary
women	athletes
standing	yogis

eating
exercise
emotion

Pathological

fever	
thyrotoxicosis	convalescence after infection
infections	pneumonia, influenza, typhoid fever.
tonsillitis	raised intracranial tension
diphtheria	heart block, jaundice
septic fever	
drugs—adrenaline	
atropine	

Table 6.3 : Character of the Nadi (Pulse) in Physiological and Pathological States of the Tridoshas

Physiological State	
Vata	- twisting
Pitta	- unstable
Kapha	- stable
imperceptible pulse as after-exertion, thirst, heat exposure, hunger, sexual intercourse	
Pathological State	
Aggravated Vata	- snake or stretched wire like on palpation
Aggravated Pitta	- unstable movement like crow-walking
Aggravated Kapha	- movement like a frog, hen
Sannipathic (tridoshaja)	- dull frog, hen strong and intermittent
Terminal stages (death)	- dull, strong, interrnittent and getting displaced in movement

2. URINE EXAMINATION (MUTRA PARIKSHA)

After examining the pulse, one has to observe the urine of the patient. Urine examination is especially done in Prameha (Diabetes and related diseases).

Changes in urine colour in different illness:

Aggravated Vata	-	blue, white or some times slight-rising sun colour.
Aggravated Pitta	-	Hot to touch, dark yellow and yellowish color.
Aggravated Kapha	-	Whitish in colour; and cold to touch with soft consistency.
Aggravated Tridosha	-	dark, reddish and smoky urine and hot to touch.
Excessive phosphate crystals excretion	-	whitish sediment
Kidney disorders	-	greenish colour
Blackwater fever	-	dark colour

In addition to routine urine examination one should also look for bile salts and bile pigments, Urobilinogen, blood, red cells, renal casts etc.

Alterations in Quantity of Urine Excreted in 24 hours

Increase urination is seen in —

- Rainy and Winter season
- Excessive intake of watery foods such as cucumber, snakegourd, etc.
- Diabetes mellitus (Madhu-meha)
- Diabetes insipidus (Vudak-meha)
- A sudden check of perspiration (Swetavarodh)

Decreased urination is seen in -

- Summer season
- Fever (Jwar)
- Perspiration (Swethadhikyatah)
- Diarrhea (Atisar)
- Vomiting (Vamanadhikyathah)
- Cholera (Visuchika)
- Ascites (Jalodhar)
- Anaemia (Pandu)
- Purgation

Urine Examination with Oil

For this test patient Midstream Urine (MSU) specimen is to be examined. In early morning the parts are cleaned and mid catch of the urine is taken in a clean bottle. The bottle is kept in good light and one drop of oil is put in urine to be tested.

1. In aggravated Vata—the oily drop floats in urine and also imparts red (Raskh) and dark colour to urine.
2. In aggravated Kapha—the oily drop mixes with the urine and settles at the bottom.
3. In aggravated Pitta—once the oily drop is put in urine one can see watery bubbles rising up to the surface.
4. When the oil is dropped in urine, if it spreads on urine, it is said to indicate curability of the disease from which the patient is suffering from, and if it does not spread on the urine surface, it indicates incurability of the disease.

3. STOOL EXAMINATION

Normal stool is yellowish brown in colour with semi-solid consistency.

1. Aggravated Vata - Stool is dry, wrinkled nature with black colour.
2. Aggravated Pitta - yellowish or grennish color with watery consistency.
3. Aggravated Kapha - Whitish colour, slimy and the stool spreads on the surface of the pan.

The character of stool in different illnesses is shown in Table 6.4.

Table 6.4 : Table Showing Character of Stool in Different Illness (Dwivedi & Pandey 1975)

Modern Name	*Ayurvedic Name*	*Character of stool*
Dyspepsia	Ajeerna	Foul smelling
Dysentry	Atisara	Bloody
Fistula	Bhagandar	Blood mixed stool
Liver disorders	Yakrit vyadhi	Clay coloured
Diarrhoea	Pravahika	Frothy
Threadworms	Spithkrimi	Mucous, watery
Rickets	Shosh	Mucous, watery
Constipation (Obstinate)	Teevre Koshtbaddatha	Mucous, hard
Enteric fever	Antric jwar	Pea soup, pus and blood mixed stool
Intestinal abscess	Aantra Vidhati	Pus containing stool
Intestinal Haemorrhage	Aantric Raktasravadikya	Tarry
Obstruction of bile	Pittavarodha	White colour
Ingestion of Iron Bismuth salts	Loha and Vismay Bakshan	Black coloured
Cholera Enteritis, Sprue	Sangarahani	Foul smelling

4. TONGUE EXAMINATION (JIHVA PARIKSHA)

It is to be remembered that tongue examination is useful not only in Alimentary disorders, but also sometimes in diseases of the Nervous system. Therefore, tongue examination should be carried out in special cases thoroughly.

Aggravated Vata - Tasteless, dry, rough and fissured

Aggravated Pitta - Red coloured, thirsty

Aggravated Kapha - Large, white coloured, red coloured

Aggravated Tridoshas - black colored

(In diseases of liver, spleen and constipation, tongue discolouration may also be seen).

The character of tongue in different illnesses is shown in the Table 6.5.

Table 6.5 : Table Shows the Character of Tongue In Different Illnesses (Dwivedi & Pandey 1975)

Character of tongue	*Diseased status*
Dry	Excessive loss of fluids from the body, nervous prostration.
Coated dry	Disorders of alimentary tract
Brown coloured, dry	Nervous people
Coated or furred	Fever, disorders of alimentary tract. Enlarged tonsils (Tundikeri vruddhi), neuralgia, pain (Nadi shool)
Flabby	Anaemia (Pandu), Glomerul-on ephritis (Vrukkh shoodh), Dyspepsia (Agni-mandya)
Red coloured. smooth shining, slimy	Diabetes (Premeha)
Blue colored Papillae covered	Heart diseases

(Contd.)

Character of tongue	*Diseased status*
Red coloured	Dyspepsia, drunkards
Immobile (Gathiheen)	Paralysis (ghath)
Ulcerated (Vranayakth)	Decayed teeth, syphilis (phirang), dyspepsia (Agnimandya).
Bitten tongue	Epilepsy (Apasmara), Tetanus (Dhanusthamb), serious disorders of stomach.
Yellow	Liver (Yakrut) disorders.

5. VOICE EXAMINATION (SHABDA PARIKSHA)

Alterations:

Vata disorder - hoarseness

Paittic disorders - clear voice

Kaphaja disorders - heavy

(Slow voice, hoarseness of voice, nasal speech are said to be incurable cases in ancient Ayurveda).

6. SKIN EXAMINATION (SPARSHA)

Vata disorders - skin is cold, rough

Paittic disorders - hot

Kaphaja disorders - cold

Fevers - skin will be hot, dry and rough

In inflammatory areas - skin will be hot.

(Sudden excessive perspiration of patients are said to be incurable).

7. EYE EXAMINATION (NETRAH)

Alterations:

Vata disorders - fearful, rough, mobile, smoky coloured

Paittic disorders - yellowish, bluish, reddish coloured, hot and lustre

Kaphaj disorders - lustreless, whitish and watery

Tridoshaja disorders - dark, rough, fearful reddish, depressed

If pupils are dilated, it probably indicates disorders of stomach (Amashaya), of small intestine (Antr.) along with disorders of brain.

If pupils are contracted it indicates inflammation of the optic nerve.

- If patient look with dilated eyes it indicated delirium
- In jaundice—conjunctiva is yellowish in colour
- If eyes are protruding, shining, red coloured—Congestion of brain and heart disorders should be suspected.
- In anaemia—eyes look pale.

8. EXAMINATION OF FACE (AAKRITI PARIKSHA)

Alterations:

Vata disorders - rough and expressionless

Paittic disorders - yellow coloured, red coloured, and hot

Kaphaj disorders - heaviness, slimy

If face is brownish coloured, nostrils reddish, eyes dilated death is to be suspected

If fever with constipation, facial expression will be sympathetic and eyes are blue coloured

If Pneumonia (Shleshmic sannipath) - flapping respiratory movements of face are seen.

SROTO PARIKSHA
SROTA SAMYA AND VYSHAMYA
(NORMAL AND ABNORMAL STATES OF SROTAS)

Ayurvedic examination of various systems of the body has been described as Sroto Pariksha. This concept of examination of the body systems is a little different from the modern clinical methods of diagnosis.

The gross and subtle forms of the existence of srotas in the body has been described in the Introductory chapter. The following is a description of the normal and abnormal states of the srotas, their causes, clinical manifestations and diagnosis of the abnormal states of the affected srotas.

All illnesses arise and manifest from the abnormal functioning of the srotas.

As long as the srotas functions are in normal state (Satmya sthithi), the sapta dhatus of the body and the various organs formed out of them, also function within their normal limits. Due to irregular and unhealthy intake of food and exercise, the srotas get vitiated and also vitiate the dhatus and the organs resulting in the production of diseases states in the body. This vitiated or pathological state of the srotas is also known as 'Khavaigunya' or 'Srotodusti.'

Causes of Srotodusti: The main causes of srotodusti are the irregular food intake and exercise. However, the various causes which affect a particular srota and cause srotodusti in that particular srotas has been described by Acharya Charaka (Ch. Vimana 5/0-22) See table 6-6. Sanjnavah and Manovah srotas get vitiated due to Asatmyendriyartha Prajnaparadha (see the chapter on Causation of disease). Of all these, Prajnaparadha is an important cause. The factors which lead to Prajnaparadha, such as, irregular food intake and exercise, cause srotodusti. Because of affection of srotas, the tridoshas which continuously flow in them also get vitiated, resulting in disease.

Table 6.6 : Causes of Srotodusti in Different Srotas

	Srotas	*Causes of srotodusti*
1.	Pranavah	destruction of dhatus, excessive exercise, starvation, excessive intake of rough diet, smoking, heat exhaustion, excessive cold and dust exposure.
2.	Vudakvah	excessive heat, Ama, alcohol intake, thirst; eating unboiled food, undue fears etc.
3.	Annavah	causes which provoke Jatharagni; irregular and excessive food intake, etc.
4.	Rasavah	excessive intake of heavy, cold and snigdha food, and water
5.	Raktavah	as in Rasavah, excess exposure to heat etc.
6.	Medovah	lack of exercise, eating food containing meda substances, alcohol intake etc.
7.	Mamsavah	daytime sleep, eating heavy, thick foods etc.
8.	Asthivah	intake of vata-vruddi producing diet excess destruction of dhatus, excess work etc.
9.	Majjavah	fracture of bones, etc.
10.	Sukravah	excess indulgence in sex and untimely sex
11.	Mutravah	excess fluid intake, destruction of dhatus, excess indulgence in sex, retention of micturition, etc.
12.	Pureeshvah	retention of defecation act, excess food intake, indigestible food intake, untimely food intake, mandagni, etc.
13.	Swedavah	exposure to heat and cold, excess sorrow, overwork, anger, weeping, and fears etc.

Note: For Sanjnavah and Manovah srotodusti, the main reasons attributed are the Asatmyendriyardah prajnaparadh, out of which Prajnaparadh is the most important cause. Prajnaparadh inturn, is affected by improper food and exercise (activity) which leads to vitiation of tridoshas and the Manasika doshas i.e. Raja and Tamas (Charaka Sutra 8/16).

Types of Srotodusti

1. Atipravrutti (overactivity)
2. Sangam (Nirodha) (Obstruction)
3. Srotograndhi (Siragrandhi) (Enlargement)
4. Vimarga gamana (Vunmarga gamana) (abnormal flow)

1. **Atipravrutti:** When the srotas are hyperactive, during healthy state, it is termed as Atipravrutti. For example, the normal respiratory rate (inspiratory-expiratory phase) of Pranavah srotas is 16 to 20 per minute. If it is excess of this, it constitutes atipravrutti. Increased heart beat, excessive movements of intestines, excessive formation of urine and stool—all indicate atipravrutti of the respective srotas.

2. **Sangam:** Partial or complete obstruction in the normal functioning of the srotas. e.g., in fever state due to obstruction of sweat glands, sweat is not secreted resulting in non perspiration. In diseases of the stomach, due to obstruction of Annavah srota, sweat is obstructed resulting in non-perspiration. In Shodh disease due to obstruction of Rasavah srota, there is swelling of skin and subcutaneous tissues. Obstruction of Mutravah srota causes, Asmari vrudddhi and Mutra bruchchi.

In this way, obstruction of srotas or sangam causes various clinical signs and symptoms. For many diseases, sangam of srotas has been found to be the main cause. That's why, the origin of all diseases has been described as due to obstruction of srotas (Sushruta Sutra 24/10).

3. **Srotagrandhi (Siragrandhi):** Some specific srotas and the related organs show pathological changes in the form of enlargement, or altered structure. e.g.,

Sleepada, Valmika grandhi, Arbuda. Vidhra dhi, Gulma etc.

4. **Vimarga gamana:** It means abnormal flow or pathologic flow. then the flow in the srotas of tridosha is abnormal, for e.g., Vamana (vomiting) is the upward movement of Annavah srotas. Vudavartam, Mudhagarbham are examples.

The above said four causes of srotodusti can occur singly or in combination resulting in diseases. Each disease may show single or multiple types of srotodusti.

In majority of instances, obstruction is the main cause of illness. This is followed in order of frequency, Atipravrutti, Srotograndhi and lastly, Vimarga gamana.

Due to atipravrutti of the particular srotas, in many cases, there occur Dhatu destruction (necrosis) and sometimes enlargement of dhatus (hyper-trophy of tissues). Srotosangam and Srotograndhi however cause hypertrophy of tissues only. The Vimarga gamana causes only abnormal function of the srotas.

From the above description it is evident that Srotodusti is the main cause of disease in any individual and the aim of any treatment should be to prevent Srotovaigunya or srotodusti because it is the root cause of any illness.

EXAMINATION OF DISEASE

Examination of the disease includes:

1. Pancha nidana (five factors)—Nidana, Purva rupa, Rupa, Upashya and Samprapti.

2. Shat Kriyakalas (six stages of disease evolution)—Chaya, Prakopa, Prasara, Sthana-samsraya, Vyakti and Bheda.

Pancha Nidana: Diseases can be diagnosed based on these five factors.

1. **Nidana (Aetiological Factors):** See the chapter on Causation of Disease.

   e.g., Pandu roga (Anaemia) due to eating of clay; dyspepsia due to untimely food intake; prameha arising due to taking of new rice etc.

2. **Purva-rupa (Prodromal symptoms):** Many diseases are due to single cause. However, one may not be able to diagnose particular disease on that cause alone. In such cases, many of the diseases may be diagnosed based on purva-rupa.

e.g., By taking foods which provoke Pitta dosha, two diseases arise

(a) Rakta pitta and (b) Amla pitta. These can be differentiated as follows:

Rakta pitta - chest pain, bloody discharge, weakness

Amla pitta - sour eructations, thirst, giddiness, nausea.

e.g., Yellowish urine mixed with blood is seen in both Raktapitta and Pittaja prameha. But, the earlier manifestations (purvarupa) of sweetish taste, heaviness of body, excessive urination, if present, constitute Prameha and if absent is the Raktapitta.

3. **Rupa (signs and symptoms):** It is easy to diagnose disease in this stage, provided the physician is well aware of the characteristic features of the illness.

Eg., Excessive body heat (Usna) is known as Jwar (fever).

Thick and whitish urine constitutes Prameha (diabetes mellitus and related diseases).

It has been said that 90 per cent of the diseases can be diagnosed based on the specific manifestations of illness.

4. **Upashaya (Homologues, Therapeutic Diagnosis):** It is a fact that two dissimilar diseases may express identical clinical features. On the otherhand, two similar (apparently) diseases may have different groups of clinical features. At that time, the diagnosis may have to be based on a trial of drugs and dietary changes to delineate the disease entities.

e.g., A patient may have the complaint of paralysis of muscle of thigh. This is seen both in Urusthamba and pure Vatic disease. Diagnosis is difficult at this stage. This can however be differentiated as follows:

If the suffering increases after performing Sneha Kriya—it is Urustham badisease.

If the suffering gets amelioration after Snehana kriya, it is Vatic illness.

This mode of differentiation is made possible because of the fact that in Urusthamba, along with the vata, kapha dominates and gets aggravated after Snehana kriya and thereby increase the suffering. The same Snehana in Vatic disease alone causes amelioration of suffering by removing rukshata. In this way, by Satmya and Asatmya (Upashaya, Anupashaya), diseases can be diagosed.

5. **Samprapti (pathogenesis):** Samprapti has been defined as the altered changes that occur in the dosha-dhatu-mala-equilibrium (dosha-dhatu-mala satmya sthi). Importance has been given to samprapti in Ayurvedic medicine and has been stressed much so that the physician can diagnose the disease accurately, if he/she perceives the clinical manifestations of illness that occur based on the underlying pathogenesis of the illness.

eg., A patient with anaemia may be diagnosed if he has the following features:

1. manifestations of excessive rasa dhatu
2. manifestations of deficient raktadhatu
3. whitish discolouration of body skin from its normal color.

The above said clinical features are seen only in Pandu roga, and the disease can be diagnosed only as Pandu roga.

From the above description it will be evident that if a physician is well acquainted with the Pancha nidana, he/she can diagnose the illness correctly and proper treatment may be instituted early in the course of the disease and the normal health restored in the shortest possible time.

Shat Kriyakalas : The six kriyakalas have already been described under clinical manifestations of disease (see the chapter on Clinical Manifestations of Disease). Nidana, Purva-rupa and Rupa are easily understood and Samprapti (the process of pathogenesis) has already been described. Upashaya (therapeutic diagnosis) needs however some explanation.

There are certain diseases, where the diagnosis become difficult or may not even be possible. In such cases certain therapeutic tests are done. This is called Upashaya. The definition of Upashaya according to Charaka is "the use of medicines, diet and regimen which are antagonistic directly or in effect to the causation factor, disease or both," (In modern Medicine, Upashaya has little application e.g., as in the case of suspected Pulmonary tuberculosis or any extra-pulmonary tuberculosis where antitubercular drugs like Isoniazid (INH), Thioacetazone are administered to see the amelioration of the illness.)

PRO-FORMA FOR EXAMINATION OF THE PATIENT

In short, the pro forma for the examination of the patient should consist of the following detailed information:

1. Prakopana Nidana (exciting factors of the disease)
2. Yoni (aetiological factors, disease origin from doshas)
3. Utthana (onset)
4. Adhisthana (localisation of the disease)
5. Sansthana (signs and symptoms)
6. Vedana (sensation of pain)
7. Shabda (sound)
8. Sparsha (touch)
9. Roopa (colour)
10. Rasa (taste)
11. Gandha (odour)
12. Upadrava (complication)
13. Vriddhi (stage of aggravation)
14. Sthana (steady continuance)
15. Kshaya (abatement)
16. Nama (name of disease i.e. diagnosis)
17. Udaraka (sequelae, prognosis)
18. Atma (nature, gravity, acute condition and so on)
19. Yoga (concomitant conditions)
20. Pratikara-pravrti and Nivrti (do's and don'ts)

The examination of the patient and the disease and the diagnosis of the disease are done on these methods but the acharyas have laid however, a great importance on the Tridosha principle in practical life. They are useful for both expert and average physician. In this respect, Charak says " When classified according to the cause, pain, colour, site, form, and nomenclature, the number of diseases become really countless. A physician need not be ashamed if he is not able to name a disease, as there can be no definite standardization of nomenclature of all the diseases. The same provoked dosas produce various diseases according to diversity of causes and its localization. Therefore, treatment should be initiated after diagnosing the nature of disease, different regions of localization and the special causative factors involved (Charak Sutra 18/42-44).

The following chart gives a complete list of parameters to be dealt, with regard to Disease:

1. Name of the Dosha
   (a) Agantu dosha
   (b) Sthanika (local) dosha
   (c) Dosha vyshamya (vitiated dosha)

   Vruddhi (excessiveness) - in quantity (pramana)
   - character (specific name of character)
   - function (specific name of function)

2. Dushya, name of the Dhatu or Mala

   Dhatu vyshamya - increase or decrease (vruddhi or kshaya)
   - in quantity
   - character
   - function

3. Srotas
   (a) The specific srotas (subdivisions/organs)
   (b) Srotodusti nature and its character
   - Atipravrutti (exaggeration of function)
   - Sangam (partial or complete obstruction or reduction in activity)
   - Srotograndhi (abnormal organic changes, excess growth)
   - Vimarga gamana (abnormal flow of the doshas in the srotas)

4. Agni-Koshtagni Vyshamya
   - (a) Manda
   - (b) Teeshna
   - (c) Vishama

   Dhatwagni vyshamya—specific dhatus affected
   - (a) Sama
   - (b) Nirama
5. Ojas—its abnormal characterr
   - (a) Visramsa
   - (b) Vyapat
   - (c) Kshaya
6. Disease character
   - (a) Pratyatmal character
   - (b) Samanya character
7. Vyadhi Bheda
   - (a) Doshanuguna - Ekadoshaja
     - Dwandaja
     - Sannipataja
     - Samanyaja
     - Nanatmaja
   - (b) Dhatu pradoshaja (character)
   - (c) The nature of character of—Ama-Pachyamana-Pakva (nirama)

(d) Vyadhivarga
   - (i) Adhyatmika, Adhibhautika, Adhidaivika
   - (ii) Balapravritta
   - (iii) Sariraka, Manasika, Mrudu, Daruna, Nija, Agantuja etc.
   - (iv) Roga and its limits—nava(new) and old
   - (v) Functions—natural, unnatural

8. Diagnosis of disease - Name of the disease
9. Curability and Incurability of diseases—their determination
   1. Number of causes—their strength
   2. Clinical feature of illness—their strength
   3. Number of doshas affected
   4. Dushyas affected and their strength
   5. Movement of disease—Abhyantara, madhyama, and bahya
   6. Ojas abnormality
   7. Nature of patient, his/her strength, mind, satmya, desha, age etc.
   8. Upadrava
   9. Dhatu gathatva (movement)
   10. Arishta and its character.
   11. Curability and incurability—degree of possibility
       (a) sadhya-asadhya, kruchchrasadhya
       (b) Asadhya-yapya, pratykyeya.

SAMPRAPTI AND ITS IMPORTANCE IN THE DIAGNOSIS OF DISEASE

With a clear idea about Samprapti, one can make a definite diagnosis of an illness. That's why, samprapti has been included as one of the Panchanidana (tools of diagnosis).

Example

The characteristic clinical features of Pandu roga (anaemia) are:

1. Pitta dominant sannipata
2. aggravation of rasa dhatu (rasa dhatu vruddhi)

3. decrease of rakta dhatu (rakta dhatu kshaya)
4. symptoms of number 3 - palpitation, weakness, and discolouration of skin (grey colour)

As said in the above example, by knowing the samprapti, a physician can have knowledge about the different illnesses and can treat the case accordingly. Defining samprapti, Vaghbhatta Acharya has mentioned that 'the manner in which the doshas are vitiated and traversing throughout the body produce the disease is termed as Samprapti (Astanga Hridaya Nidana 1). The other synonyms of samprapti are Jati (origin of disease) and Agati (establishment of disease). The Samprapti has been divided into six categories for simplification and understanding of the subject. They are:

1. Sankhya samprapti (number of a specific disease in the classification)
2. Pradhanya samprapti (pathogenesis)- predominance
3. Vikalpa samprapti (degree of permutations and combinations of doshas)
4. Balasamprapti (manifestations of symptoms during the corresponding period of doshas)
5. Kala samprapti (combined together as Balakala visesha)
6. Vidhi samprapti (types of pathogenesis)

In Charaka Samhita, there is minor change in categorisation of samprapti. He combined Bala (strength) and Kala (time) samprapti together under the label bala-kala Samprapti. He also included a new categogry known as Vidhi Samprapti.

1. **Sankhya Samprapti:** The number of ways in which a specific disease manifests itself in the body is known as Sankhya Samprapti.

e.g. Fever of 8 types
Gulma of 5 types
Kushta of 18 types

This categorisation of disease is based on the cause of illness, dosha and principal symptoms manifested.

2. **Vikalpa Samprapti:** It is known that every symptom and sign manifested in the body is the result of pathological alterations of dosha-agni-dhatu-srotas etc. By analysing the clinical manifestations and thereby understanding the vitiation of doshas etc., itself constitutes Vikalpa Samprapti. It is known as 'Amsamsa Kalpana' because of the analysis of each clinical feature carried out (Madhukosa 1/12).

   e.g., (a) the occurrence of sorrow and high temperature in fever. It is not sufficient if we know that it is due to Pitta dosha. One should also note that for rise of body temperature, the Ushna quality of pitta has been increased and that pachaka and brajaka pitta in body have also increased.

   (b) In diarrhoea (atisara), the cause of excessive watery stool is due to the excessive fluidity of the pachaka pitta.

   (c) The Amla chardi occurring in amla pitta is due to excessive liquidity of pitta dosha.

   (d) If the eyelids frequently show spasms, it indicated aggravation of Vyana vata.

   (e) If skin becomes hard, it indicated vyana vata has become aggravated due to rukshata.

   (f) If a swelling is seen anywhere in the body, it indicates aggravation of kapha in quantity.

   (g) If body skin turns greyish white indicates, aggravation of kapha due to increased activity.

(h) If limbs becomes cold, body is heavy and inability to move, it indicates aggravation of kapha due to coldness.

Similarly, the manifestationess resulting from dhatu-vruddhi should also be analysed.

By this type of study, the aggravation of dosha-dhatu has been divided into those due to Dravya (density), Guna (Character) and Karma (activity). The character and function are dependent on the substance density. Therefore once there is an absolute increase in the quantity of the dosha, then there will be corresponding increase in the function and activity of the dosha. Even then the three parameters of dosha-dhatus quality of character and function need not increase all together at a time.

For effective therapy, the Doshavyshamya (abnormality of dosha) is important. When there is only an abnormal increase in the quantity of the doshas, the treatment given to bring it to normal will not effect its character or function. Therefore, the effective treatment varies with the parameter affected for each dosha.

e.g., When there is absolute increase in the quantity of pitta, Virechana karma (purgation) is the treatment of choice;

When due to increase in Ushna character, Seethopacha (cold application); and

When there is increase in function of pitta dosha with affection of mind, then keeping happy mood and music help a lot in relieving the patient's illness.

In this way, when appropriate treatment is given, then Doshavyshamya will not arise.

3. **Pradhanya Samprapti:** When there is occurrence of disease due to vitiation of two or more doshas, then

one has to decide the predominant dosha affected. This analysis constitutes Pradhanya Samprapti. During treatment, primary attention should be laid to the vitiated predominant dosha. Sometimes, more than one disease may occur in the body. Then treatment should be directed first towards the main disease.

4. **Bala Samprapti:** During disease occurance in the body, the physician has to decide the two strengths of the samprapti, i.e. bodily strength and the disease strength. For determining bodily strength, one has to pay attention to the patient's age, gender, prakriti (constitution), mind, satmya (ahara-vihara-desha-work) etc. For determining the disease strength, its aetiology (nidana), purva rupa etc. are useful.

3. **Kala Samprapti:** In general, diseases manifest themselves depending on biological and solar rhythms (seasons). Certain diseases are evident only in certain periods of time. The aggravated doshas express themselves markedly during their prakopa state of kriya kala. In this way, the relationship between a certain period of time and the disease constitute Kala samprapti. The patient's age, the season during which the disease manifested, the day and night and food consumption times for aggravation of dosha—all these constitute kala sampra pti.

4. **Vidhi Samprapti:** The nature of the diseases which affected the body constitutes vidhi samprapti. From the classification of diseases, the manifested features of illness are compared and once confirmed, it constitutes the vidhi samprapti.

e.g., Kustha disease comes under Adibala Pravritta Rogas in the Adhyatmika Rogas. Since, Adibala

Pravritta Rogas are due to vitiated kulaja, the complete cure of these disease is impossible.

Similarly, the differentiation of Nija-Agantuja, curability and incurability; mild and severe forms of disease—all constitutes Vidhi Samprapti.

Sankhya Samprapti and others indicate the character of the disease causes whereas Vidhi Samprapti tells about the inherent character of the disease itself. In this way, the knowledge of Samprapti helps the physician to selectively treat various diseases effectively.

NOTES AND REFERENCES

1. Dwivedi R., Pandey G., Ayurvedic Pradeep (Hindi), Chowhambas Sanskrit Series Office, Varanasi, 1975.
2. Varier P.S., Principles of Ayurveda, Aryavaidyan, 1: 1: 1987.
3. Notes on Ayurveda, Ayurvedic System of Medicine, Rengarajan Siddha Tutorial College, Madurai, Tamil Nadu.
4. Narayana D.L., Roga Nirnayam' Telugu), Indian Medicine Sales House, Vijayawada, 1980.
5. Devraj T.L., Speaking of : Ayurvedic Remedies for Common Diseases, Sterling Health and Cure Series, New Delhi, 1985.

2. Vaner P.S. Principles of ayurveda, Arvindham, [illegible] 1987.

CHAPTER 7

Investigation of Patient

Investigation of Disease in Ayurveda

Investigation of the patient and the disease from which he/she is suffering from in modern parlance mean Laboratory investigation, which helps in understanding the disease states of the body and mind from a micro to macroscopic level. Nowadays, confirmation of provisional diagnosis of an illness is mostly based on laboratory investigation giving it thus a vital role in modern medicine.

However in Traditional Ayurveda investigation of the patient mean different. Charaka has mentioned that the purpose of investigation of a patient is to know about the life span and strength of the patient together with the strength of the dosha. Here we are mainly concerned with the strength of the patient and strength of doshas, since the drugs are used according to the strength of dosha and of the patient. Because without knowing the strength of the patient if drug having strong intensity is used in the patient of little strength the drug used may cause untoward effects. Subjects like children, women and of elderly persons who cannot tolerate the intensity of strong drugs may have serious complications after using them. Hence in this perspective, the investigation of the patient is essential. In the same way, if the drug of low intensity is used in a patient of good strength and having the disease of strong dosha, it may have no effect; for these reasons, patient should be examined in various aspects as given below (Dwivedi & Guru 1988).

Investigation of the patient should be done in following 10 respects to assess the strength of the patient.

Prakrititah

Prakrititah (in respect of constitution); Patient's constitution should be examined to determine the Prakriti (constitution) of the patient. Prakriti is defined as the state remaining stable throughout the whole life and originated in the intrauterine life due to predominance of specific dosha. Due to predominance of the dosha, there are three Prakriti i.e. Vatika, Paittic and Kaphaja; Due to predominance of two doshas, dwandwaja Prakritis like—Vata Paittic, Vata Kaphaja and Pitta Kaphaja and due to equal effect of all doshas there is one same Prakriti. In this context it should be known that the presence of all three doshas causing prakriti is necessary because none of the individual is of absolute Vata Prakriti or Pitta Prakriti. The characteristics and behaviour of different Prakritis have been mentioned in detail in all of the classics of Ayurveda. It is not possible to give the details of Prakriti over here. But to put briefly the characteristics and behaviour of the three prakritis like Vatika, Paittic and Kaphaja it can be said that the persons endowed with Vata Prakriti are weak having short life span, less progeny, less property and less means. Pitta Prakriti persons are of average wealth and average means. Kaphaja Prakriti persons are strong, wealthy, learned and intellectual having more progeny, vigorous, peaceful and of long life span.

Vikrittah (Inrespect to pathology of disease)

The disease from which the patient is suffering from should be examined in the perspective of etiology (hetu), dosha, and dushya (the dhatu involved), Prakriti (nature of the disease), Desha (the locality in which the disease produced), Kala (the time or season in which the disease is produced), and the signs and symptoms of the disease.

Saratah (Condition of the different dhatus of the body)

The patient should be examined by seeing his condition of saptadhatus and mental status. Eight saras (elements) have been described. Seven saras belonging to each of the dhatus viz. Rasa, Rakta, Mansa, Meda, Asthi, Majja and Shukra. The eighth sara belongs to mental status.

Thus the patient possessing all of the Saras has been said to be most strong, having all pleasures and happiness, able to tolerate pains, confident, inclined to act for well being. Their body is stable and proportionate and have a long life span. The persons possessing average saras are of average qualities as mentioned above. Persons not possessing to the above mentioned qualities are called Asarah and their characteristics are also contrary to the qualities mentioned above.

Pramanatah (Measurement of the body)

The optimum Sharira Pramana (measurement) should be of 84 angulas (finger measurement of individual's own finger). All of the different external parts of the body have a specific measurement with individual's own finger. The optimum measurement from the tip of the toe to the head is 84 Angulas. This measurement is also termed as the (Ayama). The other measurement is called as Vistar (the measurement of the body with the stretched hands horizontally). From the tip of the one hand's middle finger to the tip of the middle finger of other hand, this measurement should be of 84 Angulas (with individual's own finger). This measurement is called as the 'Vistara.' Acharya Charaka has mentioned that the measurement of

Ayama and Vistara should be equal. The persons having optimum measurement are strong, vigorous, happy and wealthy. Those who are not of optimum measurement do not possess qualities as mentioned above. To know the strength and resistance of the patient this parameter is also important.

Samhanantah

By the word Samhanana meant well knitting of joints and compactness of the body. The persons having good Samhanana have proportionate body with good contours and well knitted joints, their muscles and veins are not marked because of Well developed and nourished body, hence such individuals possess Susamhata shariram. Such persons are strong and have compact body. Persons possessing average samhanana are of average strength and those possessing less samhanana are of little strength.

Satmyatah

By continuous use and practice, whatever becomes suitable and useful for the individual concerned is called satyma. The persons who are satmya of butter, milk, oil and meat juice together with all six rasas are strong, able to tolerate pains and have long life span. Those who are Ruksha Satmya or Eka Ras Satmya are weak, able to tolerate less pains, have short life span and less means. Those who are of average satmya are of average strength and average life span.

Satwatah

Satwa is mind. The Satwa is of three types according to the mental strength. They are, Pravar Satwa, Madhya Satwa and Avar Satwa. The persons who are of Pravar Satwa (high mental status) they despite of their small body able to tolerate the pains of serious diseases caused by Agantuja or

Nija etiology. Madhya Satwa (average mental status) persons are able to tolerate the pains by their own strength or by the consolation and support of others. Heensatwa (low mental status) persons are despite of their huge body not able to tolerate even little pain and they can not be supported or consoled even by others. They are always associated with fear, worries, greed and ignorance.

Ahara Shaktitah (Capacity to digest diet intake)

The patients should be examined in this respect to assess their capacity to digest the taken food, because the diet is the basis of strength and life.

Vyayama Shaktitah (Capacity to perform work)

Vyayama shakti of the patient is assessed by the amount of work performed by him. This assessment is also a parameter to measure the strength of the individual concerned.

Vayastah (In respect of age)

The condition of the body denoting duration of life is called Vaya (age). This is divided into three viz. Bala (child), Madhya (middle age) and Jeerna (old age). Upto 16 years is Bala Vaya (childhood or boyhood). Upto 60 years is Madhya Vaya (middle age) and after this is Jeerna Vaya (old age). Vaya (age) is important in respect of administration of drug and its dose, because children and old people require drugs of low potency and in lower doses in comparison to adult people.

All these 10 above mentioned investigations in various respects relating to the patient are essential before the commencement of treatment for the proper cure of an ailing individual. Acharya Charaka has mentioned all these matters under the heading of Dasavidha Parikshya (10 groups of methods of investigation). Under the broad heading of Dasavidha Parikshya 10 things have been described in detail in the perspective of an alround examination debating each and every aspect of the disease and treatment. They are karana (Physician), Karana for Bheshaja (medicine), Karyayoni or Dhatu vaishamiya (imbalance of doshas), Karya or Dhatu Samya (to bring the imbalanced doshas balanced), Karyafala (to obtain happiness), Anubandha (life), desha (locality and the patient), Kala (year and state of illness of the patient), Pravritti (beginning of treatment) and Upaya (efficiency of physician in curing the disease) (Charaka Vimana 8/84). In the above mentioned dasavidha parikshya nothing has been left relating to the patient and the treatment of disease. Investigation of the patient is thus also included in the dasavidha parikshya.

ASSESSMENT OF PRAKRITI WITH A REVISED PRO FORMA

T. Seshagiri Rao,* Kanchana Srinivasan ** and R. Janaki.***

A pro forma has been evolved for assessing prakriti and 94 normal healthy adults were assessed for their dominant prakriti by using pro forma. The dominance in sariraka features agrees with that in Manasika traits in a majority of persons having kapha, pitta and vata dominance. Results of the X^2 test establish the validity of pro forma at $P < 0.05$ level of significance. A direct correlation is found between religiosity and gratitude; endurance and steadiness of mind and an inverse relationship between anger and endurance. This pro forma can be used to ascertain the proneness to and severity of disease.

Introduction

Ayurveda describes ten-fold methods of clinical examination of a patient to diagnose any disease. The study of prakriti (constitution and temperament) is one among them. In a patient, it enables the physician to assess Dehabala (immunological and endurance strength) and in a normal person, an insight into the Vyadhyutpadaka pratibandha katvam (resistance to disease and prophylactic capacity). As an example, case of Amlapitta (a disease due to vitiation of pitta), exhibits symptoms relevant to one of pitta prakriti in a greater form while in sleshma prakriti, the symptoms are mild. With the knowledge of doshic prakriti, in a disease individual, treatment, rehabilitation and prevention of relapses can be rationally planned. Study of prakriti here particularly refers to doshic prakriti of the diseased persons.

For the assessment of doshic prakriti, Phadia and Sharma (1967) suggested a method of cluster analysis based on some psychological tests. Singh and Dubey (1969) studied 100 cases of arthritis using the pro forma specifically prepared for the purpose. Their observations revealed that the persons suffering from rheumatic arthritis, rheumatoid arthritis and osteoarthritis are predominantly of vatic, paithic and sleishmic prakritis respectively.

Gurunatham et al (1967) prepared a pro forma to assess doshic prakriti in 178 normal healthy male adults. Utilising the same proforma, about 230 persons suffering from parinamasoola (peptic ulcer), madhumeha (diabetes), tamakaswasa (bronchial asthma) and hridhroga (myocardial infarction) were also studied to assess the dominant prakriti. The study was intended to identify, or if possible to predict its place in disease proneness in healthy individuals. The pro forma was used in about 400 cases during the last 8 years and the experience gained thereof, led to the evolving of a revised pro forma which is considered more objective and practical. This paper deals with the preparation and standardisation of the prakriti protocol.

Description of the Revised Prakriti Pro Forma

Ayurvedic Samhitas (Treatises) of Charaka, Susruta and Vaghbhatta described lakshanas (qualities) of persons belonging to vatic, paithic and sleshmic prakritis which are related to sareeral (physical) and also to manasika (psychic) prakritis (table 7-1a & 7-1b). These qualities form the basis on which the pro forma is evolved. The lakshanas, except steadiness of mind which do not find a reference to two doshas in texts, are not considered and lakshanas like adaptibility, speech, complexion etc., which pose a problem in assessment were deleted.

Manasika (Psychic) Traits

Questions with regard to the six manasika traits—Krodham, bhakthi, klesasahishnuta, kamecha, manasthairya

Table 7-1 (a) : Prakriti - Psychological Traits

Manasika (Psychological) traits	*Vata*	*Pitta*	*Kapha*
1. Klesam (endurance) (Ability to withstand stress)	Moderate	Poor Endurance (Klesashishnu)	Have the ability to withstand stress (kshamavan) (Klesasaha).
2. Kruthajnata (Gratitude)	Ungrateful (Kruthagna)	Moderate*	Very grateful (kruthajna)
3. Bhakthi (Religious beliefs)	No belief in god (Nasthika)	Belief in god is a matter of convenience and advantage*	Belief in god (Dhrudha bhaktni)
4. Manasthayryam (Steadiness of mind)	Unsteady (Chapalachithaha)	Moderately steady*	Very steady* (Sthirachithaha)
5. Krodham (Anger)	Emotionally highly irritable. Easily provoked. Emotional outbursts of long duration (Krodhaha)	Emotionally outbursts but shortlived. (Kshiprakopaha; kshipraprasamana).	Very tranquil (Shanthaha) Prone to least anger (alpakrodha).
6. Kamecha (Sexual desire)	Least *	Less (Alpakamaha)	More (Vyavayah) (Prabhootha)

Marasika (Psychological) traits that are derived are shown by asterisk* mark for the other two references are from classics.

Table 7.1(b) : Prakriti Protocol

Sariraka (Physical) Features	*Vata*	*Pitta*	*Kapha*
1. Kesam (Hair)	Dhuvsara (Dusky)*	Kapila (Brownish) Palita (Greyish)	Nila (Black)
2. Netra (Eyes)	Dhuvsara (Dusky)*	Pita (Yellow) Tamra (Copper coloured)	Sukla (White)
3. Akruti (Built)	Krusa (Slender)	Madhyama (Medium)*	Uttama (Well built)
4. Aharam (Ingestion of food)			
(i) Agni	Vishama (Irregular)	Tikshna (high)	Manda (Less)
(ii) Ahara-Rasi (Quantity)	Vishama (variable)	Mahasana (Large)	Alpasana (Less)
(iii) Ruchi (Taste preference)*	(i) Madhura (Sweet) (ii) Amla (Sour)	(i) Tikta (Bitter) (ii) Kashaya (Astringent)	(i) Katu (Pungent) (ii) Tikta (Bitter)
5. Kosta (Bowel movements)	Krura	Mrudu	Madhyama
	(i) Regularity Highly irregular	Irregular	Regular
	(ii) Consistency Hard	Not formed	Formed
	(iii) Frequency One (1)	More than four (4) after purgative.	Upto two (2) or Three (3)

6.	Nidra (sleep)	Alpa (Less) 4 hours and less	Madhyama (Medium) more than 4 but less than 8 hours	Atinidra (Excess sleep) More than 8 hours
7.	Sitalapadardha	Dveshi (dislikes)	Priyah (likes)	Samah* (neither likes nor dislikes).

Sariraka (physical) features which are derived are shown by *mark, while for the other two, references are found in classics.

and kruthagnata (anger, religious belief, endurance, sexual desire, stability of mind and ingratitude respectively) are selected after scanning a number of existing personality inventories. Each trait is considered in its totality without taking into consideration its components or dimensions. After collecting a large amount of information/data from the personality tests, the following specifications are laid down.

1. Questions are simple-worded and self-explanatory.
2. Questions, as far as possible, are illustrative of a particular situation so that the questions could be understood in their proper perspective, i.e., behavioural situation rather than hypothetical situation (e.g. 'Have you quite often missed two buses of your destination coming at the same time because you could not decide in which to get in?—This question helps to assess steadfastness of the mind in deciding.)
3. Questions, as far as possible, must relate to common daytoday situations so that the subject can pick out his answer from his own preparatory of responses instead of imaging or guessing what his reaction would be, if he were to encounter such a situation. (e.g. 'When your higher authority scolds you, do you usually express annoyance towards your wife/children/ husband subordinates?—This question reflects on proneness for anger.)
4. Questions, as far as possible, are to be socially, neutral or impartial so that the subject will not try to put himself in a socially favourable level. (e.g. 'When you are given a difficult work to do, do you like to start in and keep working on until it is completed—This question measure endurance.)

5. Importance is given in selecting the questions with the Indian background in mind. Suitable modifications are made in the questionnaire to suit the prevailing conditions, customs, modes of conduct and traditions practised in India.

6. Such questions that are applicable to all times, i.e., those which change very little with time are selected (e.g.. 'Do you feel irritated if a person of your own sex tries to push ahead of you in a ration/bus/cinema queue?—This question again helps to assess proneness for anger.)

7. Questions are framed on both sides of the continuum i.e. if some questions elicit religious belief some questions also elicit disbelief. (e.g. (a) Do you prefer your wife/husband/children to be basically religious? (b) Do you think that faith in religion is a superstition and outdated in this age of science? These questions provide an idea of mental outlook towards religious faith and belief.)

8. For traits like sexual desire, for which the subject has a feeling of delicacy, indirect question are preferred to direct question and are based on the assumption that the subject will project his own reaction/ tendencies in his reply. (e.g. (a) 'People sometimes use or listen to foul language involving sex, because they get a vicarious pleasure. Do you agree? (b) 'Most people desire to see usually those pictures wherein there is much of sex—Do you agree?—These questions help to ascertain the proneness for pornography.)

9. Format of the questions are to elicit a single unambiguous answer 'yes' or 'no.'

10. Two scores, i.e., lie score and consistency score are included to provide an overall evaluation of the test

record and also an internal check on the reliability of the subject's answer. For the lie score, 6 questions are selected from the 15 Lie (L) questions of the Minnesota Multiphasic Personality Inventory and the questions have been found to be answered in a particular direction by the general population. (Hathway and Mokinley, 1967). For example, questions like 'Do you tell lies sometimes. Do you laugh at a dirty joke sometimes? Do you sometimes postpone anything what you ought to do today? usually elicit a 'yes' or 'no' answer from the general population. 'No answer usually indicates an attempt to 'fake good' by the subject. Another validity check, provides an index of respondent consistency for which 5 questions are repeated in identical form at different locations of the pro forma and therefore, non-identical responses for the same question, usually indicate the consistency of the subject's answers. If either of these scores exceeds a specified value, the record is considered invalid and hence rejected.

Sariraka (Physical) Features

From among the Sariraka Lakshanas (physical features), seven are found useful for assessing the prakriti of individuals. These are kesa (hair), netram (eyes), akriti (body build), aharam (good habits), kostam (bowel condition), nidra (sleep), and linking for sitalapadartha (cold items). In respect of kesam and netram, physical observation of colour helps in assessment. For akriti (built), Brocas Index (Geigy and Basle, 1936) is taken as a guide to determine standard weight. Direct questioning method is adopted to type the sariraka lakshanas of agni (appetite), ruchi (liking for taste), regularity and consistency of kosta (bowel movement position) and liking for sitalapadartha (cold items). Following standards are fixed for the assessment of the remaining physical features.

Sariraka features *Ahara Rasi*		*Vata*	*Pitta*	*Kapha*
(Quantity of food)		Variable 200 gms. of pre-cooked rice.	more than 50 to 100 gms. of pre-cooked rice.	
Number of motions after taking purgatives.	1	more than 4	2 or 3	
Nidra (sleep)	upto 4 hrs	4 to 8 hrs.	More than 8 hrs.	
Akriti (Build)	Standard weight ± 5 kgs.	Standard weight ± 5 kgs.	>Standard weight ± 5 kgs.	

Methods and Materials

94 normal healthy adults of both sexes in the age range of 25-60 and stratified into 3 educational groups (primary school, high school and higher or technical education) formed the subjects for this study. Prior to prakriti assessment, each volunteer is interrogated for his/her social and clinical history. If the volunteer is declared normal and fit for assessment after a routine clinical examination, supported by laboratory investigations, he is included in the trial. Interrogation and observation are the methods adopted for filling up the prakriti pro forma.

Results and Discussion

A total of 149 cases were screened, of whom 23 were rejected on medical grounds or due to non-cooperation. The remaining 126 normal fit cases are taken for prakriti assessment of whom 32 cases are rejected on the basis of their 'Lie score' exceeding a specified value, thus invalidation the subject's other responses. Table - 7.2 presents the educational levels and rejection was based on the high 'Lie score.'

Table - 7.2

	Primary school	*High School*	*Higher or Technical Education*	*Total.*
Males	14	11	2	27
Females	4	0	1	5
	18	11	3	32

After exclusion of 32 cases that showed high 'Lie score,' 94 cases were taken for the final analysis; the education levels of these cases were 30, 30 and 34 covering higher or technical educational, high school and primary school respectively. The 34 cases in the primary school include 10 illiterates also, to make it a representative sample.

The lakshanas belonging to all the three prakritis exist in every individual in varying degree and the dominant prakriti refers to that prakrit i.e., vata, pitta or kapha which scores the highest marks according to statistical ratings. For example, if a person gets 90 marks in Kapha, 60 in Vata and 50 in Pitta, he is considered to be a kapha dominant prakriti. On analysis, it was found that 66 cases were kapha dominant prakritis, 18 pitta dominant and 10 vata dominant. Testing the validity of the pro forma is based on the assumption that the dominance in physical features will agree with that of psychological traits for a particular individual in a majority of cases.

It is observed in 77.3 per cent of kapha dominant persons, the psychological traits and physical features indicated the same dominance. The above is true in

66.6 per cent of pitta dominant persons and 50per cent of vata dominant persons. The relatively low percentage of tallying in vata dominant people might be due to the instability and variability of the psychic component in vata prakriti.

The validity of the pro forma is also tested by means of X2 test. Table 7.3 shows the observed class frequencies and expected class frequencies.

Table 7.3 : Psychic

		K		*P*		*V*		
		Observed	*Expected*	*Observed*	*Expected*	*Observed*	*Expected*	*Total*
Physical	K	36	32.8	12	14.6	7	7.6	55
	P	8	11.3	7	5.1	4	2.6	19
	V	12	11.8	6	5.3	2	2.8	20
Total		56	56.0	25	25.0	13	13.0	94

The finding that the marks obtained in physical features were not independent of marks obtained in psychological trait (P<0.05) is borne by the X 2 test, thereby establishing the validity of the pro forma. The relationship between the psychological traits, endurance-anger, religiosity-gratitude, endurance-steadiness of mind, are tested by computing correlation co-efficients. It is observed that a direct relationship exists between endurance-steadiness of mind and religiosity-gratitude and an inverse relationship between endurance-anger. These observed correlations supplemented by 'lie and 'consistency' scores, provide an internal check on the reliability of the person's answers.

The earlier pro forma of Singh and Dubey (1969) and Sharma and Phadia (1967) have got the specific purpose of assessing prakriti in specific diseases. Gurunatham et al (1967) divided the pro forma under three heads, namely (i) habits, (ii) physical features, and (iii) psychological traits. The present pro forma has got the advantage of wider application in all diseased and healthy conditions and in both sexes. It also adheres to the textual divisions in Ayurvedic classics, namely, sariraka and manasika with habits incorporated as part of the former and also employs the Ayurvedic terminology.

To have greater reliability of the subject's responses, manasika questions are mixed up along with repeated questions to avoid anticipation of the questions pertaining to a trait. The content validity (whether a question measures a particular trait) of the question is also established by five local psychologists on the basis of the concurrence of atleast three of them. This pro forma envisages rejections at clinical and statistical (lie and consistency scores) levels thus ensuing precise and objective assessment.

It is also observed that in healthy population, persons having kapha dominant prakriti are more, pitta dominant less and vata dominant least. This observation agrees with the earlier study of Gurunatham et al (1967).

Acknowledgement

The authors are grateful to Dr. M.V. Chari, Project Officer, and S.S. Rajagopalan, Asst. Director, Central Research Institute, New Delhi, for their valuable comments and suggestions. The assistance provided by Dr. K. Kuppurajan, Dr. K. Venkateswar Rao, R. Sitaraman and Mrs. R. Revathy for clinical screening and laboratory investigations is also gratefully acknowledged. The authors are thankful to the Director, Central Council for Research in Ayurveda and Siddha for his encouragement.

REFERENCES

Charaka Samhita, Vimanasthanam	:	8th Chapter, 94 verse, Niranayasagar Press, Bombay.
Phadia, E.G. and Sharma, M.D. 1967	:	On Methods of Discrimination of Constitutional Types (Prakritis). Journal of Research in Indian Medicine, Vol. 1, No. 2, pp. 261-69.
Singh, R.H. and Dubey, G.P. 1969	:	A Comprehensive Study of Pscyhosomatic Constitution (Prakriti) in Relation to Different Types of Arthritis. Journal of Research in Indian Medicine, Vol. 4, No. 1, pp 1-24.
Gurunatham, T. Chandra-sekharam, P. V. Venkataraghavan, S. Appa Rao, M.V.R. and Srinivasan, V.R. 1968	:	An Assessment of 178 Cases of Prakriti, Nagarjun, Vol. 12, No. 4, pp. 15-21.
Ashtanga Hridaya, Sarirasthana	:	3rd Chapter 84 to 104.
Susruta Samhita, Sarirasthana,	:	4th Chapter, 59 to 67 with Dalhana's Commentary, C.K. Sen & Company Ltd., Calcutta.
Hathaway, S.R. and	:	Minnesota Multiphasic Personality Inventory :
Mckinley, H.C. 1967	:	Manual for Administration and Scoring. Psychological Corporation, New York.
Edwards, A.L. 1957	:	The Social Desirability Variable in Personality Assessment and Research. New York, Dryden, (a).
Anastasi, Anne. 1968	:	Psychological Testing (3rd ed.) London : The MacMillan Company, Collier-McMiller Limited.
Geigy, J.R. and Basle, S.A. 1956	:	Documenta Geigy Scientific Tables, Page, 255.

NOTES AND REFERENCES

* Reproduced with permission from: Seshagiri Rao, T., Srinivasan Kanchna, Janaki K; Assessment of Prakriti with a Revised Pro forma, J. Res. Ayu. Siddha, CCRAS, Vol 1: No. 2: 1980.

* T. Seshagiri Rao, Asst. Director (Ay) R.R.C. Vijajanada.

** Kanchana Srinivasan, Research Asst. (Psychology)

*** K. Janaki, Research Asst. (Statistics)
(Both of Dr. A. Laxmipathi Unit for Research in Indian Medicine V.H.S. Medical Centre, Adyar, Madras - 600020).

Annexure I

Prakriti Questionnaire

Instructions to the Subject

The pro forma is aimed at knowing about the sort of a person that is under examination. The questions are read out and some questions and statements about interests, likes, reactions etc. are to be noted. The physician is to listen to each statement or question carefully and decide Whether it is true as applied to him or false. The model approach is as below:

"Do you doubt the value of prayer and worship?"

(a) Yes

(b) No

After each question there are two answers. Choose the one that applies to you.

As is obvious from the example, there may be no right or wrong answers. This is not a test of your ability. But only the way you behave. Answer the questions frankly and as quickily as possible. Give the first natural answer as it comes to you.

1. When you are given a difficult work to do, do you like to start in and keep working on until it is completed?

   (a) Yes

   (b) No

2. Most people inwardly resent when they are asked to return a favour someone has done to them. Do you agree?

   (a) Yes

   (b) No

3. Do you doubt the value of prayer and worship?

   (a) Yes

   (b) No

4. Do you often find that people can easily change you even though you thought that your mind was already made up on a subject?

   (a) Yes

   (b) No

5. Sometimes, when people are not doing well, physically, (e.g. headache, stomachacho etc.), they are irritable. Do you agree?

   (a) Yes

   (b) No

6. Sex can be enjoyed with anybody and not restricted to the married partner. Do you agree?

   (a) Yes

   (b) No

7. Do you tell lies sometimes?

   (a) Yes

   (b) No

8. Do you like to stay-up late working, in order to get a job done?

   (a) Yes

   (b) No

9. If given a chance, would you prefer to lead?

   (a) a more sheltered life with fewer difficulties to face?

(b) the same kind of life you now lead?

10. A teacher need not be remembered and respected by the pupil for teaching him for after all he is getting paid for it. Do you agree?

 (a) Yes

 (b) No

11. Would you prefer your wife/husband/children to be basically religious?

 (a) Yes

 (b) No

12. Have you quite often missed two buses of your destination, coming at the same time because you could not decide in which to get in?

 (a) Yes

 (b) No

13. In a crowded bus, if some one strikes you unintentionally with an umbrella, or steps on your barron foot, do you?

 (a) loose your temper?

 (b) take it easy?

14. People sometimes use or listen to foul language involving sex, because they get a "kick out it," Do you agree ?

 (a) Generally 'Yes'

 (b) Not at all

15. Do you get angry sometimes?

 (a) Yes

 (b) No

16. Most people inwarndly tresent when they are asked to return a favour someone has done to them. Do you agree?

 (a) Yes

 (b) No

17. When you overwork at home or office, do you?
    (a) stand the strain well?
    (b) suffer from indigestion, dirrhoea etc.?
18. Children do not owe anything to their parents for bringing them up since it is part of their duty. Do you agree?
    (a) Yes
    (b) No
19. Religious books like Gita, Bible and Quoran should not be regarded as holy and sacred. Do you agree?
    (a) Yes
    (b) No
20. On a free evening, while going to friend's place/cinema/beach etc., do you often change your mind and come home?
    (a) Yes
    (b) No
21. Do you feel irritated if a person of your own sex tries to push ahead of you in a ration/bus/cinema house queue?
    (a) Yes
    (b) No
22. When a man is with a woman (*vice versa*) he is usually thinking about things related to her sex. Do you agree?
    (a) Yes
    (b) No
23. Do you postpone anything what you ought to do today?
    (a) Yes
    (b) No

24. Do you think that prayer and worship are of no use?
    (a) Yes
    (b) No
25. When you have some difficult work to do, do you?
    (a) stick to it?
    (b) play 'sick' to get out of it?
26. When a person whom you hate very much helps you out of a crisis, do you feel thank ful to him?
    (a) Yes
    (b) No
27. Do you think that this world has evolved out of natural principles so that there is no necessity to assume a God behind it?
    (a) Yes
    (b) No
28. Having liked and bought something (dresses/shoes/some other articles) do you?
    (a) often feel like going to the shop again and changing?
    (b) stick to your original choice?
29. When your higher authority scolds you, do you usually show your annoyance on your wife/husband/children/subordinate?
    (a) Yes
    (b) No
30. If there is more sexual permissiveness in the society most people would enjoy sex without any guilt feeling. Do you agree?
    (a) Yes
    (b) No

31. Do you gossip sometimes?
    (a) Yes
    (b) No
32. Do you often find that people can easily change you even though you thought that your mind was already made up on a subject ?
    (a) Yes
    (b) No
33. With a mild body discomfort or slight rise in temperature, do you?
    (a) remain calm?
    (b) become tense and complain to others?
34. When once you are in a high position, do you think it is necessary to remember those people who have helped you to attain that position?
    (a) Yes
    (b) No
35. Do you believe that the series of failures, you have had in your life, have made you doubt the existence of God?
    (a) Yes
    (b) No
36. Do you often find that you have lost out on things because you could not make up your mind soon enough?
    (a) Yes
    (b) No
37. When you are waiting in the bus stand for a loing time, a poorly crowded bus passes by without stopping. Does it initate you?
    (a) Yes
    (b) No

38. Do you like to listen to or tell jokes in which sex plays a major part?
    (a) Yes
    (b) No
39. Do you laugh at a dirty joke sometimes?
    (a) Yes
    (b) No
40. Sometimes when people are not doing well physically (headache/stomachache etc.) they are irritable.
    (a) Generally 'Yes'
    (b) Not at all
41. When difficulties are piling up in a work, people have a general tendency to give it up or pass it on to others. Do you agree?
    (a) Yes
    (b) No
42. Do you deny help to your school teacher who comes to you for some small favour because you feel you are no longer bound to him?
    (a) Yes
    (b) No
43. Do you think that faith in religion is a superstition and outdated in this age of science?
    (a) Yes
    (b) No
44. When you make a decision on your job, children's education, buying a house etc., do you?
    (a) act on the impulse of the moment?
    (b) weight up all the *pros* and *cons*?

45. When you are seriously absorbed in an urgent work, if someone disturbs you, do you get annoyed?
    (a) Yes
    (b) No
46. Most people would like to see usually those pictures wherein there is much of sex.
    (a) Generally 'Yes'
    (b) Not at all.
47. Do you read every page of the newspaper everyday?
    (a) Yes
    (b) No

Annexure II

Prakriti Proforma

S. No. Date:

Name: Convict No.

Age: ☐ Years

Sex: ☐ Male ☐ Female

Education: ☐ Primary School

☐ High School

☐ Higher or technical education

Occupation:

Marital Status: ☐ Married ☐ Unmarried

☐ Widowed ☐ Divorced

Income per capita per month ☐

Normal ☐ Diseased ☐

Nature of disease: Peptic ulcer (*Parinamasoola*) Diabetes mellitus (*Madhumeha*), Bronchial asthma (*Tamakaswasa*) Coronary thrombosis (*Hridroga*)

Prakriti typing	Marks		
	Vata	*Pitta*	*Kapha*
I. Sariraka (physical)			
II. *Manasika* (Psychological)			
Total			

Dominant *prakriti* [ ]

Prakriti Typing

I. Manasika (Psychic) traits:

	Vata	*Pita*	*Kapha*
1. *Klesasahishnata* (endurance)	3-4	1-2	5-6
2. *Krutajanta* (gratitude)	1-2	3-4	5-6
3. *Bhakthi* (religiousity)	1-2	3-4	5-6
4. *Manastairya* (steadiness of mind)	1-2	3-4	5-6
5. *Krodham* (anger)	3-4	5-6	1-2
6. *Kameccha* (sexuality)	1-2	3-4	5-6

II. Sariraka (Physical features)

1. *Kesam* (Hair)	*Dhusara* (Blackish grey)	*Kapila* (Brownish)	*Nila* (Black)
2. *Netram* (Eyes)	*Dhusara* (Blackish grey)	*Pita* (Yellow) Tamra (copper coloured)	*Sukla* (White)

*Nos. Indicate the number of questions answered for the trait.

3. *Akriti* (Build)**	*Krusa* (slender)	*Madhyama* (medium)	*Uttama* (well built)
Height in cms.			
Weight in kgs			
Standard weight in kgs.			
4. *Aharam* (ingestion of food)	*Vata*	*Pitta*	*Kapha*
1. *Agni* (Appetite)	*Vishama* (Irregular)	*Tikshana* (High)	*Manda* (Less)
2. *Ahara rasi* (Quantity of food)**	*Vishama* (Variable)	*Mahasana* (Large)	*Alpasana* (Less)
3. *Ruchi* (Taste preference)	*Amla* (Sour)	*Madhura* (Sweet)	*Katu* (Pungent)
5. Koshtam (Bowel habits)	*Krura*	*Mrudu*	*Madhyama*
1. Regularity	(Highly irregular)	(Irregular)	(Regular)
2. Consistency	Hard	Not formed	Formed
3. Frequency after purge	1	more than 4	2-4

** A person is classified as *Krusa* if the actual weight is less than 'Standard weight—5 kgs.'
A person is classified as *Madhayama* if his actual weight is in the range of 'Standard weight+5 kgs.'
A person is classified as *Uttama* if his actual weight is more than 'Standard weight + 5 kgs.'
Standard weight is according to Broca's index:
Standard weight in kgs - Height in cms - 100.

* Appetite High—more than two meals and 1 tiffin
Less—Two meals or less

** Large—More than two *Aalaks* (400 gms). of pre-cooked rice per meal

Less—Less than 1/2 *Aalak* (100 gms.) of pre-cooked rice per meal.

6.	*Nidhra* (Sleep)	*Alpanidhra* (Less sleep) 4 hrs. and less	*Madhyama nidhra* (Medium sleep) More than 4 but less than 8 hrs.	*Atinidhra* (Excess sleep) 8 hrs. and more
7.	*Sheeta* (Cold objects)	*Dweshi* (Dislikes)	*Priylaha* (Likes)	*Samaha* (Neither likes nor dislikes)

REFERENCES

1. Dwivedi L.D., Guru L.V., Introduction to Ayurveda, Krishnadas Academy Series 20, Krishnadas Acadency, Varanasi, 1988.
2. Seshagiri Rao, Kanchana Srinivasan, Janaki K., Assessment of Prakriti with a Revised Pro Forma, J.R.S. Ayu. Siddha, CCRAS, 1: 2: 1980.

KEY FOR THE PSYCHOLOGICAL TRAITS

1	*a*	9	a	17	*a*	25	*a*	33	*a*	41	a	
	b		*b*		b		b		b		*b*	Endurance
2.	a	10	a	18	a	26	*a*	34	*a*	42	a	
	b		*b*		*b*		b		b		*b*	Gratitude
3.	a	11	*a*	19	a	27	a	35	a	43	a	
	b		*b*		*b*		*b*		*b*		*b*	Religiosity
4.	a	12	a	20	a	28	a	36	a	44	a	
	b		*b*		*b*		*b*		*b*		*b*	Steadiness of mind
5.	*a*	13	a	21	*a*	29	*a*	37	*a*	45	*a*	
	b		b		b		b		b		b	Anger
6.	*b*	14	a	22	*a*	30	*a*	38	a	46	*a*	
	b		b		b		b		b		b	Sexuality
7.	a	15	a	23	a	31	a	39	a	47	*a*	
	b		*b*		*b*		*b*		*b*		b	Lie score
8.		16	24			32		40				Consistency score

The items shown in italics measure the trait i.e. endurance, gratitude, religiosity, steadiness of mind, anger and sexuality. The one in roman items measure the opposite of the trait i.e. non-endurance, ingratitude etc.

The more the items in *italics* in the lie column, i.e. more than 2, the record is rejected as invalid. For consistency score, see questions 1, 2, 3, 4, 5, and the responses given by the subject. If the subject has given non-identical answers for more than 2 questions, the record is rejected as invalid.

CHAPTER 8

Principles of Diagnosis*

K.D. Sharma

The Ayurvedic principles of diagnosis are quite simple and easily approachable. It does not require lengthy medical laboratory investigations nor any costly sophisticated equipment. There are about 20,000 recipes which are popularly used by the Ayurvedic physicians in different parts of India. It is not necessary that all the physicians should possess all these recipes. They have broad spectrum of action. Every one recipe can cure scores of diseases simply by changing the Anupana or Vehicle which may be different for each condition (Bhagvan Dash 1981).

The following gives an outlines of the Principles of Diagnosis of the Patient and the Disease in Ayurveda. For detailed study, the relevant chapters dealing with the causation of disease, clinical manifestations of illness, case taking and examination of the patient, Investigation of the disease, in addition to the classic texts of Ayurvedic Therapeutics mentioned in the Introductory chapter of this book may be referred to.

According to the Ayurvedic principles, the diseases are not exclusively physical or psychic—but are both physical and mental. Hence, the treatment and the diet prescribed for the particular disease should have good effects on body and mind. This type of approach of Ayurveda is considered as Psychosomatic concept of the diseases and these factors are also taken in to consideration while diagnosing a patient by the Ayurvedic physician.

Ayurveda does not accept the germs as the primary factor of the causation of a disease but they are accepted as the secondary cause of the disease. The primary cause of the disease is the disturbance in the equilibrium of doshas, dhatus and malas. Ayurveda prefers to make body tissues powerful to resist the attack of the disease instead of destroying the organism. Although Ayurveda also recognises different types of germs for causation of several diseases but they are considered as secondary factors. Until the balance of equilibrium of doshas and dhatus are unchanged, no organism can produce any disease even if there is a severe infection of the germs in the body. They can not multiply in the balanced state of dhatus and doshaa but they will die to their natural death.

For a proper diagnosis of disease, ancient Ayurvedists founded the principles of Panchanidana by which all of the diseases can be diagnosed properly and treatment may be given accordingly. The five components of Panchanidana are:

1. Nidana (etiological factors),
2. Purvarupa (Premonitory or prodromal signs and symptoms),
3. Rupa (actual signs and symptoms),
4. Upashaya (exploratory or therapeutic diagnosis)
5. Samprapti (pathogenesis)

All these above five components are known as Panchanidana.

Bhattara-Harichandra in the etiological classification ascribes four possible factors as cause of illness. These are:

(i) Sannikrishta (immediate cause)

(ii) Viprakrishta (remote cause)

(iii) Vyabhichari (abortive or minor cause)

(iv) Pradhanika (potent or primary cause)

The immediate cause is disturbance of the Doshas which is due to wrong food and conduct. That does not require long stretch of time for Chaya (accumulation of dosha), the cause of the disease is the aggravation of the Malas (Astanga Hridaya 1,12). The remote cause is a delayed action, such as Kapha is accumulated in the winter season which may result in kapha diseases during spring. The abortive cause is explained by the mild or weak factor which themselves are not capable to produce the disease. The potent causes are illustrated by the direct and quick action of a Visha (poison) etc. They are strong and are therefore sure to produce the disease.

According to Charaka Samhita the main classification of causes of disease (physical or mental) is in the terms of —

(i) Asatmendriyartha Samyoga (the unwholesome association of specific sense organs with their respective objects).

(ii) Prajna Pradha (errors of judgement)

(iii) Kala or Parinama (time) (Ch. S. 1,11, 20, Nidana 1, 3)

Purva-rupa: Commenting on the character of purva-rupa, Vijay Rakshita, the commentator of Madhav Nidana, mentioned that there are two types of Purva-rupa: Samanya and Vishishta. Samanya Purva-rupa is that in which there is due to interaction of dosha and dushya (dhatu), the specific dosha involved is not known. Vishishta Purva-rupa is that in which there is more manifestation of symptoms so that the involved dosha is also known. To sum up, the purva-rupa is that by which the disease to be produced at a later state is known but which of the dosha is going to be involved is not known.

Rupa: Since all manifestations of the disease are present, hence the diagnosis of disease concerned becomes easy.

Upashaya: Another group of Upashaya has been described. In this group, the drug, diet and regimen which apparently appear alike to Hetu (aetiology), Vyadhi (disease), and Hetu Vyadhi (aetiology and disease, combined), but still they cause alleviation of disease are termed as Hetu-Vyadhi-Viparyastharthakari. In this way in the first group, nine types of Upashya and in second group also nine types totalling altogether 18 types of Upashaya with examples have been enumerated in this context.

Samprapti: Samprapti (pathogenesis) has been divided into five categories to simplify the understanding of the subject. They are:

(i) Sankhya (number) Samprapti

(ii) Vidhi (type) Samprapti

(iii) Pradhanya (predominat) Samprapti

(iv) Vikalpa (degree of permutations and combination of doshas) Samprapti

(v) Bala Kala Vishesa (more manifestations of symptoms during the corresponding period of dosha) Samprapti

For details of the components of Panchanidana, see the chapters on Clinical Manifestations of Disease.

Examination of the Patient

In the clinical examination of the patient three-fold examination is regarded:

(i) Darsana (observation)

(ii) Sparsana (palpation)

(iii) Prasna (interrogation)

The physician ascertains the progress (Sadhya-sadhyata) i.e. curability or incurability of the disease, by observing the severity and spread of the disease. Through palpation, the physical conditions like warmth, softness, hardness etc. are ascertained and from interrogation lightness, heaviness of stomach, appetite, thirst, strength and weakness etc. are examined (Astanga Hridaya 1, 2 and Bhava Prakasha I, 7, 1).

According to Bhava Prakasha, examination of eyes, tongue and urine are included in the group of observation. Of 3 fold examination under palpation, Nadi-pariksha (pulse examination) is included. The 8 fold examination was the subsequent phase and the 3 fold aspects were elaborated to accommodate the Panchendriya Pariksha (examination by five senses) (Yoga Ratnakara I, 35, 131).

Thus in the Ayurvedic texts, 3 fold examinations, 5 fold examinations, 6 fold examinations, 8 fold, and 10 fold examinations are described. But in short, all can be summarised in three-fold examination mentioned above. Five-fold examination is performed through five senses and 6 fold includes the interrogation with it.

To conclude, the following eight points should be carefully examined by the physician:

1. Nadi (pulse)
2. Mutra (urine)
3. Mala (stool)

4. Jihva (tongue)
5. Svara (voice)
6. Sparsa (touch or palpation)
7. Chaksu (eyes) and
8. Akriti (general appearance)

Examination by the above methods provides a comprehensive picture of health or illness and also indicates the normality or abnormality of the three doshas and seven Dhatus and Malas etc.

The patient should be investigated from the following point of viewin order to determine the bala (strength) of the patient).

1. Prakriti (habitus)
2. Vikriti (pathological condition)
3. Swara (tone of the system)
4. Samhanana (compactness)
5. Pramana (proportion)
6. Satmya (homologation)
7. Satva (psycho condition)
8. Ahara (capacity for food)
9. Vyayama (capacity for exercise)
10. Vayah (age)

To assess the degree of the strength in a diseased person above examination is therefore very essential. Because, a strong person suffering with a strong disease, weak medicines administered without examination are useless. Similarly a weak patient should be first treated with non-distressing, mild and generally delicate remedies and later on, gradually by heavy remedies which do not upset the patient nor produce any complications.

Examination of the Diseases

To determine the exact nature of disease, it is necessary to ascertain the nature of doshas, dhatus, Malas, Srotamsi and Agni involved in manifestation of illness. As, already pointed out before, in respect of each disease whether named or not, Patient must be examined carefully by the Pancha nidana methods. It is mentioned in Ayurvedic texts that a physician should not be very particular about the names of the disease. Names are given to some commonly occurring important diseases only by way of illustration (Charaka Vimana 8/94).

While examining the patient a physician must ascertain the following details for each and every disease:

(i) Prakopana (exciting factors of the disease)

(ii) Yoni (origin of the disease from doshas)

(iii) Utthana (the mode of manifestation)

(iv) Atma (nature, gravity, acute condition and so on)

(v) Adhishtana (localisation of the disease)

(vi) Vedana (sensation of pain)

(vii) Samsthana (configuration of symptoms)

(viii) Upadrava (complications)

(ix) Vruddhi (condition of aggravation)

(x) Sthana (continuation)

(xi) Kshaya (abatement)

(xii) Udarka (prognosis)

(xiii) Nama (nomenclature of the disease)

(xiv) Yoga (concomitant conditions)

The treatment of the disease is an attempt to correct the imbalance of the doshas by using the methods of Sodhana and Samana. These details as well as the prescriptions and prohibitions advocated must be followed scrupulously in order to achieve the normal dosha equilibrium and thus the health of the individual.

* Contributed by Dr. K.D. Sharma, M.S. AIM (Jam.), Bhishgacharya, Ayurvedacharya.

NOTES AND REFERENCES

1. Agnivesh, Charaka Samhita.
2. Vaghbhatta, Ashtanga Hridaya.
3. Anonymous, Yogaratnakara.
4. Bhava Prakasha, Bhava Prakasha.
5. Bhagwan Dash, Diagnosis and Treatment of Diseases in Ayurveda.
6. (Ed) Prof. Ramachandra Rao S.K., Encyclopaedia of Indian Medicine.

CHAPTER 9

Classification of Diseases

Although there are innumerable diseases but still they are classified according to the choice of the person classifying them seeing and considering their importance and specificity for an easy diagnosis, treatment and for other practical purposes. In the context of the classification of diseases, Acharya Sushruta has mentioned that as all of the universal objects, animate or inanimate, have their origin from Trigunas (Satwa, Rajas, and Tamas) and nothing can remain apart from them, in the same way, all of the diseases are embraced by Tridoshas and cannot remain apart from them. The variations in diseases are according to their association with dhatus, malas, etc., and according to different seats of involvement and different etiology. It will be termed as Rasaja, Raktaja, Mansaja etc., according to the hetus involved (Sushruta Sutra 24/8). In this way diseases may be of innumerable number. Therefore, the ancient Acharyas of Ayurveda gave much more stress on the principle of Tridoshas rather than the nature and nomenclature of various diseases. Acharya Charaka also has the same point of view. He says that when classified according to the cause, pain, colour, site, form, and nomenclature, the number of diseases become really countless. A physician need not be ashamed if he is not able to name a disease, as there can be no definite standardization of nomenclature of all diseases. The same provoked doshas produce various diseases according to diversity of causes and its localisation. Therefore, treatment should be initiated after diagnosing the nature of disease, different regions of localization and the special causative factors (Charaka Sutra 18/42-44). Though Charaka and Sushruta, both of the Acharyas have mentioned the names and etiology of more than thousand of diseases, still their main thrust on the principle of Tridoshas is spectacular. Thus, to sum up the classification of diseases, it can be said that, all of classifications have been made on the basis of Tridoshas and the treatment of all diseases have been also furnished in the light of tridoshas. It is the Tridosha which acting like an axis of the wheel support all of the functions associated with the physiology, pathology together with effects of therapy to maintain the life of the individual (Table 9.1).

Table 9 - 1 Classification of Diseases

Sushruta (Sushruta Sutra 24/5-7)

I. Category

1. Adibhautika—aetiology pertaining to physical powers outside the body.
2. Adhyatmika—aetiology pertaining to the body of the individual.
3. Adhidaivika—aetiology petaining to devas or deities.

II. Category

1. Adival pravritta diseases (fault in the reproductive climate, shukra (sperm) and shonita (ovum)
   - i. Matrija—defect in mother.
   - ii. Pitrija—defect in father.
2. Janmabala Pravritta—faulty habits of mother during the gestation period, e.g., lameness, blindness, deafness, stuttering, short stature.
3. Doshabala Pravritta—faulty diets and regimens.

(a) (i) Amashaya Samutha—faulty functions of Amashaya (Stomach)

(ii) Pakvashaya Samutha—faulty functions of small intestine

(b) (i) Sharira—those involving body

(ii) Manasm—those involving mind

1, 2, and 3 combined together are included under Adhayatmika.

4. Sanghatbala Pravritta—these diseases are also called Agantuhja i.e. of external causes origin like, trauma.

   (i) Shastrakrita (due to trauma caused by instruments or weapons).

   (ii) Vyatadidrita (due to trauma caused by wild animals).

4. (i), (ii). combined together are included under Adhibanutika.

5. Kala bala Paravritta—due to seasons, winter, rainy, summer alongwith the wind.

6. Daivibala Pravritta—due to animosity of deities.

   (i) Vidyautashini krita (due to trauma caused by electric shock).

   (ii) Pishachadi krita—due to demons.

7. Swabhava bala Pravritta—occurs spontaneously like natural instincts hunger, sleep, senility etc.

(i) Parirakshana krit—can be prevented for longer periods.

(ii) Aparirakshana krit—which occur before hand to their usual time 'hence called Akaladrita.

5,6, and 7 are together included under Adhidaivika diseases.

Charaka (Sutra Sthana (20th Chapter) and Vimana Sthana (6th Chapter)

I. Category

   1. based on aetiology.

      (i) agantuja (external causes)

(ii) vataja

(iii) pittaja

(iv) kaphaja

Since (i), (ii), (iii) and (iv) cause pain, these are called Rogas.

2. According to the presence of causes outside the body and inside the body.
   i. Agan—exogenous
   ii. Nija—endogenous
3. According to the seat of involvement
   i. bodily seated
   ii. mentally seated

II. Category

1. Samanyaja vyadhi - arise from vitiation of tridoshas; jointly as described in 19th chapter of sutra sthana.
2. Nanatmaja - originate independently from one dosha (20th chapter sutra sthana).

Total number of disease described :

(i)	Vatic diseases	80
(ii)	Paittic diseases	40
(iii)	Kaphaja diseases	20

Names of Diseases: In ancient texts, no methodology of nomenclature of diseases has been mentioned. Even then, if we study the texts carefully we find that some orderliness has been followed to name and classify various diseases. The salient points that may be noted are:

1. Nomenclature based on prominent symptoms—Majority of diseases are named on this basis. e.g. Jwara (fever), Pandu (anaemia), Atisara (diarrhoea) etc.
2. Based on disease causation—Krimija hridroga Bhutonmada, Dhaurudra chardi etc.

3. Based on Samprapti (pathogenesis)—Raktapitta, Amlapitta, Amavata, Vatarakta, Urdvavata, etc.
4. Vikruta anga suchaka (diseased organs)—Hridroga, Grahani, Siroroga, Nasaroga etc.
5. Anya vastu sadrusenana—Gulma roga, Valmikan, Dhanusthamba, etc.
6. Based on Itihasa—Rajayakshma (tuberculosis), Bhutonmada etc.
7. Rudha nama—Grudhrasi, Bhippa etc.
8. Based on prabhava - Sathagni, Darunaka, Kantha kulja, etc.

Recently, another classification of diseases according to the systems of the body affected has been attempted. Since, Ayurvedic classification of diseases is very detailed, it is difficult to regroup them according to the modern medical school of thought. However, an earnest attempt has been made by Ramnath, Dwivedi and Gurudeep Singh who gave such a description and classification of diseases in their book "Classification of Diseases (Hindi Version) published by Chowkamba Surabharathi Prakashan, Varanasi, 1977. From the study of the classification of diseases of the ancient Ayurvedic physicians, one does not hesitate to appreciate their genius in understanding the concept of Health and Disease in its totality unaided by the present day medical laboratory technology.

NOTES AND REFERENCES

1. Dwivedi L.D., Guru L.V., Introduction to Ayurveda, Krishnadas Academy, Varanasi, 1988.
2. Dwivedi R., Singh G., Ayurvedic Rog Ka Vargeekaranam (Hindi), Chowkhamba Surabharati Prakashan, Varanasi, 1977.
3. Murthy A.R.V., A Systematic Classification of Diseases, Personal Communication.

A SYSTEMATIC APPROACH TO THE CLASSIFICATION OF DISEASES

Dr. A.R.V. Murthy, M.D. (Ay)

Ayurvedic texts have adopted multiple approaches to the classification of diseases. Charaka while choosing a binary classification in Vimana Sthana declares that the classifications may be numerable and innumerable basing on the criteria chosen for such a classification. He gives full liberty to the individual to go in for newer and newer classifications, provided the criteria are different. Taking cue from this statements an attempt has been made at categorizing the diseases mentioned in Ayurvedic texts under different systems in keeping with the current practice in the Western Medical Science.

Introduction

Ayurvedic texts have given a detailed account of many diseases that were prevalent in those times. The etiology, pathogenesis varieties, symptomatology, prognosis and Therapeutics—all have been detailed quite descriptively. However it seems that very little effort was made by them in categorizing the diseases in a systematic way. Classification was mainly restricted to give an account of the varieties of the disease and also an individual disease was classified with different view points. For example Prameha was classified based on the constitution of patient in to two groups as afflicting Sthula and krisa patients.[1] Again two types of pramehas—Sahaja and Jatottaraja have been mentioned in respect of time of origin[2]. Basing on the involvement of Dosas 20 varieties were described.[3]

Besides this, diseases have been classified into innumerable groups on the basis of a different criteria[4] like prognosis, intensity etc., which would be discussed in the coming pages. After going through the texts carefully one cannot but appreciate the tremendous flair the ancient Indian Masters had, for classification and their vast array of nomenclature. However with due regards and apologies one has to accept that an approach to systematise the diseases based on the system involved is lacking. May be it was not necessary for them under the prevalent conditions. 'System' here refers for a group of organs having similar functions e.g. Respiratory System G.I.T. etc. The present write up makes an initial attempt in that direction.

Classification is defined as the ordering or arrangement of objects (in the context, diseases) in to groups or sets based on the relationships. (These relationships can be based on observed or inferred properties). Nomenclature is the naming of the pathological conditions. The concepts of classification and nomenclature are closely related. The element of grouping distinguishes classification from nomenclature.

Classification is an important aspect of most sciences and the subject of classification in Medicine continues to engage the minds of many thinking people. Each classification should have a basis and should have a purpose and some utility which varies depending upon the basis of the classification. Classification is based on recognition of similarities and recognition or the 'nature' of this similarity distinguishes one classification from another.

Ayurvedic texts have described more than 200 diseases and an equal number of pathological conditions. The diseases have been classified with various viewpoints which facilitate the understanding of the disease in various contexts.

Charaka has tried various classification at different sites in the course of his incestrious text Charaka Samhita. For example he adopts binary classification in Roganika Vimana—Vimana Chapter 6/3. He classifies diseases into two groups each on the basis of 5 different criteria.[5]

	Criteria of classification	*Grouping*
1.	Prognosis	Curable Incurable
2.	Intensity	Mild Severe
3.	Location	Mental Physical
4.	Site of origin	Amāsaya Pakwāsaya
5.	Nature of the causative factors	Endogenous Exogenous

First two types of classifications help in clinical decision making as to how one has to proceed—whether to accept the case or simply refer to a specialist. Third group helps in deciding the type of treatment to be chosen either Satwāvajaya or Yukti—Vyapāsraya. Fourth one gives a clear idea about the dosha to be treated either Kapha or Vāta and the type of the purifactive procedure to be adopted either Vamana or Virechana. The fifth classification helps in deciding as to which cause should be treated first either exogenous or endogenous. Not stopping at this Charaka puts diseases in to one group based on the "Similarity of `Pain.'[6] He adds—"Multiplicity of classification of diseases may be numerable or innumerable."[7] In fact the numerability of the diseases has been described in the Nineteenth chapter of Sutrasthana.[8] The peculiarity of this classification is that, here Charaka classifies diseases based on the number of varieties, each disease is having. For Ex. he puts all these diseases having eight suybtypes in one group. Similarly those diseases having 7, 6, 5, 4, 2, 1 and 20 varities have been put in to different groups. Innumerability of the disease classification has been described in 18th and 20th chapters of Sutrasthana. The most important classification appears in the 20th chapter of Sutrasthana where Nānatmaja (specific) and Sāmanyaja (Non-specific) classification has been made.[9] Probably this is the most useful classification inasmuch as it is most scientific and systematic. Specific diseases/pathological conditions belonging to three body systems—Vāta system, Pitta system and Kapha system have been enumerated. This classification clearly identifies the dosha involved and treatment becomes easier. This in one way is over simplification of the therapeutic procedure as the dosha involved is single and treatment becomes very specific. Susruta's classification of diseases in to Adhyatmika. Adidaivika, Adibhoutika, is peculiar in it's own way as it takes into consideration, the acts of past life too.[10]

Thus we find multiplicity of the classification based on different criteria. Charaka defends such variation by stating that the individual has the liberty to classify the things as he likes.[11] In fact the two terms numerable and innumerable having mutually contradictory meaning have been applied to the samething, i.e., disease. But the criteria followed for classification are different, resulting in change in the number of groupings and this is justified. Charaka adds: 'If something is already classified into some groups in a particular manner one may classify it on the basis of different criteria which may result in changes in the number of groups in different ways.[12] Thus an attempt at a new classification herewith carries Charaka's permission and blessings both.

Systematic approach to disease classification has two components.

(1) Enumeration of diseases belonging to different systems.

(2) Subgrouping of these diseases having similar symptomatology.

The present classification takes care of both these things. However there can be one more component of this systematization—Once systems are outlined/defined, a subgrouping depending upon the organ involved. Example Diseases of the stomach, colon etc. In fact glimpses of this classification are available in our texts. Charaka's binary classification—Āmāsaya Samutha and Pakwāsaya Samutha is an example. Terms like Amasayāgatavata, Pakwāsayagata vata Gudagatavāta point toward such an approach. Terms like 'Hridroga,' 'Grahani,' Ṇetraroga, Karnaroga give a clue towards attempts at topological classification. This approach too has been adopted in classifying the diseases or GIT where it has become a necessity.

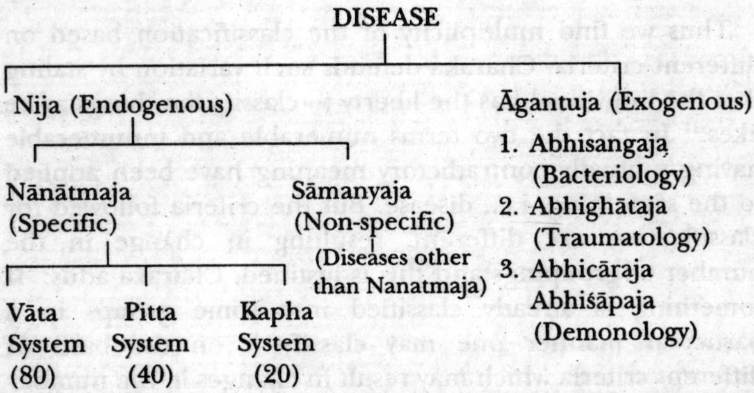

CLASSIFICATION BASED ON THE SYSTEMS

1. Respiratory System

Swāsa
Kāsa
Swara Bhedha
Rajayakṣma
Urakṣata
Kṣīna

2. Cardio Vascular System

Hṛidroga—5 types
Hṛiddrava
Hṛidgraha
Hrinmoha
Dhamini praticaya
Raṣagatavāta
Raktagatavāta
Siragatavāta

3. Gastro Intestinal System

Anorexias

Abhaktachhanda
Anannabhilasha
Arocaka
Bakta Dwesa

Dyspepsias

Vidagdajir na
Vishtabdajirna
Amajirna
Rasaśeṣajirna
Dinapaki Ajirna
Prakṛita Ajirna
Amlapitta

Diarrhoeas	-			
	-	Acute	-	Atisara (6 types)
	-			Pravāhikā
				Visucika
	-	Chronic		
			-	Grahani
				Jirnatisāra
Constipation				
	-	Acute	-	Alasaka
	-	Chronic	-	Vibanda
				Vilambikā

Vomitings	Nija	-	5 types
	Agantija		5 types
Hiccoughs	Annajā		
	Yamalā		
	Kṣudrā		
	Gambhirā		
	Mahatī		
Pain abdomen/ Colics	Udaraśoola 8 types		
	Parināmaśula		
	Annadravaśūla		
	Tūni		
	Pratitūni		
Abdominal distentions -	Localised		
		-	Gulma
			Pleehodara
			Yakritodara
			Baddodara
			Kṣatodara
-	Generalised		
		-	Udarasamānya (V.P.K.S.)
			Jalodara

Diseases of the GIT can also be classified as under:

Diseases of the mouth including Oropharynx	Osṭagata - 8	8
	Dantagata - 10	10
	Dantamulagata	15
	Jiwahāgata	5
	Talugata	9

	Kanthagata	17
	Sarvagata	3
Diseases of the Stomach & Duodenum	Amlapitta	
	Chardhi	
	Hikkā	
	Amaśayagatavāta	
	Alsaka	
	Annadravaśuḷa	
	Pacināmāśula	
	Grahani	
Diseases of the Intestines	Gulma	
	Roṣtagatavāta	
	Pakwāśayagatavāta	
	Atisāra	
	Pravāhikā	
	Vilambikā	
	Visucika	
	Raddodara	
	Cidrodara	
	Aṇtravidradhi	
Diseases of the Rectum	Arśas	
	Guda Brahmsa	
	Gudapaka	
	Sanniruddhaguda	
	Gudagatavāta	
	Bhagandara	

4. Hepatobiliary System

Kāmala	-	Śakhaśrita
		Koshṭa Sākhaśrita

Kumbhakamala
Halimaka
Panaki

5. Haemopoeitic System

Pāndu
Raktapitta
Pleehodara

6. Urogenital System

Mutrakricra	Parivartikā
Mutrāghata	Avapatikā
Mutrāsmari	Niruddha Prakasa
Prameha	Sephastamba
Napumsakatā	Medrapaka
Vriddhi	Sooka Doṣa
Sukragatavāta	Vrishnakshepa

7. Helminthiasis/ Parasitology

Krimi	Bahya	(2)
	Kaphaja	(7)
	Purișaja	(6)
	Raktaja	(5)

8. Metabolic and Endocrinal Disorders

Madhumeha
Medoroga
Atisthūla
Atikṛisa
Atiloma
Aloma
Atigowra

Atikrișna
Atidīrga
Atihraswa - Kubjatwa
Vāmanatwa

9. Diseases of the Connective - Tissua, Bones and Joints

Sandhivāta	Urusthamba
Amavāta	Urusāda
Vātarakta	Snayugatavāta
Kroṣṭukasirśa	Māmsa madogatavāta
Janu Bheda	Asthikṣaya
Janu Visleṣa	Asthiśoṣa
Vātakantaka	Astnimajjāgatavāta
Gulpagraha	Asthi Bhagna
Vātakhuddata	Sandhimukta (Cyuti)
Apabahuka	Hanugraha
Amsaśoṣa	

10. Diseases of the Nervous System

Pakṣāghāta	Antarāyama
Ekangavāta	Bahirāyama
Sarvangavāta	Grīvasthamba
Pangu	Manyāsthamba
Khañja	Jihwāsthamba
Kalayakañja	Vaksanga
Gṛidrasi	Mukatwa
Viswāci	Minminatwa
Ardita	Gadgadatwa
Kampavata	Jnanendriyangatavāta
Akṣepaka	Sirahsoola—11 types
Apatānaka	Padadāha
Apatantraka	Padaharṣa

11. Psychiatry

Unmāda
Apasmāra
Atatwābhiniveṣa
Tandrā
Klama
Bhrama
Anawasthikacittatwa
Aswapna
Atipralāpa
Mada
Murca
Sanyāsa

12. Diseases of the Organs of Special Sense
Diseases of the Eye

Diseases of the Eyelashes (2)	Pakṣmakopa Upapakṣma Māla
Diseases of Lids (19)	All Vartmagata diseases except Pakshmakopa
Diseases of the Lacrimal Apparatus (6)	Srāvas—4 Pūyalasaka Upanāha
Diseases of the Conjunctiva (12)	Abhiṣyanda—4 Arma —5 Suktika Arjuna Piṣtaka

Diseases of the Sclera (3)	Balāsagrathitha Sirajāla Sirājapidika
Diseases of Cornea (4)	Savranasukla Avranasukla Ajakājata Akṣipakatyaya
Diseases of Refractive Media (17)	Timiras—6 Dhumadarsi Nakulandyam Hṛaswajadyam Pittavidagdha Dṛiṣti Kapha Vidagdha Dṛiṣti Gambhirika Vataviparyaya Anyatovāta Shuṣkha Akshipaka Bāhyaroga - 2
Diseases of Uveal Tract (7)	Adimantha - 4 Hatādimantha Akṣipāka Śasopha Aśopha
Miscellaneous	Sirotpāta Sirāharṣa Amladyuṣita Parvani Alaji Krimigranthi

(b) Diseases of the Ear

Diseases of the Pinna

Durvidda	Paripota
(Dukhavardana)	Tantrikā
Kucikarṇika	Utpāta
Karnapippali	Unmantha
Māmsamkura	(Gallira)
Paliśoṣa	Vidārika
Parilehi	Syāva
(Lehya)	

Diseases of the External Auditory Meatus

Pạnasika	Karnahallika
Karnārśa	Karnakandu
Karnarbhudha	Karnavidradhi
Karnagutha	
(Karnavatika)	

Diseases of the Middle Ear Cavity

Pūtikarna	Karnaśotha	Krimikarnika
Karnapāka	Karnasrāva	
Karnapratinaha	Karnaśula—5 types	

Diseases like Karnaśotha, Karna Vidradhi, Karnapāka, Karnārbuda, Karnasrāva can occur both at Middle ear and External Auditory Meatus. Similarly Krimi Karnika can affect any part of the ear.

Diseases of the root of the ear
(Karna Moolagata rogas)—5 types
Diseases of Vestibulo - Chochlear appratus
(Internal Ear)

Bādiryam
Pranāda
Karnakṣedam

Bādivam can be due to Karnagūtha, a disease of external auditory meatus and may also due to diseases other than those of ear.

(c) Diseases of the Nose

Diseases of the External Nose including Vestibule

Arbuda
Nāsāpāka
Śopha

Diseases of the Internal Nose

Arṣhas	Nāsasrāva
Bramsathu	Putaka
Dīpta	Pūyasonita
Kshḥawathu	Sonitapitta

Diseases of P.N.S.

Pīnasa
Pratisyāya
Putinasya

Diseases of the Nasal Septum

Nasānaha
Nasaśosa

13. Diseases of the Skin and its Appendages Including Venerology

Kuṣta - Kṣudra—11	Ajagallika
Mahā — 7	Gardabhika
Sītapitta	Vivṛata
Udarda	Gandamala
Kotha	Agnirohini

Visarpa	Kakṣā
Jālagardabha	Anusāyi
Khālitya	Yavvaṇa Pidika
Pālitya	Padminīkantaka
Indralupta	Chippa
Aruṃṣikā	Khunaka
Irivellikā	Nakhabhedha
Dārunaka	Pādadāri
Yavaprakhyā	Kadara
Maśaka	Alasaka
Vyanga	Indravidda
Nilika	Ahipūtana
Nyaccha	Vanara Damstra
Tilakālaka	Jatumani
	Twa Kgatavatam
Phiranga	
Upadamsa	

14. Fevers

Doṣhaja
Viṣama Jwara
Dhatugata Jwara
Pidakamaya Jwara

15. Neoplasms

Granthi
Arbuda
Gandamāla
Apaci
Galaganda
Ashtila
Pratyastila
Vatasthila
Vidari
Pāṣānagardabha

Valmika
Sarkara

16. Wounds and Ulcers

(A) Nija

Vyadhijanya (Specific Infective)
Śosajanya (Tubercular)
Madhumehajanya (Diabetic)
Kuṣhtajanya (Lapromatous)
Phirangajanya (Syphylitic)
Tropical
Malignant

Vidradhijanya (Non-specific Infective)

- Sadharaṅa (Dosaja)
- Nādivrana

(B) Agantuja

Chinna
Bhinna
Viddha
Gṛiṣta
Picchita
Kṣata
Agni Dagda

17. Toxicology

Sthāvara Viṣa
Jāñgama Viṣa

18. Diseases of the Children

Ulbaka	Mahāpadmaka
Kulunaka	Ahipūtanā
Jalaśirṣaka	Utphullikā
Mastulunga Kṣaya	Coraka
Nābhi Roga (6 types)	Pāridagdhaccayi

Ostha Bhedha	Pārigarbika
Talu Vikriti	Phakka
Bālagraha	Sayyamutra
Kṣiralasaka	

19. Diseases of the Women

Yonivyāpat	Mūdagarbha
Yonikanda	Sūtika Roga
Pradara	Sthana Roga
Somaroga	Kṣira Dosa
Garbaśayagatavāta	Vandyatwa
Garbhiniroga	

20. Miscellaneous

Congenital diseases*

Kubja
Kuni
Pangu
Mūka
Minmina

Diseases of intrauterine life

Upavishtaka
Nagodara
Linagarbha
Mritagarbha
Mritajata
Jatamatramrita

Others

Sotha
Daha
Snāyuka
Vidradhi

*. Except Kuni all congenital diseases have appeared under the sub-group Diseases of Nervous System, inasmuch as they can also be acquired.

Once we have come to the end of classification a few words are necessary. No classification is complete. Each classification has it's own advantages and disadvantages; omissions and commissions. American College of Pathologists classifies the diseases on the basis of four modalities viz., Topology, Morphology, Etiology and Function. W.H.O. has developed ICD (International Classification of Diseases) based on systems involved. Of late W.H.O. is encouraging a RFE (Reason For Encounter) Classification which classifies the reasons for seeking health care from the perspective of the patient and this is patient oriented. Ayurvedic approach seems to have many things in common with this. In all these classifications there are some lacunae/drawbacks. The present classification is no exception. Certainly there are some overlappings, which cannot be avoided. e.g. Pleehodara comes both at Abdominal Swellings and Blood Disorders. Āmavata and Vātarakta, in spite of being metabolic by nature have been put under Musculo skeletal system basing on the site of appearance, involvement. Two separate classifications have been adopted for GIT based on different criteria. By this an attempt had been made to include all disease conditions both—medical and Surgical in to the system. Further Yakritodara, Baddodara and Kshatodara have been kept under localised Abdominal swellings, because the swelling in these cases is localised. Vatodara, Pittodara, Kaphodara, Sannipatodara and Jalodara have been considered as generalised swellings. Vṛiddhi has been considered specific for Scrotal swelling and hence has been kept under Urogenital system. Antravṛidhi (Hernia) however has been put into GIT. Madhumeha has been separated from Pramehas to include among metabolic disorders basing on the view that all Pramehas except Madhumeha are urinary abnormalities while Madhumeha is a metabolic disorder similar to D.M. (Refer to author's article under publication—Ancient Science of Life). A separate unit is allotted to skin and its appendages. In it are included all Kushtas and most of Kshudra rogas. However Vrana though manifests in skin has been given different unit because of the importance it enjoys, in the system. Many Vatavyadhis appear in different systems based on the organ involved, though all of them come under Vata system. Thus Pakshāghāta, Pangu etc., move under Nervous System; Urusthamba and Urusāda are included under the diseases of connective tissue and Gudabramsa enters GIT; so on and so forth. In the organs of special sense Netra Rogas and Karna Rogas and even Nāsā Rogas have been classified based on the anatomical locations.

Diseases seen exclusively in women and children have been kept under different heads. No further classification has been attempted under these units. A separate head is maintained for Neoplasms where all 'mass'es have been included. Ulcers and Fevers have been given independent units. Toxicology includes the whole Viṣa Tantra. Swellings find their place under many heads based on the organ involved. However, Oedemas (Sothas) have been kept under miscellaneous group. Vidradhi too has been kept under this group. Some more diseases which cannot be grouped under any other system have been included under this miscellaneous group.

The initial division of diseases into Nija and Agantuja varieties and subsequent divisions into Nija and Agantuja should be considered as basic classification. When diseases are grouped into systems all the divisions overlap and this does not invalidate the classification, inasmuch as the criteria for categorization is different.

The current endeavour as said earlier is a new step in this direction and as such no claims for perfection are being made. However sincere efforts have been made to minimise overlappings, repetitions and other shortcomings.

ICD classification and classification based on topology are slowly loosing their importance. Current trend is to focus on biomolecular and ultra structural origins of disease, on the alteration at cellular and subcellular levels. At this level the doctrine of specific causes looses its ground because various types of insults may produce the same result in terms of biochemical changes produced. The emphasis in classification of diseases probably should be on underlying disturbance of control of mechanism which has to be treated rather than on a given disease belonging to a particular system. What Charaka and Suśhruta thought about a disease was disequilibrium of normal body constituents (tridosas), which of late have been found to operate at cellular and sub-cellular levels. Restore the equilibrium of doṣas and the disease is cured. In other words restore the normalcy of cellular function/structure, and the disease disappears on its own!

NOTES AND REFERENCES

1. Caraka Cikitsā 6/15
2. Suśruta Cikitsā 1/3
3. Caraka Cikitsā 6/6

4\. & 5. Caraka Vimāna 6/3

6\. & 7. Caraka Vimāna 6/3

8. Caraka Sūtra 19/3
9. Caraka Sūtra 20/10
10. Suśruta Sūtra 24/4

11\. & 12. Caraka Vimāna 6/4

13. Astanga Hṛidaya
14. Kaśyapa Saṃhita

15. Mādhava Nidāna
16. Sarangadhara Saṃhitā
17. Ayurveda and Modern Medicine M.V. Lehe.
18. Davidson's Text Book of Medicine
19. API's Text Book of Medicine
20. Love and Baily's Short Practice of Surgery.

CHAPTER 10

Principles of Treatment

T.N. Pande

According to Acharya Vagbhatta, a person who desires longevity which is the suitable vehicle for achievement of Dharma (religious virtues), Artha (wealth and satisfaction of the senses) and sukha (happiness) should observe with great respect the instructions prescribed in Ayurveda (Asthanga Hrudiya Sutra 1/2).

Kayachikitsa (Internal Medicine) is one of the eight major branches or disciplines of Ayurveda. The term chikitsa is usually joined with the term kaya that is to say, this term is specific to Ayurveda. Kaya means body. Three different words has been used for body viz., Deha, Sarira and Kaya. The term deha means that which is nourished thus carrying the sense of anabolism. Sarira means that which undergoes degeneration and decay thus the sense of catabolism. The term kaya means selection of suitable nutrition i.e. to absorb useful substances and eliminate the non-usefuleness. This carries the sense of both anabolism and catabolism i.e. metabolism. The process of metabolism takes place with the help of digestive juices, enzymes and hormones; so, some explain kaya as Agni or digestive fire i.e., enzymes.

Chikitsa covers up a vast field. It not only means relief from disease but also to bring the patient to his normal individual condition. It includes relief from stress and strain. It does not only include medicines but also things like diet, daily routine, atmosphere and mental health.

Thus the term kaya chikitsa means the treatment of whole body including Agni i.e., digestion and metabolism. (Realms of Ayurveda).

In the context of chikitsa, Acharya Charaka defined it as the measures by which the imbalanced doshas become balanced. The word chikitsa has been derived from the root verb 'Kit'. To achieve the dhạtu samya (homeostasis) Charaka has mentioned that by avoiding the aetiology which causes imbalance of doshas and using measures to maintain the dhatu samya—should be the objective of the physician (Charak Sutra 16/34-36).

Kriyakala (The Time for Treatment)

Every disease, mild or severe, acute or chronic has to pass through certain stages and these stages are called Kriya Kala (the time for treatment) and these are six in numbers, viz. Samchaya (accumulation of morbid dosha), Prakopa (vitiation of dosha), Prasara (spread of dosha), Sthana Sansraya (localisation of dosha), Vyakti (manifestation of disease), and lastly, Bheda (chronicity, complications, etc.) (Table 10 -1a, 1b).

Table 10-1a Kriya Kala and Its Management

Aims and Objectives of Treatment		
1. Swasthasya Swathya Rakshanam	(i)	Promotion of health
	(ii)	Prevention of disease
	(iii)	Rejuvenation
2. Aturasya Vyadhipariomokshah	(i)	To cure or relieve from disease
	(ii)	Rehabilitation
	(iii)	Rejuvenation

Table 10-1b : Kriya Kala and Its Management

Interaction of Host and Environment	*Sanchaya (Pre-pathogenesis)*	*Prakopa and Prasar (Early Pathogenesis)*	*Sthana Sansraya (Demonstrable early Disease)*	*Vyakti (Advanced manifest disease)*	*Bheda (chronicity)*	*Convalescence*
Management	Promotion of Health	Specific protection	Early Diagnosis and prompt treatment	Specific Treatment	Limitation of disability and Rehabilitation	Rehabilitation and Rejuvenation

Samprapti (Process of Pathogenesis)

At any step of kriya kala and specially at the level of sthana sansraya i.e. localisation, the vitiated dosha combine with dushyas i.e. body tissues and vitiate them. This process is known as Dosha Dushya Sammurchana. The spread of the dosha and the dhatus takes place through srotas i.e. blood vessels, lymph vessels, and cellular spaces etc. At some level in the beginning or during the process of pathogenesis, the Agni or digestion and metabolism gets disturbed resulting in indigestion, impaired metabolism or impaired assimilation and formation of a new unwanted product known as 'Āma.' Ama may be produced at any level of digestion or intermediary metabolism or at the end, when the body tissues are formed. Thus there are five factors of pathogenesis:

1. Vitiated dosha.
2. Dushya and the combination of dosha-dushya (Dosha Dushya Sammurchana).
3. Srotas or body channels (through which nutrient material and waste matter or metabolic products flow).
4. Agni (digestive juices and/or hormones and enzymes).
5. Ama (impaired and unwanted product of digestion and metabolism).

Vyadhi Kshamatwa (Immunity/Resistance)

It is the most important factor considered for the production or prevention of disease and/or reducing the severity of disease. Thus the aim of Ayurveda is to promote health (Swasthysya swasthya raksana) improve immunity and resistance (vyadhi kshamatwa) and to cure a disease (vyadhi parimoksha).

The knowledge of pathogenic process is thus very essential to check the spread of the vitiated doshas and the disease at different stages of kriya kala. The same is explained in the table.

Important Factors to be Considerd Before Initation of treatment

The following few factors should be examined before starting the treatment.

1. Study of the Individual's Individuality

It is necessary to understand that two individuals are not equal in all respects. Theoretically the forms of man can be described as a range of values to be accepted as a standard found to be the average in persons who generally appear healthy and free from disability or disease. But practically, the study of the individual will be necessary to bring accuracy in diagnosis, treatment and assessment of results. Sushruta, while describing the norms of the individual states that "it is not possible to standardize exact measures of dosha, dhatu (body tissues) and mala (waste matter) due to their varying nature (Asthayitwata) as well as individual variation (vailaksanyat) of the body constitution. He further says "if a physician wants to know the state of equilibrium (samatwam) of all these, he can only do it by finding the signs of perfect health in that individual. The expert physician makes diagnosis or infers indirectly (Anumanam), the imbalanced condition of these body elements by finding the person not in perfect mood (aprasannedriyan)." Even the word disease means absence of ease; this can't be established by laboratory methods or by any other clinical signs. Actually it is at this stage that pathology begins. It is the duty of the physician to recognise this stage and start treatment (Realms of Ayurveda).

2. Study of the Individual Wholistically

It is necessary to study the individual as a whole before starting treatment. It is also essential to study other factors which affect an individual viz. Dushya (vitiated body tissues). Desha (habitat), Bala (strength, vitality or resistance), kala (season), Agni (digestion), Prakriti (individual constitution), Vayas(age), Satva (psyche), Satmya (wholesome or suitable diet etc.), and Ahara (food or nutrition) (Charaka Vimana 8).

Detailed Rogi and Roga Pariksha is necessary before the treatment (see the chapter Rogi Pariksha) is carried out for the sake of knowledge of his life span (Ayushah-pramana), strength (Bala), and intensity of morbidity (Dosha-pramana) (Charaka) Vimana (8/91).

Assessment of Bala and Dosha

The following ten factors should be examined for assessment of Bala, and Dosha of the patient:

1. Prakriti (constitution)
2. Vikriti (pathological condition)
3. Sara (perfectness of body tissues)
4. Sandhanana (compactness)
5. Pramana (proportions of the limbs and element)
6. Satmya (homologations or suitability)
7. Satwa (psyche)
8. Ahara-shakti (capacity for food and its digestion)
9. Vyayama shakti (capacity for work and exercise)
10. Vaya (age of the patient) (Charaka Vimana 8)

The above factors can be classified as Pravara (high), Madhya (medium), and Avara (low). The knowledge of these factors and etiology helps in clinical course, in the prognosis of a disease and also as practical therapeutics.

Roga pariksha is also necessary for the diagnosis of the disease (Charaka Sutra 10). This can be carried out by the five methods (panchanidana)—nidana (etiological factors), purva-rupa (prodromal symptoms), rupa (clinical manifestations, signs and symptoms), Upashaya (homologus, thereapeutic diagnosis), and Samprapti (pathogenesis) (see the chapter 6)

The diagnosis of disease is done on these methods but the Acharayas have laid a very great importance of tridosha in practical life. They are useful for both the expert and average physician. In this respect Charaka says, when classified according to the cause, pain, colour, site, form and nomenclature, the number of diseases become really countless. A physician need not be ashamed if he is not able to name a disease, as there can be no definite standardization of nomenclature of all the diseases. The same provoked doshas provide the various diseases according to diversity of causes and its localization. Therefore treatment should be initiated after diagnosing the nature of disease, different regions of localization and the special causative factors (Charaka Sutra 18/42-44).

Assessment of the Effect of Treatment

The effect of treatment can be assessed by the signs and symptoms of cure from a disease as mentioned in Charaka Vimmanasuthra 8:

1. Rupa-upasaman (relief from pain and disease)
2. Swara Varna Yoga (accession of voice and complexion)
3. Sharira-Upacharya (increase in body weight)
4. Bala Vriddhi (regaining or increase of vitality and strength)
5. Abhyavatharya abhilasa (desire for blood)

6. Ruchi-ahara-kala (relish while eating)
7. Samyak Jaranam (timely and proper digestion of food)
8. Nidra-labhah yatha-kalam (sleep at proper time)
9. Vaikarikanama Swapnam Adarshanam (not seeing frightful dreams)
10. Skhen Pratibhodhanam (happy awakening)
11. Vata-Mutra-Purisha-Retasam Mukti (elimination of flatus, urine, stool and semen)
12. Sarvgakaraihi mano-buddhi-indriyanam avya atti (freedom from impairement of any kind of the mind, intellect and sense (organs).

The above mentioned are the criteria for cure, in short, which indicates not only relief from pain but also ensure proper functioning of the body, body organs, increase in vitality, digestion and proper functioning of the mind and intellect.

Methods of Treatment

Five factors of pathogenesis e.g. Dosha, Dushya, Srotas, Agni, and Ama, have already been described. The treatment is also based on the predominance of the above factors. Thus, the lines of treatment to be adopted are as under:

1. Shodhana and Shamana
2. Six Upakarmas
3. Panch Karmas—its Purva and Paschat karma
4. Santarpana and Apatarpana Chikista
5. Niramkarana
6. Daiva-Vyapasraya, Yukti-vyapasraya and Satvawaya

7. Antaah-parimarjana and bahir Parimajana and Shastra parridhana
8. Dosha - prasamana and dhatu prasamana
9. Vyadhi - Pratyanika chikitsa
10. Srotas - Shuddhikar chikitsa
11. Swasthya - Ojaskara chikitsa
12. Rasayana and Vajikarana Chikitsa
13. Pathya-Apathya chikitsa
14. Vihar chikitsa

The details of the above lines of teatment are given as under:

1. **Shodhana and Shamana** (Purification and Subsidence Line of Treatment)

Shodhana mean purificaton of the body by eliminating morbid doshas and dushyas (body tissues) from the body through Vamana (emetics), Virechana (purgation), Basti (enema), Sirovirechana (nasal medication), and Raktmokshana (blood letting). It is also called Panch Karma or five-fold line of treatment.

Samana means subsidence of disease and symptoms. It is stated that the morbid doshas, eliminated by shodhana therapy do not recur, but there are chance of recurrence of doshas and disease treated by samana due to various factors. In such cases Samana therapy is prescribed. Samana are: (1) Lahut or Langhana (fasting or light diet), (2) Trit nigraha (restriction of fluids), (3) Vyayama (exercise including yogic exercises). Atapa sevana (use of sun rays, Maruta sevana (breeze of air) and also the symptomatic and the other treatment for subsiding disease, Deepana and Pachana (digestive and increasing metabolism process).

2. **Six Upakarmas** (Methods of Treatment) :

The following upakarmas comprise the entire field of the therapeutics.

UPAKARMAS

Aptarpana (For the reduction of body Kapha and fat)			Santarpana (to increase body weight)		
Langhana	Rukshana	Swedana	Brimhana	Snehana	Sthambhana

I. **Langhana:** It produces lightness of the body. It is prescribed in the diseases caused by Ama and weak digestion. It includes four types of purificatory processes, viz. Vamana (emetics), Virechana (purgation), Asthapana Basti (enemata with decoction of medicinal plants), and Sirovirechana (removal of Doshas from the head with the use of medicine administered through the nose), Trit-nigraha (restriction of fluids), Maruta sevana (wind and air), and Atapsevana (sun rays exposure), Pachana (digestives), Upavasaya (fasting), and Vyayama (exercises including yogic exercises). But of these ten, the first four are included in Shodhana therapy and the remaining six under Samana therapy.

Ib. **Rukshana:** This is a therapy by which the unctuous, sticky and fatty constituents of the body are dried up or rendered dry.

Ic. **Swedana:** It is a process of inducing perspiration or sweating which can be brought about by heat or fire with agni or without application of heat (niragni sweda). The types of swedana where heat is necessary are of four types viz. Tap swedana (application of dry heat), Ypanah sweda (application of poultices), and Drava sweda (use of hot liquids). These four types are futher divided into fourteen, according to the method and articles used for swedana.

IIa. **Brimhana:** This is reverse of langhana. The line oftreatment which increases body weight is called Brimhana.

IIb. **Snehana:** This is reverse of Rukshana. The body elements which are dry are rendered oily on unctuous by snehana. It is conducted with four types of fatty substaness viz. ghrita, taila, vasa (muscle, fat, mazza, (bone marrow). The methods of administration of snehana are as below:

(i) by drinks and foods

(ii) by enemata with oil and

(iii) by massage through skin.

IIc. **Sthamba:** The procedure by which the flow of fluid on the body is lessened or checked is called Stambhana (e.g. use of grahi (astringents) in diarrhoea or polyuria and such other conditions (Charaka Sutra 22).

Pancha Karma
(Five types of Treatment)

The Panchakarma line of treatment is to eliminate or excrete the vitiated doshas from the body thereby whole body gets purified. The diseases in which the doshas localised in Saka (dhatu and skin) are brought into the Kostha (alimentary tract) and then eliminated. The five-fold line of treatment according to Charaka school of thought are: (1) Vamana (emesis), (ii) Virechana (purgation), (iii) Anuvasana or Sneh vasti (enemata with oil or fat), (iv) Asthapana or Niruha (enemata with decoctions of medicinal plants) and Sirovirechana Nasya (removal of Doshas by medicines through nose). Pancha karma according to Sushruta school of thought are: (i) Vamana (emesis), (ii) Virechana (purgation), (iii) Basti (enemata of both anuvasana and asthapana) (iv) Sirovirechana (use of medicines through the nose) and (v) Rakta mokhshna (blood-letting).

All the above methods except Anuvasana basti are also included under Shodhana therapy. (Charaka Siddhi 1-6-7-10-12).

Poorva-Karma (Pre-elimination Treatment)

The patient is prepared for elimination before starting any of the five-fold elimination therapies. This preparation is called Poorva-Karma. This includes two procedures viz. Snehana (oleation) and Swedana (sudation) (Charaka Sutra 10).

Paschat-Karma (Post-elimination Treatment)

After any of the Panchakarma, the patient gets exhausted and feels weak. For this reason as well as for improvement of digestion he is administered a diet gradually so that his digestion and metabolism may improve, and his stamina may also increase. This is called Paschat karma or Sansaryana karma (Charaka Siddhi 1-12).

Santarpana and Apatarpana Line of Treatment

Santarpana indicates the food taken to satisfaction of the patient. It may or may not contain fat. Apatarpana, indicates the quantity of food which is not enough to fill the belly completely (Charaka Sutra 23).

Niramkarana

Āma has been discussed on previous pages. It is the product of improper digestion or metabolism. Niramkarana means the treatment to digest or remove these products of impaired digestion and metabolism. This is mainly done by langhana (fasting or light diet), Pachana (digestive medicines), warm water etc.

Daiva-Vyāpasaraya-Chikitsa (Divine Therapy)

Diseases are not only physical or psychological, but there may be certain other aetiological factors also, which cannot be explained by any of the known methods. Such diseases are believed to be due to the curses of saints etc., or due to the entrance of some unformed bodies like ghosts etc.; Charaka, the pioneer of scientific medicine does not believe such causes. He says neither gods, nor the gandharvas, neither the goblins (pishacha) nor the demons nor ought else, torment man, who is not tormented of himself (Charaka nidana 7). Thus, he classifies these diseases to be psychological in origin, but still he gives the line of treatment in such disorders.

Divine therapy consists of the following:

1. Mantras (Incantation)
2. Certain divine herbs
3. Gems
4. Mangala (rituals)
5. Bali (oblation)
6. Upahara (offerings)
7. Homa (sacrifice)
8. Prayaschitta (ceremonial penitance)
9. Upavasa (fasting)
10. Pranipat (prostration)
11. Gamana (pilgrimages)
12. Niyama (bows)
13. Swati Ayana (auspicious rites) (Charaka Sutra 11/54).

Yukti-Vyapasraya Chikitsa (Scientific Medicine)

This line of treatment consists of medicines and dietic regimens.

Satwa-avajaya (Mental Control)

Mental control or psychological treatment consists of restraining oneself from the desire for ahita (un-wholesome) objects etc.

The Daiva vyapasraya and Satwa-avajaga lines of treatment are psychic treatments performed in ancient India. It is performed even today at some places not only in India but also in several other countries (Charaka Sutra 11/54).

Antah-Parimarjana, Bahiha-Parimarjana and Sastrapranidhana—Lines of Treatment

Antah-parimarjana: Means internal purification. This consists of medicines taken orallly or internally for relief or cure of the diseases.

Bahiha-Parimarjana: Means external application of medicines. This procedure consist of Abhyanta (oil massage), Swedana (sudation), Pradeha (applications), Pariseka (afflusions), Mardana (massage), and such other lines applied to the external surface.

Sastra-pranidhana: Means operative treatment. This consists of Chedana (excision), Bhedana (incision), Vyana (puncturing), Dharana (rupturing), Lekhana (scrapping or erasion), Seevana (suturing), Eshana (sounding and the application of leeches and caustics) etc. (Charaka Sutra 11/55).

Dosha Pratyanika, Dhatu Prashamana and Vyadhi Line of Treatment

Dosha Pratyanika: Pratyanika means antagonistic to provoked doshas e.g. use of oil and/or basti in vata disorders, use of ghrita and/or Virechana in pitta disorders and the use of honey and or vamana in kapha disorders.

Dhatu-prashamana: The line of treatment which acts on vitiated Dhatu (tissues) e.g. blood-letting in diseases of blood and skin.

Vyadhi-pratyanika Chikitsa: It is the line of treatment which directly acts on diseases. Charaka has given fifty decoctions, each containing ten medicinal herbs for fifty diseases according to the action of medicines (Charaka Sutra 4).

Srotas - Suddhikara Chikitsa

As described earlier in the factors of pathogenesis, the srotas (body channels) become pathogenic. Srotas are innumerable but for the purpose of practical applications, they have been classified in to thirteen main types according to the flow of material through them. The characteristics of the morbidity of srotas are: (i) Ati-pravritti (increased flow), ii) Sanga (obstruction), (iii) Siragranthi (knotted condition), and (iv) Vimarga gamana (flow in reverse direction).

The line of the treatment to purify the srotas, to get normal flow of the flowing material and to make the morbidity subside is called "Srotas-shuddhikara Chikitsa" (Charaka Vimana 5).

Pathya-Apathya (See Table 10.2)

Pathya means the diet and other regimen which are suitable in health and disease.

Apathya means the diet and other regimen which are not suitable for health and may provoke the disease.

Ayurveda lays a great emphasis on pathya-apathya in regulation of diet etc. It is to that extent that Acharyas say "If a man uses pathya (wholesome diet etc.), there is no need of any medicine. And if the patient does not observe pathya and indulges in apathya, the medicine will not act."

Table 10-2 : Showing day and night division, English and Hindi Calendar Months, Season, Three Stages of Tridosas, Dosapratyarika Cikitsa and Ahar-Vihar Regimen in Different Seasons

Day & Night Division	*English Calendar Months*	*Hindi Calendar Months*	*Seasons (C.S. 6/4)*	*Three stages of tridosas and Dosha Pratyanika Cikitsa (C.S. 4)* Pitta	Kapha	Vata	*Ahara (C.S. 6)*	*Vihara (C.S.6)*
Pradosa (evening)	Aug-Sep. Sep-Oct.	Bhadrapada Asvayuja	Varsa (Rainy-Sea.)	Accumulation	—	—	Honey-sours and unctuous diet.	Avoid day sleep, excessive exercise—moving in the sun indulgence in sexual intercourse.
Ardharatri Mid-Night	Oct-Nov. Nov.-Dec.	Kartika Margashira	Sharad Autumn	Provoked	—	Pacified	Madhura, Kasay, Ras, ghee, milk, rice, and its preparations, sweets	To sit in moon light in the Ist quarter of night, exercise, avoid curd and acrid diet. etc.
(Pratyusas early morning)	Dec.-Jan. Jan.-Feb.	Pausha Magha	Hemanta (Early-winter)	—	Accumulation	—	Madhur, amle & lavana rasa, Nutrious diet.	Massage, exercise, woollen blanket, protection against cold.
(Survahna Morning)	Feb.-Mar. Mar.-Apr.	Falguna Chaitra	Vasanta (Spring)	—	Provoked	—	Laghu, ruksa, laja-canaka, (Bengal-gram)	Massage, exercise, fomentations

Madhyanha (Noon)	Apr-May May-Jun.	Vaishakha Jaishta	Grisma (Summer)	—	Pacified	Accumu-lation	Laghu, madhura, snigdha, light in digestion, sita and seasonal fruits, Jamhu	Cold air and air passing through usira (Khasa)
Aparanha (Afternoon)	Jun-Jul. Jul-Aug.	Asadha Shravana	Praurit (early-rainy)	—	Provoked		Kasay, madhura rasa, amla, lavan, nigdha, drava light chief, coil, clean water, curd and kshara, lemon	avoid sleeping on the ground, clear the dirty monsoon water from the area around.

Dosa Pratyamika Cikitsa	-	ghrta and or Vineeana and Rakt mokshana	-	madhu and or Tail or Basti vaman

Hence it may be said that the treatment can be carried out only by regulated and wholesome diet without the use of medicine.

Vihara means the procedures and routine to be observed during health and disease e.g., in condition of fever of recent origin, one should avoid sleeping during the day, bath oil message, food, sex act, anger and excitement, direct breeze, exercise etc. He should on the contrary take complete rest, keep mental control, fasting and so on. In this way, lVihara includes the procedures to be followed during disease and health (Charaka Sutra 25).

Rasayana or Swasthya—Ojaskar Chikitsa

Swastha means physically, psychologically and spiritualy healthy person. Oja is considered to be responsible for vitality resistance, complexion etc. The line of treatment which increases physical, mental and spiritual strength is called Swasthya-Ojaskar treatment.

Rasayana means that kind of treatment which controls and prevents disease, increase vitality and brings healthy long life. In short it may be said that Rasayana may not add years to one's life but may add life to years (Charaka Chikitsa 1).

Vajikarana means the line of treatment which increase pleasure in sex act. It is very near to aphrodesiacs (Charaka Chikitsa 2).

However, it is for the physician to select which line of treatment will be suitable to the patient for the relief or cure of the disease. The Physician has to treat the man as a whole and not just the organ or systems of the body. He/she has to see the body, mind and spirit during diagnosis and treatment. Table 10.2 shows day and night divisions, English and Hindi calendar months, seasons, three stages of tridoshas, doshas, dosha pratyanika chikitsa and Ahara vihara regimen in different seasons. The table showing day and night divisions etc. is given to understand the line of treatment in various doshas and its provocation along with Ahara vihara regions according to seasons of the year etc.

To sum up, one should not forget the caution given by Charaka. "The learned physician who is unable to win his way into a patient's heart by the light of his scientific understanding is not entitled to treat disease." (Charak Vimana 4).

NOTES AND REFERENCES

1. Ashtanga Hridaya Sutra 1/2
2. Susruta Sutra 1/19.
3. Sabda - Kalpadruma.
4. Sabda - Kalpadruma, Charana Vyuha
5. Realms of Ayurveda
6. Charaka Vimana 8/91
7. Charaka Vimana 8.
8. Charaka Sutra 18/42-44
9. Charaka Sutra 22.
10. Charaka Siddhi 1-6-7-10-12.
11. Idem 1-12.
12. Charaka Sutra 23
13. Charaka Sutra 11/54
14. Charaka Sutra 11/55
15. Charaka Sutra 4
16. Charaka Sutra 5
17. Charaka Sutra 25
18. Charaka Chikitsa 1
19. Charaka Chikitsa 2
20. Charaka Vimana 4
21. Charaka Sutra 2
22. Charaka Sutra 10
23. Charaka Nidana 7

CHAPTER 11

Pharmaco Therapeutics in Ayurveda

M. Paramkush Rao

Introduction

Ayurveda is a science of human life developed through ages and fabricated with profound preclinical, and clinical subjects. Pharamacological aspects have been dealt by Dravyaguna, a branch concerned with drug's study. Dravyaguna chiefly concentrates on medicinal plants and their therapeutic uses. Mineral drugs prescribed in Ayurveda are also processed or/and combined with herbs. Hence Ayurvedic pharmacology is the study of medicinal plants. Its approach to explore the therapeutic benefits of medicinal plants is unique.

Ayurvedic study of the drugs is prevalently aimed for therapeutic benefit. The integral approach adopted to analyse and apprehend the human body will also actuate the Principles behind the study of the drugs. The viability and utility of Ayurvedic style of drugs' study is evident with the current researches in the field of medicinal plants.

Ayurveda prefers prescribing the herbs in totality over the active ingredients. The approach fetches the following advantages.

(i) Drugs used in totality remain in natural state. Alike foods, drugs procured from natural sources are more homogenous and readily accepted by the human body. Isolated active ingredients of the same plant will be devoid of naturality and become heterogenous to the human body. They produce unwanted effects resulted by the rejection mechanism. The synthetic forms of these ingredients produce more side effects. Reserpine isolated from Rauwolfia serpentina Benth exokurz is possessing certain undesired effects. But whole drug is still safely prescribed by Ayurvedicians in the name of Sarpagandha.

(ii) Using the drug as a whole provides extra, rather side benefits, while avoiding side effects. An active ingredient in a plant drug is bound to be associated with certain other chemicals. All together, they exhibit a cumulative effect on the human body. One ingredient among them acts as a balancing agent against the other in order to exert the desired effect in a controlled fashion. For instance the chemical analysis of Rauwolfia serpentina, Benthexkurz and Papaver somniferum L. is presented in Table No. 11.1.

The different chemical ingredients with divergent Pharmacological effects support the concept of cumulative effect of the drug. Nowadays the concept of whole drug and its cumulative effect is gaining popularity.

Ayurvedic pharmacology is designed to understand the cumulative effect of the medicinal plants. The basic pharmacological principles developed and practised by ancient seers for the study of medicinal plants are derived from the theory of "Panca Maha Bhutas" or "Five Proto elements."

Table 11-1 : Chemical Ingredients and Their Pharmacological Effects of Rauwolfia Serpentina and Papaver Somniferum

Sl. No.	*Name of the plant*		*Active ingredient*	*Pharmacological effect*
1.	Rauwolfia serpentina Benth ex kurz.	(a)	Reserpine	Reduces the Blood pressure
		(b)	Rawolfine	Increases the Blood pressure
		(c)	Azmaline	No effect on Blood pressure.
2.	Papaver somniferum L.	(a)	Morphine	Narcotic and Depresses the respiratory rate.
		(b)	Narcotine	Accelerates the respiratory rate
		(c)	Papaverine	No marked narcotic effect. Relaxes the smooth muscles.

Human body is said as the epitome of the Universe. All the constiuents of Universe are also present in the human body. A specific state of equilibrium or a sort of homeostasis, among the Bhautic components of human body is needed for the maintenance of health. During different stages of life, due to activities of life force, there is a natural consequence of the Panca Maha Bhutas being consumed for the manifestation of energy. The transient depletion of bhautic content will be replenished by the consumption of corresponding bhautic components from the Universe, in the form of food, drinks and air. Excessive intake of a particular substance will lead to imbalance, and continuous indulgence leads to prolonged disturbance. Imbalance of the Bhautic components in the human body is called as disease.

Imbalance in principle is of two types (1) Enhancement and (2) Depletion. Correction of imbalance is achieved by reducing the enhanced and supplementing the depleted in the form of drugs. Restoration of the balance among the body constituents is called therapy in Ayurveda.

Supplementation of depleted constituents is done by using similar components. Reduction of enhanced is done by using opposite substances. Hence the Panca Maha Bhutas are again grouped to facilitate the identification of similar and opposite substances. Vayu and Agni belong to one group as they always flow upwards. Pruthvi and Jalam belongs to another group as they always fall downwards. These two groups are opposite to each other. Akasa is said as neutral. In another classification of substances, those associated predominantly with Agni are called Agneya, kind with lesser ratio of Agni Bhuta are called Soumya. These groups are relatively opposite in nature.

In principle, the foregoing description forms the basis of therapy in tune with the theory of Panc Maha Bhutas. The theory of Panca Maha Bhutas being purely a physical theory, its biological application necessitated to propose two more theories in regard with Man and drug. The theory of "Tridosas" is promulgated to understand the human body in its physiological and pathological states and to diagnose the disease in the terms of Bhautic imbalance. The drug's bhautic composition and its changing pattern of bhautic composition during the effective phase in the body is interpreted by the theory of "Rasa Pancaka."

Rasa Pancaka and the Drug

The drug in Ayurveda is called as Dravya. Dravya Guna is the pharmacological branch dealing with the drugs, their properties and effects. The composition and effects of the drug are analysed in a wholistic perspective as said earlier.

Alike human body, drugs are composed of Panca Maha Bhutas. In order to study the bhautic composition of the drugs "Rasa Pancaka" or the Theory of "Five Pharmacological" principles is proposed. It comprises the following:

(1)	Rasa	(Taste of the drug)
(2)	Guna	(Attribute or property)
(3)	Vipaka	(Post-digestive form of Rasa)
(4)	Virya	(Potency)
and (5)	Prabhava	(Specific effect)

These five principles constitute the conceptual part of the Dravya Guna.

(1) Rasa (The Taste of the Drug)

Rasa means the taste of the drug. It will also indicate the bhautic composition, and probable effect. Effects on Dosas ascribed to the taste of the drug will be exhibited by majority of the drugs except few. Effect of such exceptional drugs is understood on the basis of its Vipaka or Guna or Virya, of the corresponding drug.

Every Rasa is the resultant of Bhautic composition of the substrate substance. Variation in the predominance gave rise to the formation of Six Rasas. Six types of Rasa in fact, can be called as the pharmacological classification of the tastes of the Drugs.

The types of Rasa, Bhautic predominance and their effect on Dosas are summarized in Table No. 11-2.

Table 11-2 : Rasas, Bhautic Predominance and Effect on Dosas

S.No.	*RASA*	*Bhautic Predominance*	*Effects on Dosas*		
			Vata	*Pitta*	*Kapha*
1.	Madhura (Sweet)	Jalam & Prthvi	↓	↓	↑
2.	Amla (Sour)	Agni & Jalam	↓	↑	↑
3.	Lavana (Saline)	Agni & Prthvi	↓	↑	↑
4.	Katu (Pungent)	Vayu & Agni	↑	↑	↓
5.	Tikta (Bitter)	Vayu & Akasa	↑	↓	↓
6.	Kasaya (Astringent)	Vayu & Prithvi	↑	↓	↓

↑ = Aggravates or increases
↓ = Pacifies or decreases

(2) Vipaka (Taste of the Drug Emerging After Digestion)

Every substance consumed orally has to change its Bhautic composition after processing through digestion in the human body. This change is due to breakdown and resynthesis of the substances during digestion. This change will also influence the taste of the drug. The changed form or post-digestive form of the taste is called Vipaka. Unlike Rasa, it is to be inferred on the basis of its effect on Dosas. In accordance to Tridosas three types of Vipaka are formed from six tastes. Majority of the drugs follow a definite changing pattern as mentioned in Table No. 11.3. But few drugs escape this pattern due to altered arrangement of bhautic molecules in resynthesis caused by digestion. In order to identify such variables and for logical explanation of their effects concept of Vipaka is proposed.

Table 11- 3 : Changing Pattern of Rasa-Vipaka, and Effect on Dosas

S.No.	*RASA*	*Bhautic Predominance*	*Effects on Dosas*		
			Vata	*Pitta*	*Kapha*
1.	Madhura Lavana	Madhura (Prithvi & Kala)	↓	↓	↑
2.	Amla	Amla (Agni & Jalam)	↓	↑	↑
3.	Katu Tikta Kasaya	Katu (Vayu & Akasa)	↑	↑	↓

↑ = Increases
↓ = Decreases

(3) Guna (Physico-Pharmacological Properties of the Drug)

Every substance is having certain properties. Ayurveda says such properties denote its bhautic composition. These are the secondary properties of Bhutas manifested due to interactions among them. These physico-chemical properties often exhibit a definite influence on their pharmacological effect, and nurture similar properties in the human body. e.g. Guru (Heavy). The heavier substances are heavy to digest and more nutritious. They help in gaining the body weight. The substances light to digest are called Laghu. They are not much nutritious and reduces the body weight. They oppose each other in action. Ten such pairs of properties are identified. They are relatively opposite to each other. Few of them are perceptable hence can be called as physical properties. The remaining are inferred by their effects on the body.

A summarised form of Ten pairs of Gunas, their Bhautic predominance and effect on Dosas is presented in Table No. 11.4.

Table 11-4 : Pairs of 20 Gunas : Bhautic Predominance and Effect on Dosas

S.No.	*GUNĀS (in Pairs)*	*Bhautic Predominance*	*Effect on Dosas*		
			Vata	*Pitta*	*Kapha*
1.	Guru (Heavy)	Jalam & Pṛthvi	↓	–	↑
	x				
	Laghu (light)	Ākaśa; Vāyu & Agni	↑	–	↓
2.	Śīta (Cold)	Jalam	↑	↓	↑
	x				
	Uṣna (Hot)	Agni	↓	↑	↓
3.	Snigdha (Unctuous)	Jalam	↓	–	↑
	x				
	Rukṣa (Un Unctuous)	Vayu, Agni & Pṛthvi	↑	–	↓
4.	Manda (Dull)	Jalam & Pṛthvi	–	↓	↑
	x				
	Tikṣna (Sharp)	Agni	–	↑	↓

5. Sthira (Stable)	Pṛthvi	–	–	↑
x				
Sara (Mobile)	Vāyu & Jalam	↓	–	–
6. Mṛdu (Soft)	Akasa &	–	–	↑
x				
Khaṭina (Hard)	Pṛthvi	–	–	–
7. Picchila (Slimy)	Jalam	–	–	↑
Viśda (Non-Slmry)	Ākāśa, Vāyu Agni & Pṛthvi	↑	–	–
8. Slakana (Smooth)	Agni	–	↑	–
x				
Khara (Rough)	Vāyu	↑	–	–
9. Sthūla (Gross)	Pṛthvi	–	–	↑
Sūkṣma (Sublte)	Ākāśi; Vāyu & Agni	↑	–	–
10. Sāndra (Dense)	Pṛthvi	–	↓	↑
x				
Dravya (Fluidity)	Jalam	–	↑	↑

↑= Increases ↓ = Decreases – = Neutral effect.
x = Opposes

(4) Virya (Potency or Efficiency of the Drug)

Rasa, Vipaka and Guna are the properties existing in the drug. Few of them are perceptable and others are inferred basing on their effects. In turn properties once known will help to identify a drug for a probable pharmacological effect. In real sense, that is the drug which exerts effect by the virtue of its own efficiency. This particular efficiency of the drug is called Virya or 'Potency.' A drug may become effectless as it looses potency though the taste and certain physical properties are still present in it.

The term Virya means power and potency. Ayurveda defines it as the power which performs action. No action is possible without Virya. All actions are performed only due to the presence of Virya in the drug. This definition and description of Virya will remind the modern definition of energy i.e. the energy of a matter is its capacity for doing work and the measure of energy is work. Energy may be potential or kinetic. The chemical energy locked up or potentially held in the food or drugs represents Sita Virya. Substances from which energy is readily released during digestion and metabolic reactions in the body, involving oxidation are Usna in Virya. Thus the energy transformations which take place during the process of life have been grouped into two categories and named after the names of Guna, i.e. Usna and Sita Viryas. Dravyas of Usna Virya promote or undergo catabolic reactions. On the other hand Dravyas of Sita Virya promote or undergo anabolic reactions, resulting in conservation of energy in a potential form. Though these energies are said to be of 8 types according to another school, Usna and Sita types are more popularly used in the Ayurvedic texts.

Bhautic predominance and effect on Dosas of Viryas is mentioned in Table No. 11-5.

Table 11 -5 : Viryas—Bhautic Predominance and Effect on Dosas

S.No.	*Virya*	*Bhautic predominance*	*Effect on Doshas*		
			Vata	*Pitta*	*Kapha*
1.	Usna (Hot)	Agni	↓	↑	↓
2.	Sita (Cold)	Prthvi & Jalam	↑	↓	↑

= Increases

= Decreases

(5) Prabhava (Specific Effect)

Prabhava a form of energy causes unexplainable effect by the drug. It can also be called as the nature (Svabhava) of the drug. The effect of the drug, which is explained logically on the basis of Rasa, Guna and Vipaka, existing in that drug, is caused by virya or rational energy (Cintya Sakti). (In other words Virya is the result of bhautic composition of a drug). And if the action of a drug is not explainable on the basis of Bhautic composition or Rasa etc., it is believed as caused by an empirical form of energy (Acintya Sakti) or Prabhava.

The definition and description of Prabhava can be appreciated well on the analogy of 'Isomerism' explained in modern physical chemistry. Rasa, Guna, Vipaka and Virya are indicative of Bhautic composition of a drug. Certain drugs in spite of possessing similar Rasa etc., produce a different effect.

Therefore it is evident that the special relation (Dik) among the constituent bhautic molecules will also play a major role in deciding the drug effect. All such drugs escaped from the theory of Bhutas, are identified and explained individually basing on their specific actions. Efforts are also being made to provide a rational explanation to such drugs with the help of current researches.

All the foregoing explanations theoretically may look like dealing with the pharmaco dynamic aspects of the drug. Still this solution oriented approach in the study of the drugs gives greater importance to its therapeutical utility. Hence pharma cotherapeutics has more importance in Ayurveda.

The theory of Rasa Pancaka thus evolved is also helpful in understanding the actions of newer drugs. Current researches on Ayurvedic medicinal plants are re-establishing the drug effects previously identified on the basis of Rasa Pancaka. Besides, many drugs newly found effective in a particular ailment, by the modern research methodology, show no common relation explainable by modern sciences. But all such pharmacological effects of new drugs can be conveniently understood on the basis of Rasa Pancaka Siddhanta. For example, there are about 62 plants have been identified with hypoglycemic effect in experimental screening. Few of them have also been confirmed clinically. Their effect is explainable neither on phytochemical similarity nor taxonomical proximity. But majority of these plants possess bitter and astringent tastes. Their action is evident as they are anti-Kapha.

More over if any disease is analysed and diagnosed on the basis of Tridosas, there are numerous drugs provide relief with their conspicuous influence on Dosas. Therefore it is apparent that the contemplation of medicinal plants through the time tested methodology propounded by Ayurveda will always provide desired therapeutic benefits.

NOTES AND REFERENCES

1. Anonymous, *Wealth of India (Raw Material)*, Vol. VII & VIII. C.S.I.R., New Delhi, 1966 & 1972, p. 242 (Vol. VII). 387 (Vol. VIII).

2. Bhagavan Dash, Introductory Notes, *Ayurveda Saukhyam of Todarananda*, Volume I & II, Concept Public Company, New Delhi, 1987.

3. Dhyani, S.C. *Dravya Guna Siddhanta* (Hindi), Krishnadas Academy, Varanasi, 1986, pp. 58.

4. Ibid, p. 28.

5. Dwarkanath. C. *The Fundamental Principles of Ayurveda,* Part III, Hindustan Press, Mysore, 1954, pp. 46-50.

6. Ibid p. 43.

7. Ibid pp. 151 & 152.

8. Ibid p. 171.

9. Gilman, A..G.; Goodman, L.S.; and Gilman, A. *The Pharmacological Basis of Therapeutics,* MacMillan Publishing Co. Inc. New York, 1980, pp. 203.

10. Phunjalal, B.R. *The Susruta Samhita,* An English translation. The Chowkhamba Sanskrit Series, Varanasi, 1963. (Chapter XII; Verse 2), p. 375.

11. Satyavati,. et. al. *Medicinal Plants of India,* Vol. I & II, Indian Council of Medicinal Research, New Delhi. 1976, 1987.

12. Sharma, R.K., Bhagawan Dash, *Caraka Samhita,* English Translation, Vol. I, Chaukhamba Sanskrit Series, Varanasi, *1983.* (Chapter XXVI, Verse 10) p. 451.

13. Ibid. (Chapter II; Verse 4), p. 184.

14. Ibid. (Chapter XVI; Verse 34), p. 307.

15. Ibid. (Chapter I, Verse 44), p. 26.

16. Ibid. (Chapter XXVI; Verse 41), p. 465.

17. Ibid. (Chapter I; Verse 64), p. 39.

18. Ibid. (Chapter XXVI; Verse 40), p. 463.

19. Ibid. (Chapter I; Verses 65 & 66), p. 46 & 47.

20. Ibid. (Chapter XXVI; Verse 58), p. 473.

21. Ibid. (Chapter XXVI; Verse 65). p. 476.

22. Sharma, R.K., Bhagawan Dash, *Caraka Samhita (Sarirasthana)* English Translation, Chaukhamba Sansrkrit Series, Varanasi *1979,* (Chapter V; Verse 2), pp. 414.

23. Ibid. (Chapter VI; Verse 3), p. 427.

24. Sharma, P.V. *Introduction to Dravyaguna,* Chaukhamba Orientalia, Varanasi, *1976,* p. 45.

25. Sharma, S. Realms of Ayurveda, Arnold Heineman Publishers (India) Pvt. Ltd. New Delhi, 1979, p. 38.

26. Tripati, R. *Astanga Sangraham (Ṣutrasthānam),* Hindi Commentary, Chaukamba Sanskrit Pratisthan, Delhi, 1988, (Chapter 19; Verse 1), p. 325.

27. Ibid. (Chapter 19; Verse 13), p. 331.

PRINCIPLES OF PANCHAKARMA THERAPY

Dr. A.R.V. Murthy

Ayurveda the ancient system of medicine has a special concept of health and disease. The disease is caused by the derangement of '*Tridoshas*' (vayu, pitta and kapha) and the healthy state is brought back by restoring the equilibrium of these *doshas.* To restore the equilibrium Ayurveda advocates two categories of approaches: *Samana* (palliative measures) and *Shodhana* (eradicative measures).

The former approach is adopted when the magnitude of derangement is mild to moderate and when the derangement is of a higher magnitude the latter course is resorted to. When *Samana* is done the chances of recurrence persist while *Sodhana* ensures a complete cure inasmuch as it roots out the cause. The speciality of Shodhana is that, as the word '*Shodhana*' itself denotes is 'cleansing' of the body and elimination of the vitiated *dosas* from the body. The procedures used for this elimination of *doshas* are collectively called '*panchakarma*'. *Pancha* means five and *Karma* has four meanings in 'Acts of past life, action, effort and Therapeutic measure', out of these 'Therapeutic measure' seems to be the most appropriate one. Thus *Panchakarma* means 'five Major Therapeutic measures.' 'Major, because there are many minor procedures which do not qualify for this usage because of their inferior quality of elimination of *doshas.* Controversies not withstanding, the following five procedures are considered as *Panchakarmas.*

Vamana	Emesis
Virechana	Purgation
Niruna Vasti	Medicated Enema with decoction
Anuvasana Vasti	Medicated Enema with oil
Nasya	Errhine

The extra-ordinary efficiency of *Rakta Mokshana* (Blood-letting) in the eradication process of *doshas* has prompted some scholars to suggest its inclusion among *Panchakarmas* in place of *Anuvasana vasti* whose efficacy in elimination of *doshas* is not of high standards. If this is conceded then we have the following as *panchakarmas.*

Vamana
Virechana
Vasti
Nasya
Rakta Mokshana

Panchakarma has a special place in Ayurvedic therapeutics. It is an unique approach to the science of healing. Though considered as a part of *Kayacikitsa* (Medical branch) it is potentially useful in all the other branches of the Medical science. It is a major force in the management of almost all the chronic and even incurable diseases.

Panchakarmas are preceded by *purvakarmas* which assist *panchakarmas* in proper elimination of the morbid *doshas* and are followed by *Samsarjana karma* which ensure a steady but gradual recovery. Chart-I gives a schematic representation of different components of panchakarma.

Only a brief description is being made here of the *panchakarmas* because the purpose of the article is only to acquaint the readers with the principles of *Panchakarma* Therapy.

Purvakarma

It includes *pachana* which is done to check indigestion. Drugs like Sunthi (Zingeber officionalis) which are capable of augmenting the digestive juices are used.

Table 10-3 : Schematic Presentation of Classification of Panchakarma

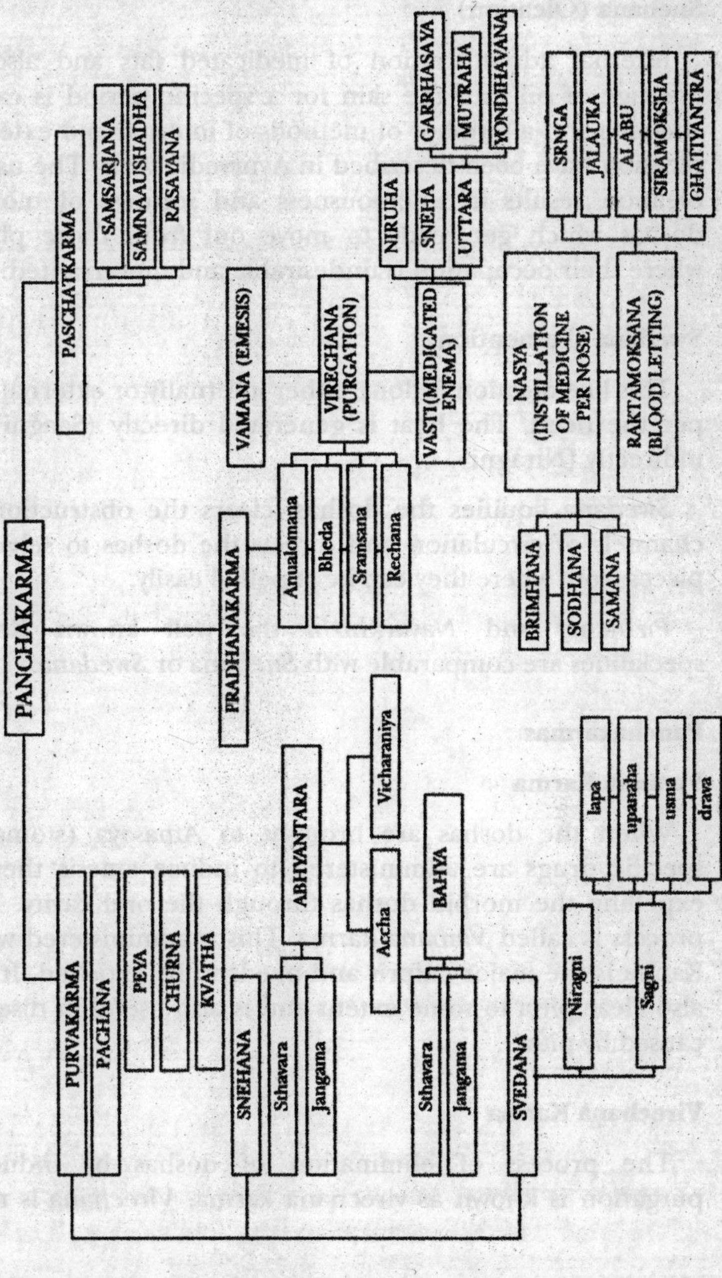

Snehana (Oleation)

Internal administration of medicated fats and also of massage of oil into the skin for a specific period is called *snehana* and a number of methods of internal and external oleation have been described in Ayurvedic texts. The use of oleation results in unctuousness and softness of morbid doshas which get ready to move out from those places where their occupation is undesirable and unwarranted.

Swedana (Fomention)

This like oleation is done either internally or externally as per the need. The heat is generated directly (Saagni) or indirectly (Niragni).

Swedana liquifies the doshas, clears the obstruction of channels of circulation and directs the doshas to selective places from where they can be expelled easily.

Pizhichal and *Navarkhizhi* the well known Kerala specialities are comparable with *Snehana* or *Swedana*.

Panchakarmas

Vamana Karma

When the doshas are brought to *Amasaya* (stomach) specific drugs are administered to induce emesis thereby expelling the morbid doshas through the oral cavity. This process is called *Vamana karma.* This is administered when Kapha is the major culprit and needs to be expelled. It can also clear pitta to some extent and is also useful in diseases caused by pitta.

Virechana Karma

The process of elimination of doshas by inducing purgation is known as virechana karma. *Virechana* is most suitable to alleviate the diseases caused by pitta. However its potency in the diseases of kapha origin is equally remarkable. *Anulomana, Sramsana, Bhedhana* and *Rechana* are the four varieties of *virechana.*

Vasti is the process of elimination of doshas from lower part of the body. Though the site of action is stated to be pakwasaya (large intestine) it is presumed that it attracts the doshas to its site of action from each nook and corner of the body before expelling them through the an orifice. '*Vata*' is the most important of the three doshas accounting for the major share of the diseases caused by them and *vasti* is the best treatment for *vata.* In fact *vasti* is said to be half and even full Therapy for any disease.

Based on the drug used *vasti* is of two types *Niruha* & *Anuvasana.* When the decoction of the herbs forms the major component of medicated enema then it is called *Niruha vasthi.* In Anuvasana oil is the major component. In general the route of administration of vasti is anus, (packwasayagata vasti). However depending on the need it is also administered through the urethral orifice (Mutras-sayagata vasthi) and Vagina (Garbhasayagata vasthi.)

Nasya

Installation of medicine per nose is called Nasya. This process is said to eliminate the doshas from different organs of head.

Raktamokshana

Vitiated blood is let out of the body in many ways. A direct puncture of the blood vessel (siravyadha) or a few incisions over the skin (pracchana) or the use of *Jalouka* (Leech) to suck the blood from the affected site are the common measures resorted to. Alabu, Shringa and Ghatiyantra are the other instruments used for this purpose.

Samsarjana Karma

The patients digestive power should be restored to normalcy gradually and he is administered foods of lighter quality after performing panchakarma. He is given liquid diet first, semi-solid later before finally giving normal diet. This process of gradual restoration is called Samsarjana karma.

Properly performed *panchakarma* results in the following beneficial effects.

1. Cure of the disease
2. Augmentation of general metabolism
3. Promotion of strength and bulk.
4. Pleasentness of senses
5. Improvement of mental and intellectual faculties
6. Improved quality of Semen and good progeny
7. Delayed aging and healthful longivity.

Utility of Panchakarma

Panchakarma has three major objectives

Preventive

Curative

Promotive

Preventive aspect of *Panchakarma* is visible in the form of its use in the daily regimen. Pratimarsha—a variety of Nasya is administered daily for the maintenance of health. Matravasthi—a form of vasti is also used daily for the same purpose. Natural aggravation of *doshas* occur during particular seasons—e.g. *pitta* in *Sharat Ritu*, and if they are eliminated by means of *Panchakarmas* the possibility of one getting the disease is minimised. Similarly the diseases caused by the suppression of natural urges can be prevented by performing *panchakarmas.*

Curative nature of *panchakarmas* is well known. Any disease, with the exception of '*urusthambha*' (a disease characterised by stiffness and heaviness of thighs) can be cured by *panchakarma*. Ayurvedic texts have specified the variety of the Karma to be used in each disease.

Promotive role of *panchakarma* is mainly because of its effectiveness in cleaning the body of the impurities and preparing it for the administration of *Rasayana* (Science of Nutrition) and *Vajikarana* (Aphrodesiology) therapy. It is said that *Rasayana* and *Vajikarana* therapy should not be administered to those who have not undergone *panchakarmas*.

Scope of Panchakarma

Panchakarma is a special branch of Ayurvedic medicine which has a unique approach towards the management of diseases. It has a big role to play in this new era when newer and newer diseases are cropping up and when the older diseases are becoming incurable. There are many causes for such a development but the most important of the culprits are—Food habits and life style. Improperly digested food, because of improper activity accumulates in the tissues in the form of toxic materials ('Ama' as Ayurveda calls it) and causes all the diseases. Such toxic materials unless and until thrown out of the body, continue to irritate and insult the tissues causing all the trouble. *Panchakarma* is the only answer to such a situation inasmuch as it expels all the toxic materials from the body thus rooting out the cause and restoring the health. *Panchakarma* is being successfully used to cure such incurable diseases like Hemiplegia, Poliomylitis, Rheumatoid Arthritis and many more dreaded conditions.

Table 10-4 gives the details of the effectivness of *panchakarmas* in different diseases.

Table 10-4 : Essence of Clinical Research Condu.ted in Panchakarma in Past Two Decades

Type of Panchakarma Studied	*On...... Disease No. of Cases IN ()*	*No. of Cases Relieved Cured + Partial Relief*	*Reference*
Pinda sveda	Polio Myelitis (376)	69	Kasture H.S. et al. Rhenumatism vol. 3 No.1 - 1969.
Pinda sveda & Matravasti	Polio Myelitis (196)	69 + 82	Kasture et al. 1973
Pinddasveda	Rheumatism (Amavata) (20)	20	Singh R.H. et al. Journal of Research in India Medicine vol. 7 No. 4 1972
Pizhichil	Hemiplegia (12)	12	Kurup P.N.V. Kasture et al. Ayurvedalok July, 1965.
Patrapindasveda	Shoulder pain (15)	13	Kasture et al. Sachitra Ayurveda May - September 1967.
	Sciatica (30)	21	
Vamana	Hemilegia (9)	6	Mehta et al. 1975-76 Poddar Ayurvedic College, Bombay
Virechan	Eczema (300)	210	Giri D.D. et al. 10 Akhandanand Ayurvedic Hospital, Ahmedabad
Vasti	Paralysis (16)	10	Mehta et al. Poddar Ay.c. Bombay
Vasti	Peptic ulcer syndrome (157)	83 + 48	Kasture et al. 1974
Vasti	Backache (28)	22 +5	Kasture et al. Rheumatism vol. 3, issue 4, 1964.
Vasti	Joint pains (30)	10 + 14	Kature et al. Rheumatism, vol. 8, No. 2, 1974.

In spite of all it's effectivity *Panchakarma* has it's own limitations. Complex nature of the procedures, enormous time it involves (A course of *panchakarma* requiries exactly 129 days) are the two major hurdles. *Panchakarma* needs to be revived and popularised to suit the needs of present day conditions. Nevertheless prompt efforts are being made to simplify the procedures for their use in general practice. This would go a longway in taking *panchakarma* to the masses—thus providing the mankind the help it needs today.

NOTES AND REFERENCES

H.S. Kastur, Ayurveda Panchakarma Vignnan, Baidyanath Ayurveda Bhavan Limited, 1979.

V. Nagaraju,Role of Panchakarma in Ayurveda, Hospital Health Journal NLC.

CHAPTER 12

Principles of Drug (Dravya) Administration

Among four basic factors of treatment, drug (dravya, Aushadh) occupies a second place to physician (Sutr. 9/3). All the drugs with basic elemental (panchabhautic) composition have effect on the three humors (tri-doshas) in human body—As regards the drug administration and preparation in respect to their action and properties, Charaka conceives "that should be known as the proper medication, which requires to be taken in small doses, which is quick in action and is effective even in excessive degree of morbidity, which is easy to take, which is easily diagestible, palatable, pleasing, curative of the specific disease, not harmful even if complications arise, not very depressant and possesses the most agreeable smell, colour and taste (Sutra 6/15-16). Rules were also framed to bring about an uniformity in use of drugs containing the opposite properties in the preparation, whenever found necessary to add such a drug for the taste, smell, appearance or any other factor. The antagonism of the drug potency does not vitally impair the main effect of the principal drugs, while admixturing the drugs of similar potency—intensifies its action in case of administration of compound preparations. The use of articles that are of antagonistic potency to the disease is allowed for the purpose of imparting to the medication, pleasant colour, touch and odour suitable to the condition of a disease (Kalpa 12/43-46).

Incompatible drugs: Charaka gave due consideration with regard to the drugs having incompatibility with the illness in question. He says that substance is unwholesome which is incompatible from the point of view of country, season, gastric fire (jatharagni), measure, homologation, vata and other body humors, preparation, potency, bowel tendency, state of the patient, time of eating, things to be avoided or observed, cookery combination, palatability, richness of quality and rules of eating (Sutra 26/86, 87).

Dosage: Charaka states that "the art of prescription depends upon the knowledge of dosage and time and on this art, in return, depends success of merely a theoretical knowledge of drugs (Sutra 2/16). Though treating with right prescription, yet if the physician be ignorant of the knowledge of place etc., he cannot achieve success in treatment. There exist many differences in the nature of men as regards age, vitality, constitution etc. ('Chikitsa 30/320). The dose depends upon the condition of the patient, the stage of the disease, the age of the patient, his/her habits etc. Vagbhatta says in Ashtanga Kalpa Ch. "there is no general rule as to the dose, the dose must be determined by a consideration of the disease, the constitution of the patient, his strength, his age, the character of the country and time." Charaka says "there can be no compounding of drugs without taking into view the measure, the measure of dosage. The dosage of medicine is dependent upon individual patient (Sutra 15/10). An underdose of medication cannot cure the disease just as a small quantity of water cannot extinguish great fire and medicine given in over dose will prove harmful just as excessive watering harms the crops. So after carefully considering the severity of disease and the strength of the medication, the physician should administer it, neither in too small dose (Chikitsa 30/313-314).

The criterion for fixing the dosage has definite base as per Charaka"; the dosage of drugs given in the section is with reference to moderate-build persons and of average strength. This should be regarded as the standard for pharmaceutical purposes and larger smaller doses have to be prepared accordingly (Kalpa 12/86). The drugs should be administered after a full investigation of the morbid-humors, the medications, time and season homologation of the patient, his digestive power, psychic condition, age and vitality (Siddhi 3/6) (Table 12-1a, 16).

Table 12 - 1a : The Scale of Dosage Generally Advocated According to the Age of the Individual (Sandu 1986)

Age	*Dose*
1 month	1/20
3 years	1/15
6 years	1/10
9 years	1/9
1 year	1/7
2 years	1/6
3 years	1/5
4 ,years	1/4
5 - 6 years	1/3
7 - 8 years	1/2
10 - 12 years	2/3
13 - 15 years	3/4
16 - 20 years	5/6
21 - 45 years	1
46 - 50 years	5/6
51 - 70 years	3/4
71 - 91 years	2/3
91 - 100 years	1/2

As already pointed out before, the action of medicines is modified by many factors both preparations of medicines and physiological states of the body. Women being possessed of more delicate organisation than men rarely require the same doses. Old age and childhood do not bear doses, proportionately to manhood, youth. Avoid also during pregnancy, and mercury during anaemic conditions. Except under urgent circumstances, an opiate should never be administered to an infant; while mercury is better borne in childhood and old age than in middle life. Inquire always as to idiosyncrasies, especially towards mercury and opium. Town dwellers particularly in overcrowded quarters, cannot bear doses which are quite suitable for those of rural or outdoor life. Note this especially in children. Passions and affections of the mind markedly influence the action of remedies (especially narcotics). Faith in the prescription or in the prescriber, may remove many hurdles. Every means should be used to implant confidence and stimulate hope.

The doses of any given medicine, particularly a narcotic or purgative should be regulated in accordance with the effect produced in each individual, rather than with published data, which are merely guides and are not infallible. The character, period, and form of disease influence the action of medicines administered in no slight degree. For example, in epidemics, a remedy which is highly beneficial at one period, appears to possess no efficacy at another. Usually, while the onset and climate of an epidemic are marked by numerous deaths, with its wane recoveries are the rule; hence the period of an epidemic influence the action of medicines.

Diet exercises a marked influence. Antiphlogistics (medicines that subdue inflammation or fever), refuse to act in the presence of an excess of animal foods along with stimulants; and the latter notoriously interfere with the action of mercurials; and iron salts are inoperative, when confronted with vegetable acids during febrile conditions. Light, air and exercise possess great therapeutic powers, and are very essential adjuvant to drugs. Confinement in close, dark, ill-ventilated apartments, counteracts any benefit that might be had from tonics, and violent physical action retard the effect of diuretics.

Seasons also have a modifying effect; some diseses independent of remedial measures improve at certain seasons, and relapse at other; tuberculous patients almost invariably improve in summer, remain stationary in winter, and decline in spring.

Mode of Administration: Thc modc of administra-tion of drugs and ancient pharmaceutial concepts are described by Charaka. Charaka says "In diseases of stomach, the medicine be administered by mouth; in diseases of head-nasal medication, and in diseases affecting abdomen, the medication given by the rectum, act most readily". In local diseases arising in the various regions of the body and in acute spreading affections; pimples and similar lesions, local applications suitable to the part afflicted, will prove specially efficatious (Chikitsa 30/294,295).

Time of Administration: The time of administration of medicines is important because it affects the action of medicines. Charaka gives various time schedules for administration of medicines which are basically indicated in accordance with morbidity, constitution and age or season as these have to assist in alleviation of any ailing conditions, by application of medicine at suitable times which may hasten the pharmacological activity of drug administered.

Narcotics, emetics and diaphoretics act to most favourably when administered an hour or two before bedtime. Diuretics are best given during the day when the body may be kept cool. Resinous cathartics such neutral salts, oil and those whose operation is speedy, be administered early in the morning; Arsenic acts best on full stomach.

The time of administration is generally twice a day, in the morning and evening, an hour or two before meals. In some cases, dose is administered thrice aday or even at an interval of one hour or two according to the nature of the disease.

In case of persons accustomed to take opium and other similar narcotics, the ordinary dose will not produce any action. Almost any medicine acts differently when given in large or small quantity. Narach churna, for example, is laxative when administered in 20 grain doses; while the same acts as a purgative with double the quantity. The dose should be regulated in accordance with the effect produced in each individual under different conditions. Kadhas, Rasas, Aristas have to be diluted with water in order to reduce their potency according to the strength of the patient. The scale of dosage found generally useful in almost all cases (the full dose being prescribed as Unit one) is shown in table 12.1a. Another dosage scale generally advocated is as shown in table 12-1b. The proportionate dose for any age (twenty years or less) may also be found by taking one-twentieth (1/20) of the full therapeutic dose, and multiplying the reuslt by the age in years. The doses may require lessening for patients advanced in life, but no exact rules can be laid down.

Modern Vaidyas (Ayurvedic physicians) do not stick to the old regulations of the Shastras (ancient texts) of prescribing in tolas etc. Formulating Ayurvedic medicines and dosage is advised according to the current system of measurement i.e. C.G.S. (centimetre, gram, second) or F.P.S. (foot, pound, second) systems.

Therefore, for comparison purpose and for ease of understanding of dosage, tables of Indian and English measures have been included in the appendix.

Anupan (Vehicle) (Table 12-2)

Anupan is an excipient (or agent) added to a medicine in order to increase its potency and gives it a proper form. It is regarded in Ayurvedic treatment as a most important factor in the administration of remedies. A medicine prescribed with a proper anupan is more effective than when administered singly as the anupan helps to bring about the desired effect more quickly. The best example is in 'Rasa Chikitsa' (Chemotherapy). The advantages of Rasa-chikitsa being the efficacy to cure diseases, its preservation for a longer period, use in small doses to get the desired effect, enhance potency due to proceedings and their use in various diseases with the change of Anupan (adjuvant or vehicle). The main speciality of Ras Yoga (Mercurial compound) being its quality of catalytic agent (yogavahi). Due to yogavahi quality (catalytic agent), even a small number of Rasayogas can cure large number of diseases of different nature. Whatever effect of Rasayoga is desired that can be obtained only with the change of Anupana. As for example, Makaradwaja, an important Rasayoga, can be used in various diseases to potentiate the action of any drug with the change of Anupana. Even, this can be used for lowering the temperature of the body in hyperpyrexia with the anupana of antipyretic drug; and may be used also to increase the temperature of the body in cases of shock.

Therefore, it is evident from the above description of Anupana that Anupana is as necessary for the effect of a medicine to act as water is for the proper digestion of food. It has become therefore a general rule in Ayurveda that a physician should not prescribe a medicine without an Anupana. Table 12.2 shows some of the most common Anupana (liquids or solids) which should be mixed with the medicines in respective ailments. Some of these can be used independently also.

It is true that one sometimes has to prescribe a mixture of drugs for a particular disease, but that is because each ingredient has a certain relation to the disease, and not because it has any relation with the other drugs prescribed. It is therefore generally specified in what media the drug should be taken such as decoction honey, ghrita, milk, sugar or water. When nothing is stated, simple water is the medium for intake of the drug.

Diet: It has become a custom to give general hints as to what type of food to be taken while the patient is on treatment. But, in general diet has relation more with the disease than with the medicine. It is true however that in some very 'hot' (ushna) medicines like marking nuts, some particular food substances are especially prohibited, e.g. when marking nuts are being taken, capsicum and even exposure to sun leads to eruptions. But, such drugs are few and far between, and even in their case, if taken in proper dose, there is not much danger. But is some diseases e.g. diabetes mellitus, diet has a special significance.

Thus diet has special relations with diseases and in some cases is a very important element in the treatment of diseases, but ordinary general hints appear to be a useless burden on the patient. It is needless for example, when prescribing a particular drug, to advise avoidance of over eating; over-eating is bad in all cases and does not need a special precaution in any particular disease.

Few common examples are given below regarding diet in various diseased conditions:

Hyperacidity

Allowed - emetics, purgation, moong, cooled water, sugar, wheat-bread, green vegetables, fruits, milk, ghee, honey.

Forbidden - sour and salty things, curds, butter, oils, wine.

Fevers

Allowed - Moong water, orange juice, kanji etc. Generally milk is not allowed by traditional Vaidyas for 7 days but in allopathy it is allowed from the beginning of fever.

Forbidden - cold baths, exertion, ghee, pulses, sweets, heavy foods, generally all solids until after crisis; in typhoid, solid food should not be given until after a week after the temperature becomes constantly normal.

Obesity

Allowed - wheat, bajra, jowar (in small quantity), moong water, butters (in moderation), water hot or cold (plentiful), milk (skimmed), fruit is, i.e. grapes, organges, green vegetables such as caulir lower, cabbage, tomatoes etc.

Forbidden - ghee, thick pulses, rice, sagom potatoes, pastry and sweets, cream, milk (except in moderation), sugar.

General directions - 1. An active life with full occupation, short hours of sleep, and the most vigorous exercise, compatible with the physical condition. Cycling, fencing etc. are valuable but the form and amount of exertion must be carefully adapted to each case.

2. Free action of the bowels and skin, with regular vapour baths is advisable.

Table 12 - 1b : The Scale of Dosage Generally Advocated with Respect to the Adult Dose

If the adult dose of any given drug be 24 grains or about 13 gunjas -

a patient under 6 months of age		would	need	1 grain	(gr.)	or	1/2	gunja
	6 months - 1 year	,,	,,	1/ 1/2	gr.	or	3./4	,,
from	1 year - 2 years	,,	,,	2	gr.	or	1	,,
	2 - 3	,,	,,	3	gr.	or	1 1/2	,,
	3 - 4	,,	,,	4	gr.	or	2	,,
	4 - 6	,,	,,	6	gr.	or	3	,,
	6 - 10	,,	,,	8	gr.	or	4	,,
	10 - 13	,,	,,	10	gr.	or	5	,,
	13 - 16	,,	,,	12	gr.	or	6	,,
	16 - 18	,,	,,	16	gr.	or	8 1/2	,,
	18 - 20	,,	,,	20	gr.	or	10 1/2	,,
	21 and above	,,	,,	24	gr.	or	13	,,

Note : The proportionate dose for any age (twenty years or less) may be also be found by taking one- twentieth (1/20) of the full therapeutic dose and multiplying the result by the age in years. The doses may require lessening for patients advanced in life, but no exact rules can be laid down.

Table 12.2. Some of the Most Common Anupanas which Should be meant with the Medicines in Respective Ailments (Some of These Can Be Used Independently Also)

Disease	*Anupan required*
Acidity	Avalkathi, ghee and sugar
Anaemia	Butter and sugar candy
Anorexia	Ginger juice and honey
Asthma (bronchial)	Bharang-root churna and ginger
Bronchitis	Adulsa churna, honey, ghee
Dysentry Colic	Asafoetida, ghee
Epilepsy	Butter milk
Facial palsy	Vakhand, akkalkadha, honcy
Gout	Udid preparations and butter
Leucoderma	Cow's urine, castor oil
Lumbago	Barchi
Obesity	Pushkar-root
Renal calculus	Honey and hot water
Rheumatism	Shilajit and gokhru
Tumors	Gulvel, castor oil
	Lemon juice, castor oil

NOTES AND REFERRNCES

1. Sandu D.V., Indian Therapeutics, Sri Satguru Publications, Delhi, 1987.

2. Devaraj T.L., Speaking of : Ayurvedic Remedies for Common Diseases, Sterling Health and Cure Series, New Delhi, 1985.

3. Panel of Vaidyas, Clinical Application of Ayurvedic Remedies, Sri Satguru Publications, Delhi, 1986.

4. Pandey G., Contribution of Charaka to Indian Pharmacy, I.R.S. Ayu. Siddha, CCRAS.

CHAPTER 13

Ayurveda and Yoga

Yoga - 'Definition & Antiquity' and Utility

Dr. A.R.V. Murthy, M.D. (Ay.).

Yuj	-	'Yogi'
Yuj	-	'Samadhau'
Yujir	-	'Yoga'
Yujir	-	'Yogana'

The word Yoga is derived from the roots *'Yuj'* and '*Yujir.*' *'Yuj'* is applied to mean *'samadhi'* and *'Yujir'* to mean '*Yojana.*' It is interesting that '*Yuj*', though seems to convey two different meanings in '*Yoga*' and '*Samadhi,*' in fact conveys a singular meaning. For Yoga and Samadhi are termed synonymous—'*Yogah Samadhih*' (Vyasa Bhashya) as both of them refer to the unified state of the individual soul (Jivatma) with the universal soul (Paramatma).

The '*Yogaja*' meaning of the root *Yujir* has frequently appeared in the ancient science of medicine—Ayurveda in reference to medicinal preparations which are the *'Combinations'* of various herbs and minerals. The term '*Yokta*' has also been used with reference to the physician, who analyses 'Combinations' of various factors, before finally preparing a 'Combination' of various herbs to suit, combat the clinical condition. Thus, '*Yuj*' and '*Yujir*' both refer to union, or combination.

Whenever one says union, it implies that more than one factor is involved. In it's most popular sense, and in it's true sense too, Yoga refers to the means by which the Jivatma can be united with the paramatma and so secure liberation (Moksha). *Hatha Yoga* feels it is the union of '*Surya*' with '*Chandra*' or '*Prana*' with '*apana*.' It is also said Yoga refers to mean to 'Joining' of *Siva* with *Shakti* or *Retas* with *Raja*. Thus it is the union of two opposite forces, forming a stable force. Yoga is the union of our will with the will of God. Sri Mahadeva Desai, in his Introduction to Gita, according to Mahatma Gandhi says. 'It is the yoking of all the powers of the body, mind and soul to the God, it means the disciplining of the 'intellect,' the mind, the emotions, the will, which that Yoga presupposes, it means a poise of the soul which enables one to look at life in all it's aspects evenly.'

The word 'Yoga' has appeared in *Upanisads, Gita* and ofcourse in *Patanjala Yoga Sutras*, and in many a treatise on Indian Philosophy. The definition in each context differs, but still is applied to mean the same objective, the union or the communion. As a well cut diamond has many facets, each deflecting a different shade of light, so does the word Yoga, each facet reflecting a different shade of meaning and revealing different aspects of the entire range of human endeavour to win inner peace and happiness. Hereunder are given different definitions of Yoga, found in various Indian classics.

The theory and practice of Yoga is dealt in almost all Upanisads, though the word Yoga appears in very few of them. The Katha Upanisad and Sandilya Upanisad even define Yoga. The utility of Yoga according to Upanisads is personal development and expansion of consciousness.

(1) *Yada paneavatisthante Jnanani manasa saha/Buddhis Cana vicestati tam auh paramam gatim/Tam yogam iti manyante sthiramindriadharan pramattah tada bhavati yogoni prabhava pyayau.*

(Katha Upanisad)

Yoga is the highest state when the five senses of knoweldge together with the mind are stilled, and the intellect itself does not stir. Yoga truly is the origin and the end.

(2) *Yogah Samatavastha Jivatma Paramatmanah.*

Yoga is stage where the individual soul (Jivatma) elevates itself to find it on par with universal soul (Paramatma).

(3) *Jivatma Paramatmaikyavastha Yogah.*

(Sandilyopanisad)

Yoga is the true union of Jivatma and Paramatma.

The word Yoga appears very frequently in Bhagavad Gita. Infact the name of the each chapter ends with the word Yoga. E.g. *Sankhya Yoga, Vibhuti Yoga* etc. Yoga has also been defined at different contexts to mean differently.

(4) *Dukhah Samyoga Viyogam Yoga Samjnitam.*

(Gita 9/23)

Detachment from the union with sorrow or pain is Yoga.

(5) *Yogah Karmasu Kausalam.*

(Gita 9/48)

Yoga is wisdom in work or skilful living.

(6) *Samatvam Yogamucyate.*

(Gita 9/48)

It is a state at which the Yogin finds no difference between happiness and misery, gain and loss and the like.

Patanjali, the ancient Indian authority on Yoga, and also the man who systematised the science, for the first time, defines Yoga thus—

(7) *Yogah Citta Vritti Nirodah.*

(Yoga Sutra I/2)

Yoga is the inhibition (Nirodhah) of the fluctuations (Vritti) of consciousness (Citta). In other words it is the restraint of mental modifications. This is the most authoritative definition of Yoga and the most popular too. The word *'Citta'* denotes the mind in it's total or collective sense as being composed of three categories (a) Mind (*Manas*) (b) Intellect (*Buddhi*) and (c) Ego (*Ahamkara*). The word *Vritti* is derived from the Sanskrit root *Vrt* to mean to turn or to revolve. Yoga is the state where the *Purusa* rests in his own state (*Tada derashtuh Swaroope avasthanam—Yogasutra* 2/3) in other state he is identified as its modifications which are five in number (*Pramana, Viparayaya, Vikarpa, Nivera, Smriti)*, a few of which are painful and the few not painful. Thus Yoga teaches the means by which mind can be controlled, so that it can be directed to constructive channels. In fact Patanjali advocates two methods to control the mind—'*Abhyasa Vairagyam Tannirodhah.*' (Yoga Sutra 1/2) (Mind has to be controlled by constant practice and detachment. Lord Krishna too has prescribed the same two methods to train the mind. *Abhyasenatu Kaunteya Vairagyenaca grihyate* (Gita 6/31).

More definitions are available for Yoga in Bhashyas.

Sankara Bhashya says.

(8) *Yogah Apraptasya prapanam.*

Achieving the one that has not been achieved. The goal here is once again Salvation in the form of union of Jivatma and Paramatma. Vyasabhashya gives definitions Yoga thus:

(9) *Jnanendriyani Sarvani Nigrahya manasa sah Ekatwa bhavana eva Yogah.*

Yoga is a state where all the five senses of knowledge together with mind aim at a singular focus —achieving the communion with paramatma.

Vyasabhashya also gives a very interesting definition for Yoga.

(10) *Yogah Samadhih'* -

'Yoga is nothing but *Samadhi*' as it means, the definition looks strange because *Samadhi* has been considered a part of octapartite Yoga.

The root Yuj has two meanings.

Yuj - *'Yogas'*

Yuj - *'Samadhau'*

Further,

Yujyate Cittamanena iti Yogah and
Samidheeyate cittamanena iti Samadhih.

carry similar meaning. In fact it is only at the 'Samadhi state' that one can achieve 'Yoga State.' In other words No Yoga without *Samadhi*. Yoga is the true knoweldge and '*Samadhi* is the means of achieving it. Attainment of *Samadhi* signals the attainment of true knowledge. The two definitions given down below make it crystal clear that Yoga and Samadhi are synonymous.

- *Dhayayato Yoginah sarva manovrittis vinasyati*
- Samadhih Satu Vigneyah Sarvavrittirvivarjitah

  Bramha Sampadyate Yogi Na bhuyah Samsrutim Vrajet.

(Trisikha Bramhana Upanisad)

This is what Patanjali says about yoga.

and is said to have been taught by the Lord Vishnu to Surya who passed it on to Manu and Manu transferred it to Ikshwaku.

Siva tradition which was told by the Lord to his wife Parvathi was later on passed out to Brahma, Narada, Vasistha and others.

One more tradition is also in vague. It is known as *Dattatreya Sampradaya* or *Nadra Sampradaya.* Matsyendranath, Goraknath, Jalandaranath had been the promoters after having learnt it from Dattatreya. Swatvarama, one of the ardent followers of this school of thought is believed to have authored the book *Hathayoga Pradipika.*

In the recent years Yoga was revived and rejuvenated by Swami Vivekananda (Raja Yoga), Sri Aurobindo, (Integral Yoga), Mahatma Gandhi (Anasakti Yoga), Krishna Murthy (Yoga of Choiceless Awareness) and others.

Uses of yoga are multidimensional. There has been a significant change in the outlook of Yoga over the years.

In ancient times the science of Yoga was developed as a method of mental transformation and expansion of consciousness. Therapy was never a field of Yoga in it's proper sense. However in modern times the revival of interest in Yoga is predominantly aimed to apply this science for the promotion of health and treatment of diseases. Yoga certainty today has grown to reach the masses from the ancient individualistic approach and has even entered the international arena from the National stands, but the subtler spiritual links of Yoga are slowly loosing their ground to give way to grosser physical and metaphysical approaches.

(The yogic path of self knowledge and of Yoga vidhi (Rules of Yoga) while the *Swetaswatara Upanisad* refers to *Dhyana yoga* (the yogic path of meditation).

Bhagavad Gita gives various definitions for Yoga and advocates three basic paths of Yoga—*Jnana Yoga, Karmayoga* and *Bhakti Yoga.* The usages *Imam Vivaswate Yogaṃ*' and *'Yogam Yogeswarat Krishnat*' means to say that Gita in itself is a science of Yoga. Lord Krishna in the very beginning of the fourth chapter of Bhagavad Gita says that it was he who taught Yoga to Lord Surya and the samething is being told again to Arjuna.

Imam Vivaswate Yogam Proktavanahamavyayam
Vivaswarmanava praha Manurikshwakavebravit

(Gita 4/1)

Patanjali was the first person to author a book on Yoga, in which he has systematised and co-ordinated the science of Yoga. The Patanjala *Yoga Sutra* consists of 185 Yogic aphorisms which deal with all aspects of Yoga. '*Astanga Yoga*' consisting of eight parts or stages to achieve the final goal of emancipation, has been described very systematically here. The *Astanga Yoga* is more popularly known as *Raja Yoga*—to mean the king of Yogas—Yoga of highest order. Later the *Asana* and *Pranayama* part of this *Raja Yoga* were separated and along with *'Mudra'* and '*Nadanusandana*' were formed into a specialised branch of Yoga called *Hathayoga,* which mainly deals with the physical and metaphysical aspects of yoga. *Hathayoga Pradipika, Gheranda Saṁhita* and a few others deal exclusively with the branch of Yoga.

Yoga as it is available today seems to be based on three separate traditions. The first one is *Vishnu Sampradaya,*

- *Yogah citta Vritti Nirodah.*

(Yoga Sutra I/2)

The word Yoga has been applied to mean different things altogether in some of the ancient Indian classics. Thus in *Nitisastra,* Yoga is used to mean 'Perfection' (*Praveenya*). In Ayurveda, the ancient science of medicine, medicinal combinations are called *Yogas.* In *Jyotissastra*—the science of Astronomy and Astrology different '*Yogas*' of Sun, Stars and Planets have been explained. In Bhagavad Gita Yoga is also used to refer to ways, methods and practises adopted consciously by the votaries of Yoga to attain this ultimate objective and even intermediate goals. In fact, Lord Krishna prescribe three 'Yogas' (Ways) in *Jnanayoga, Karmayoga* and *Bhakti Yoga* for attaining the final emancipation.

The antiquity of Yoga dates back to *Vedas.* Though the exact word 'Yoga' has not appeared in *Vedas,* the concept of union of the individual soul with that of the universal is well conceived.

Yujevam Bramhapurvyam
Bramhana Te Bramyujayunajmi
Yunjonah pratamam menastatva savitadhiah
Agne Jyotir nijavya prithivya Adya Bharat

(Yajurveda)

Most of the Upanisads have dealt both the theory and practice of Yoga. Yoga is defined as the highest state of mind, where it is absolutely stilled, signifying the identification of *Jivatma* with *paramatma.* The two early Upanisads *Katha* and *Swetaswatara* specifically deal with many aspects of Yoga. The *Katha* speaks of *Adyatma Yoga.*

Yoga as it is conceived today is a combination of some physical postures and Breathing exercises. In fact these constitute only two of eight steps of Yoga as explained in the Yogic texts. Eight parts of Yoga are:

Yama Niyama	Ethical practises
Asana Pranayama	Physical practises
Pratyahara Dharana	Sensorial practises
Dhyana Samadhi	Meditative practises

Asana (physical posture) and Pranayama (rhythmic breathing) are collectively known as yoga today and are being taught and practiced by many. What is being achieved as therapyt is being achieved just by practising, these two. But in spite of being practised in part, Yoga has not failed, to show it's utility. The performance has been consistent and significant. Many diseases are being successfully treated today either with Yoga alone or in combination with medicines. The list of diseases being managed by Yoga is growing at enormous pace and it's no wonder, if in a short period all the existing diseases are included in the list. Studies are being conducted at different centres to identify specific Yogic procedures for specific diseases. In addition to clinical studies Biochemical and pharmacological studies are being conducted to understand the mechanisms involved with the effect of Yoga.

Utility of Yoga in medicine today has two components.

1. Positive health
2. Therapy

Positive health aspect of Yoga is well known. Regular practice of Yoga—in the form of postures and systematic breathing prevents one from falling ill frequently and also promotes one's health. Physiological studies conducted on Yoga volunteers at different centres gives ample proof of this aspect of Yoga. The exact mechanism of action; of course, is not clear. But it has been suggested that the practice of Yoga helps to achieve stable autonomic balance and also to develop a relative hypometabolic state and improve physical efficiency. Efficiency of cardio respiratory functions and endocrine systems are of significant importance.

The efficacy of Yoga in curing diseases is well documented. Text books on Yoga like Hathpradipika have mentioned the use of few Yogic postures in curing certain ailments. This forms the basis for the present trends in yoga. Though most of the diseases are being tried with Yoga, extensive trials have been made in recent years in reference to Bronchial Asthma, Diabetis Mellitus and Hypertension. It has been suggested that Yoga helps Asthmatics by way of improving broncho pulmonary functions, regularising the method of breathing, cleansing the air passages, and tranquillity of mind. Yoga is said to help diabetics by reconditioning the Hypothalamopituitary-adrenal axis with the control of Insulin scretion and it's metabolism. In hypertension Yoga is believed to raise the arousability of cerebral cortex and helps in sending decreased impulses to the hypothalamus in brain which in turns reduces the sympathetic tone reducing the peripheral resistance and thus reducing blood pressure.

Studies conducted at different centres on effectivity of Yoga practises in the management of certain diseases are quite encouraging. While the results obtained in cases of Bronchial Asthma, Hypertension, chronic GIT disorders and anxiety neurosis have been significantly good, satisfactory improvement has been observed in cases of Rheumatoid Arthritis, Diabetis mellitus, chronic back ache and a few other diseases. There certainly is a good scope for exploring Yoga as a Therapy in various diseases, but it appears that while it can play a good role in the management of chronic and functional disorders, it's applicability in the management of acute disease is limited. The following chart can be used as a guideline in the management of few diseases.

AYURVEDA AND YOGA

Dr. A.R.V. Murthy,
M.D. (Ay.)

Introduction

The science of Ayurveda and Yoga are the centres of attraction today. The entire world has focused its attention on these two products of ancient wisdom. To a common man Ayurveda is known for the medicaments which are absolutely safe having no side effects and Yoga is known as a positive health measure, which can also cure many diseases. This is true in one sense, but there is more to it than that meets the eye. This is only a tip of the Iceberg. These two are not merely simple medical sciences. To be more precise therapeutic aspect forms only a minor part of the system, more so for Yoga than Ayurveda. For Yoga, 'therapy' aspect is only an extraneous outgrowth under the pressures of modern civilization, because it became a necessity for its survival. At the time of origin, and for certain period of its development, Yoga, was restricted to help attain Salvation (*Mokṣha*). As for as Ayurveda is concerned it is more of a science of life, than a science of Medicine. It tells how to live and how to keep ourselves healthy. Treating a disease is only secondary.

Ayurveda and Yoga have many things in common. Both of them are derived out of ancient wisdom and represent ancient culture. They are based on similar principles and aim at a similar focus—attainment of *Mokṣha*. The write-up endeavours to throw some light on the relationship/ similarities between the two sciences.

Yoga and Ayurveda were developed by the ancient seers for the benefit of the human race, to relieve the homosapiens from worldly miseries (*Dukha*) and to take him to the pleasures of the eternal bliss by teaching him the means of mental transformation, personality development and expansion of consciousness, while keeping himself healthy and free from diseases. In fact Yoga seems to be a part of Ayurveda. Ayurveda is the science of life (*Āyu*) and this '*Āyu*' is defined as a composite combination of *Sarira* (Body), *Indriya* (Senses), *Satwa* (Psyche) and *Ātma* (Soul).[1] While Ayurveda concentrates on the related aspects of the '*Jiva*' (living being) who is a product of peculiar combination of the four—*Sarira*, Indriya, *Satwa* and *Ātma*, Yoga limits itself to evolve the means for the proper understanding of Psyche and Soul. Besides it thrusts on the expansion of consciousness and attainment of Salvation. It concentrates on the health of Psyche, but remains a part of Ayurveda. Probably Yoga was evolved to as an applied aspect of Ayurvedic doctrines on Psyche and Soul. It is believed that Caraka Saṁhita (Ayurveda) *Pátañjala Sutra* (*Yoga*) and *Vyākarana-Mahabāshya* (Grammar) - all three texts were written by the same seer - *Pātañjali.*[2] Besides the origins of both these sciences can be traced back to *Vedas.* Just as Ayurveda has different schools of thought such as Charaka School, Susruta School etc., Yoga too has *Siva* School of thought, *Vishṇu* School of thought and so on and so forth. The *Guru-Sishya* '*Paramparā*' or the preceptor-descriple Tradition—had been the order of promotion for both the systems. While Ayurveda is said to have been told by *Brahman*—the Lord of Creation to *Prajāpati* who transferred it to his successor,[3] Yoga too is said to have been taught at first by *Hari* the Lord of Promotion, to *Manu.*[4] Thus *Karnaparamparā* or 'hearsay' has been the route of promotion for both. The aims and objectives are also similar. Āyurveda says, the ultimate goal of a human being is to attain *Moksha* and Yoga aims at communion of *Jivātma* with *Paramātma* which is nothing but Salvation. While Ayurveda advocates Yoga to promote mental health and to cure psychological disorders Yoga banks on Ayurvedic methods to acquire sound physique. In turn both aim at achieving a healthful longivity. Ayurveda defines disease thus—'*Tad Dukḥa Saṃyogā Vyādhayah.*'[5] Gita defines Yoga, '*Dukah Saṃyoga Viyogam Yoga Sanjñitam.*'[6] Ayurveda aims at attainment of Mokṣha and it is said Yoga is promoter of Mokṣha.[7]

Ayurveda and Yoga share identical concepts. In the very definition of health (*Swasthya*) Ayurveda incorporates the absolute pleasantness of mind (and Soul).[8] Pātañjali says 'At the time of absolute concentration of mind the seat rests in his own (*Swa-Roopa*) state.'[9] *Vikāra* (disease) is a state where man is other than his own being.' Cure means restoring him to his true normal self ('*Swa-stha*'). Thus the terms '*Swāsthya*' and *Swa-Roopa Avasthana*' have similar intensions. Ayurveda prescribe four disciplines for the physician—Friendship (*Maitri*), Sympathy (*Karunā*), Concern (*Sakye pritih*) and indifference (*Upekshanam*).[10] The same four are termed as attitudes of mind towards different subjects that come before it, by Patanjali.[11]

Both Yoga and Ayurveda are Octapartite. Each Section of this Octapartite Yoga seems to have its origin in Ayurveda texts, although in a modified way. It appears as though relevant material is gleaned from Ayurvedic texts and presented in a concised way to form different parts of Yoga.

The first two steps of Yoga—*Yama* and *Niyama* have been directly derived from the Ayurvedic *Sadvritta* of the ______ *Yamas, Ahimsā, Saṭya* and *Astheya*—all have appeared among Dasavidha *Pāpakarmas.*[12] *Brahmacharya* is counted among the three supporting factors of life.[13] Ayurveda advocates a modified form of celibacy in *Vaivahikja Brahmacharya.* Importance of *Brahmacharya* has been stressed in the management of many a disease. *Aparigraha* is also a part of *Sadvritta. Souca, Santosa* and *Swādyaya* are among the basic qualities of a physician. *Daiva Vyapāsraya Cikitsa* incorporates *Tapa* and *Iswara Pranidhana.* In short, the concept of *Yama* and *Niyama* is akin to the concept of

Mitāyu (useful life—to the society) and *Sukhāyu* (Happy life to the individual).[14]

Āyurveda has conceived *Āsana* in the form of *Vyāyama*. *Asana* (Physical posture) as such is a modified, rather systematised form of *Vyayāma*.

'*Pranāyama*' the fourth of Octapartite Yoga is the control of breath (Respiration)[15] in general sense and channellization of pranic energy in a specific sense. Though the exact term *Prānayama* has not been used in the Āyurveda Samhitas there are many references related to this. The word '*Prāna*' has been used to mean both 'Breath' and pranic energy. *Prānavayu* is said to vitalise *Citta, Buddhi, Indriyas* and *Hridaya*[16] and so does *Pranāyama* according to Yogic texts. The usage '*Vayu Nigraha*[17] (control of breath) is available in Caraka Samhita. Further '*Hersher-shoschwaa Sayodat*' indirectly refers to the breathing exercise taking to *pranāyama* in the management of *Swāsa* (Bronchial Asthma). According to Yoga too, *pranāyama* results in the cure of many diseases.[18] Vrinda Madhava's 'Siddhayoga' directly refers to *Prānayāma* advocating it in the management of *Sulka Kambalavrita gātrasya prānayāmam prakurvate.'*

Dhārana, Dhyāna and *Samādhi* form a part of internal' Yoga and as such refer to different stages of concentration, with Samādhi referring to absolute stillness of mind. Āyurveda advocates similar procedures for the management of psychological disorders. Application of mind in *Dhee, Dhṛiti* and *Ātmadi Vignana* in other terms indicates *Dhyāna* and *Dhārana.*[19] '*Samādhi*' in Ayurvedic form can be a milder form of 'Mind control' as against complete command over the 'Will,' depicted in Yogic texts.

Ayurveda and Yoga share identical views in necessitating the 'purification of body' at regular intervals. Here Yoga incorporates Ayurvedic concept on *Doṣa, Dhātu* and *Mala,* and stresses on the expulsion of '*Malas*' from the body. We get a clear reference to this effect in 'Hathayoga Pradipika' a treatise on Yoga, while dealing with '*Shatkarmas.*' The text says the *Shatkarmas* have to be performed only by those who have *Meda, Kapha* and *Mala* in excess, for the removal of these impurities from the body.[20] *Prānayama* has to be indulged in, only after shatkarmas are performed. The *Shatkarmas* are *Dhouti, Neti, Vasti, Nouli, Trāteka* and *Kapālabhāthi.* Ayurveda too believes in purification procedures and these are collectively called '*Panca karmas.*' (*Vamana, Virecana, Vasti,* (*Anavasana, Niruha*) *Sirovirecana*)). '*Vasti*' is common to both the systems. While Ayurveda prescribes medicated preparations for the advocation of *Vasti,* Yoga makes use of plain water (with a pinch of salt). While in Yoga, *Vasti* is administered by the Yogi himself, physician has to administer the *Vasti* to patient according to Ayurveda. *Dhouti* and *Vamana* are the similar procedures and should be understood as above.

Finally a word about Yoga proper, in Āyurveda. In Caraka Saṃhita, the most ancient extant treatise on Āyurveda, described, Yoga of highest order. Large part of the first chapter of Sarira Sthana (Kathidhapurusiya) deals with Yoga and related topics. Yoga, Caraka says is the promoter of *Mokṣha*—the ultimate goal of one's life.[21] Caraka defines Yoga as a state where the sensation of happiness and miseries disappear. This state he says can happen when mind is absolutely concentrated, and contained in the soul.[22] Gita says '*Samatvaṁ Yogamuchyate*' Kathopanishad tells, '*Yogam Sthiramindriya Dhāranam*', Patañjali preaches '*Yogah Cittavritti Nirodhah.*' It is clear that Caraka's definition of Yoga is akin to definitions given at various contexts. Caraka talks about eight supernatural powers[23] that are achieved by a Yogin. He calls them '*Eiswaras*'. Patañjali's '*Astasiddis*' have many things in common with these '*Eiswaras.*' Very interestingly Susruta, the ancient

Indian authority on Surgery says the *Eiswaras* can be achieved with the help of a divine herb named '*Soma*.'[24] Caraka's authority on Yoga is reflected in the fifth chapter of Sarirasthana, where he gives his views on 'Individual and Universe.' Here he identifies the individual as an epitome of the Universe. He talks about a state of mind where it is pure, in possession of true wisdom, free from vanity and detached from miseries, conducive to attainment of Yogic power and which serves for the attainment of *Brahman*, the Eternal, Tranquil, Immutable and Indestructible. This state, he says can be achieved when the *Puruṣa* (Individual) identified himself with *loka* (Universe). He calls this true knowledge *Satyā Buddhi*.'[25] This *Satyābuddhi* is what Patañjali names *Ṛtambara Prajña*, and that Gitā calls '*Sthitha Prajña*.' The concept of *Satyābuddhi* is very simple and more practical as compared to the rest. In other words it is an applied form of the two.

Thus Yoga and Ayurveda have many things in common. Both had singular origin and similar course of development. They share many an identical concept. By seeking mutual help they complement each other. The ultimate goal of both the sciences is attainment of final emancipation. The difference is, while Ayurveda insists on the true knowledge of all the four components of life (*Sarira, Indriya, Satwa* and *Ātma*), Yoga-concentrates only on the latter two, to reach the ultimate goal of Salvation.

NOTES AND REFERENCES

1. Caraka Saṁhita Sutrasthāna 1/49
2. Caraka Sutra (Cakradatta) 1/1
3. Astānga Hṛidaya Sutra Sthāna 1/3
4. Bhagavad Gita 4/1
5. Susruta Sutra 24/4
6. Bhagavad Gita 9/23
7. Caraka Sareera 1/136
8. Suśruta Sutra 15/41
9. Patañjali Yoga Sutra 1/3
10. Caraka Sutra 9/36
11. Patañjali Yoga Sutra 1/33
12. Astānga Hṛidaya Sutra 2/21-22
13. Caraka Sutra 11/35
14. Caraka Sutra 1/41
15. Patañjali Yoga Sutra 2/49
16. Astānga Hṛidaya Sutra 12/4
17. Caraka Sutra 18/43
18. Hathayoga Pradipikā 2/16
19. Caraka Sutra 1/58
20. Hathayoga Pradipikā 2/2, 37
21. Caraka Sareera 1/136
22. Caraka Sareera 1/138-9
23. Caraka Sareera 1/140-1
24. Caraka Sareera 5/7, 16-19

Table 13 -1 : Schedule of Yoga Therapy

	Asana	Pranayama	Kriya
Hypertension	Sarira Sancalana, Pavan-Muktasana, Khujanga, Salbha, Savasana, Sirsa.	Ujjayi, Sitali, Candra Bhedana	Kapalabhati
Bronchial asthma	Bhujanga, Salbha, Pascimatt-ana, Vakrasana, Maha Mudra, Trikona, Hala, Cakra, Matsya, Matsendra, Dhanura, Sarwanga, Sirsa, Yoga Mudra.	Ujjayi, Sitali, Bhastrika	Kapalabhati, Neti, Dhauti, Uddivana.
Anxiety Neurosis	Bhujanga, Salbha, Pascimatt-ana, Vakrasana, Trikona, Savasana, Hala, Viparita, Pavana, Mukta, Sarwanga, Matsya, Savasana, Matsendra.	Ujjayi, Bhastrika	Kapalabhati
Diabetes Mellitus	Bhujanga, Salbha, Pascima-ttana, Vakra, Trikona, Hasta Pada, Pavana Mukta, Hala, Sarwanga, Matsya, Nauka, Cakra, Dhanura, Mayura, Yoga Mudra, Savasana.	Bhastrika, Agnisara	Uddiyana Dhauri Nauli

Rheumatic Disorders	Bhujanga, Salbha, Sarira-sancalana, Brahama Mudra, Akarma Dhanura, Dhanura, Cakra, Hala Matsya, Sarwanga, Gomukha, Sava.		Kapalabhati, Dhauti
Thyrotoxicosis	Salbha, Trikona, Vakra, Pascimattana, Bhujanga, Hala, Sarwanga, Matsya, Sarira Sancalana, Jalandhara, Matsendra, Brahma Mudra.	Ujjayi	Kapalabhati
Gastro-intestinal tract disorders	Pascimattana, Pavan, Mukta, Trikona, Vakra, Bhujanga, Salbha, Pada Hasta, Hala, Sarwanga, Dhanura, Cakra, Matsendra, Mayura, Sirsa, Padma, Yoga, Mudra.	Sitali, Sitakari, Candra Bhedana	Uddiyana, Nauli Dhauti
Headache	Savasana, Pavan Mukta, Trikona, Bhujanga, Salbha, Pascimattana, Matsya, Brahama Mudra.	Sitali, Ujjayi	Neti

Table - 13-2 : For individual ailments the practises to be avoided and emphasized from the basic set along with additional practises is given below

	FROM THE BASIC SESSION		
Ailment	*Avoid*	*Emphasize*	*Add*
Nasalallergy	-	Breathe & stretch Jogging, Rapid abdominal breathing	Alternative nostril Kapalabathi
Bronchial Asthma	-	Trangle, cobra, bow shoulder stand, fish forward stretch, Pavana-muktasana, Pranayama emotion culture.	Alternative nostril Kapalabhati
Chronic bronchitis emphysema	Loosening up	Pranayama	
DIGESTION diarrhoea	Loosening up	Half shoulder stand, Relaxation, Pranayama emotion culturing.	Uddiyana

Hyperacidity	Sitting	Loosening up, sun-salute asanas, standing asanas, nadisudhi, emotion culture yoga diet.	Uddiyana Vamandhouti
Constipation Haemorrhoids	Jogging	Half shoulder stand (Viparitakarani)	Uddiyana Agnisara Shankha-prakshalana once in 2-4 weeks.
METABOLIC Diabetes (DM)	Yogamudra	Bow, half spinal twist, relaxation, Pranayama, meditation.	Uddiyana Agnisara
DM with eye haemorrhage	All asanas loosening up	Arm stretch breathing hand stretch breathing Tree breathing, DRT QRT, Pranayama	
Obesity		Jogging, Loosening up Diet.	Makarasana

Hyper Thyrodism	Loosening up Sarvangasana, Halasana, Kriyas	Standing asanas, Pranayama DRT, QRT, CM Bhramari	Ujjayi
Hypothyroid		Loosening up Sarvanagasana, Halasana AA, UU, MM.	Shanmukhi Mudra
WHOLE BODY			
Fatigue, Insomnia	Loosening up	DRT, Pranayama and meditation before going to bed.	
Cancer	All Loosening up Asanas	Breathing practises DRT, Pranayama	Yoganidra
AIDS	All those difficut tc practice because of debility	DRT-Pranayama emotion culture	Vamamadhouti, Alternate nostril Kapalabathi, Yoga nidra

CIRCULATION			
Hypertension-Moderate & Severe	Loosening up Sun-salute, Prone asanas, supine asanas, Kapalabhati	DRT, Pranayama Om meditation 2 times a day	
-as above–Mild	Loosening up Sun-Salute, Bow, supine asanas	- as above -	
IHD Coronary Artery disease	Loosening up, All asanas	Relaxation Pranayama Meditation, emotion culture	Cyclic Meditation
Varicose Veins	Jogging	Viparitakaram, Sarvangasana. Halasana, Pranayama	

NERVOUS SYSTEM

Head Ache	Bow, Fish, Moon Cakrasana	Breathing and stretch Pranayama	Neck Roling
Epilepsy	All fast deep breathing-cat stretch, Rabbit breathing Kapalabhati	Back bending, shoulder stand, Nadisudhi Meditation	Neck, Rolling Sirsasana
Anxiety	Any practice if tiring	Loosening up, emotion culture	
Obscession		Loosening up Kapalabhati	Worry bead Meditation (Jāpa with Rosery) Ujjayi
Depression	Meditation	Loosening up Sun-salute, Sectional breathing, Relax in sitting and standing postures	Singing of Corpse Dynamic music

Psychosis	Meditation Shavasana	Loosening up Inverted postures	Veda Chanting Vamanadouti
Addiction		Loosening up Seetali, Seetkari	Worry bead meditation, Vamanadhouti Shankhaprakshalana
REPRODUCTION			
Pre-menstrual Perimenopausal syndrome		Triangle, bow Viparitkarani, Sitting asanas, Relaxation, Meditation Pranayama	Butterfly (Badhakonasana)
Painful periods	Camel, Cakrasana Bow for one week before periods	Standing Asanas, Shoulder stand, Halsana, emotion culture.	Badhakonasana

Excess flow in periods	Loosening up, Sitting postures	Inverted postures, Deep relaxation Meditation	Ashwini Mudra
Scanty and irregular periods		Loosening up Standing postures	Badhakonasana
Prolapse uterus-grade I & II, Stress incontinence	Loosening up Standing Sun Salute	Inverted postures Viparitkarani Sarvangasana Halasana, Relaxation emotion culture	Agnisara Uddiyana Ashwini Mudra in Viparitakarani
MALE REPRODUCTION			
Premature ejaculation	Loosening up Standing Postures	Viparitakarani Halasana Pranayama, AA Chanting	Alternate nostril Kapalabhati, Ashwini Mudra Chandranuloma
Impotence		Loosening up Pranayama	Ashwini Mudra Mahamudra

			Ujjayi Agnisara, Nauli Suryanuloma
Male Infertility (low sperm count)		Inverted postures Sectional breathing	Nadisudhi with Anthar-kumbhaka with 3 Bandhas, Mahamudra.

Now there is enough scientific evidence to show that yoga is helpful in all the above mentioned ailments.

Now there is enough scientific evidence to show that yoga is helpful in all the above mentioned ailments.

EXERCISES	Rotating Excercises 1	2	Time (Minute) Full Session	Short Session	Emphasize
BREATHE & STRETCH					
Befor you start	#	•	1	2	2
Ann-Stretch Breathing	#	•	2	-	2
Hand Stretch Breathing	#	•	2	-	1
Tree Breathing	#	•	1/2	-	1/2
Cat Streach	#	•	1	1/2	2
Rabbit Breathing	#	•	1/2	-	1/2
Single Leg Raising	#	•	2	11/2	2
LOOSENING UP AND SUN SALUTE					
Jogging	#	•	2	1	2
Forward-Backward Bending	#	•	1/2	1/2	1/2
Sideways Bending	#	•	1/2	-	1/2
Twisting	#	•	1/2	1/2	1/2
Embryo	#	•	1	-	1
Sun Saluto*	#	•	3-1/2	1-1/2	10
Instant Relaxatation Technique	#	•	2	2	2
STANDING					
ASANAS					
Lateral Arc	#	-	4	4	4
Hands to Feet Pose	#	-	3	3	3
Backward Bend	#	-	2	2	2
Triangle*	#	-	1/2	-	1/2
PRONE					
Cobra	-	•	2	1	4
Locust	-	•	2	1	4
Bow	-	•	1	1/2	3
Crocodile	-	•	1	1/2	3
SLIPINE					
Half Shoulderstand or	-	•	2	2	5
Shoulderstand	-	•	2	2	5
Plough	-	•	1	-	3
Bridge	-	•	1	-	3
Fish*	-	•	1	1	3
SITTING					
Kneeling Pose	#	-	1	1/2	2
Moon	#	-	2	-	3
Camel*	#	-	2	-	3
Spinsl Twist	-	•	3	-	4
Forward Stretch	-	•	2	1	4
Supine Kneebend*	-	•	1	-	4
RELAXATION					
Relaxation					
Quick Relaxtion Techniqe (QRT) or	#	•	5	5	10
Deep Relaxtion Techniqe (DRT)	#	•	10	5	20
PRANAYAMA & MEDITATION					
Pranayama & Meditation					
Sectional Breathing	#	•	4	1	5
Rapid Abdominal Breathing*	#	•	4	2	10
Alternate Nostril Breathing*	#	•	4	2	10
Folded-Tongue Breathing*	-	•	1	-	2
Sounds Breathing	#	-	2	-	3
Meditaion	-	•	5	5	15

= Rotating Excercise Day 1   • = Rotating Excercise Day 2   * = Difficult Excercise

CHAPTER 14

Appendix

The following is a list of Diseases and their Ayurvedic equivalents.

Abortion	Garbhapat
Abscess	Vidradhi
Acne	Youvanpitka
Acidity	Amlapitta
After-Pains	Makkal
Albuminuria	Lalameha
Alcoholism	Madatyaya
Amenorrhoea	Artav-Dosh Kashinartav
Anaemia	Pandu-Roga
Angina Pectoris	Hradgraha Hrad-Roga
Anorexia	Arochak
Aphonia	Mookatva
Aphthae	Sarvasarmukh-Roga
Apolexy	Sanyas
Ascites	Jalodar
Asthma	Shwas (Tamaka)
Bites & Stings	Dansha
Blepha-Ritis	Pakshmashat
Boils	Pitika
Bronchitis	Kasbheda (Cough-Janya)

Bubo	Braghna
Burning of the Feet	Pada-Daha
Calculi Biliary Or Gall Stones	Ashmari (Pittatmak)
Gravel Calculi Renal	Sharkara
Calculi (Urinary)	Ashmari
Cancer	Mansarbud
Carbuncle	Vinata Prameha Pitaka
Chicken-Pox	Krodnarava Sneelekla
Chlorosis	Pandu-Roga
Cholera	Vishoochika
Cholera Infantum	Vishoochika (Balanam)
Chyluria	Pistha Meha
Cirrhosis of the Liver	Yakrit-Dalyudar
Colic	Shoola
Conjunctivitis	Abhishyanda
Constipation	Anaha
Convulsions (Infantile)	Akshepak
Corns	Kadar
Cough	Kasa
Coryza (Catarrh)	Pratishyaya
Croup	Swaraghna
Cystitis (Inflammation of the bladder)	Mutrou-Kasad
Deafness	Badhirya
Debility	Kshina-Roga
Debility (Sexual)	Kshina Shukra Klaibya
Diabetes Insipidus	Udakmeha
Diabetes Mellitus	Madhu Meha
Diarrhoea	Atisar
Diarrhoea Chronic	Pakwa-Atisar
Dirrhoea Infantile	Balaroga-Atisar
Diphtheria	Kanth-Rohini
Dropsy	Shoaf Shwayathu
Dysentery	Pravahika
Dysentery Chronic	Pravahika

Dysmenorrhoea	Artav-Dosh-Kratchharajaska
Dyspepsia	Agnimandya
Dysuria	Mutrakrichha
Ear-Ache	Karnashoola
Ear (Inflammmation of the)	Karnashoath
Eczema	Kitibh
Elephantiasis	Shlipad
Epilepsy	Apasmar
Epistaxis	Nasarakta, Raktapitta, Urdhwagata
Erysipelas	Visarpa
Fainting	Moorchha
Fever	Jwara
Fever (Intermittent)	Sheetjwar
Fever (Puerperal)	Sutikajwara
Fever (Relapsing)	Parivarti Jwara-Sannipatbheda
Fever (Remittent)	Jwara Santat
Fever (Typhoid)	Sannipat Jwara (Pralapak)
Fistula Et Ano	Bhagandar
Giddiness	Bhrama
Goitre	Galgand
Gonorrhoea	Oupsargik-Meha
Gout	Vatarakta
Heart-Burn	Hradayadah
Hematemesis	Pittajanya-Chhardi-Oordhwagat Raktapitta
Haematuria	Shonit Meha
Haemoptysis	Oordhwagata Raktapitta Oorakshat
Headache	Shirah-Shool
Heart (Diseases of)	Hridrog
Hemicrania	Ardhav-Bhedak
Hemiplegia	Pakshaghat-Pakshavadha
Hepatitis	Yakrit-Dalyudar
Hernia	Antra Vridhhi
Herpes Zoster	Kaksha

Hiccough	Hikka
Hoarseness-Laryngitis	Swara-Bheda
Hydrophobia	Jaltras
Hysteria	Aptantrak
Incontinence of Urine	Hasti-Meha
Indigestion	Ajirna
Influenza	Dushta Pratishyaya
Insomnia	Aswapna-Nidranash
Intestinal Obstruction	Baddhantrodar
Jaundice	Kamla
Lactation	Stanya
Lactation Fever	Stanyottha Jwar
Leprosy	Mahakushtha
Leucorrhoea	Pradar (Shwer)
Lichen-Planus	Rajika
Lumbago	Katigraha-Trikagraha
Mania (Acute)	Unmad
Mastitis	Stanshoath
Measles	Romantika
Melaena (Intestinal Haemorrhage)	Raktapitta-Adhogat
Menorrhagia	Asragdar-Rakta Pradar
Mumps	Pashangardab
Nausea	Hrullas
Nephritis	Urikka-Shoath
Neuralgia	Shoola
Night-Blindness	Shleshma, Vidagdha, Drishti, Naktandhya
Obesity	Medo-Vriddhi
Orchitis	Vriddhi
Otorrhoea	Karnasrav
Ozaena	Peenas
Paralysis (Agitans)	Vepathoo
Paralysis (Facial)	Ardit
Paralysis (General)	Atatvabhi-Nivesh
Paraplegia	Urustambha

Perspiration (Night Sweats)	Prasveda-Arisweda
Peritonitis	Chhinna-Antrodar
Phithisis	Shoash-Rajyakshma
Phosphaturia	Kshar-Meha
Piles—Bleeding	Raktarsha
Piles	Shushkarsha
Pityriasis	Sidhma
Plague (Bubonic)	Vidarika
Pleurisy	Puppusavaram shod
Pneumonia	Raktasthivi-Sannipat
Pregnancy	Sagarbh-Avastha
Prolapsus Ani	Guda-Bhransha
Prostate Gland (Enlargement of)	Asthila (Mutraghat)
Pruritus & Prurigo	Alasak-Rakasa
Pruritus Ani	Ahiputna
Pruritus Vulvae	Yonikandu
Psoriasis	Vicharchika
Retention of Urine	Vat-Basti
Rheumatism	Sandhigat-Vatroga Amvat
Ringworm of the body	Dadroo
Ringworm of the scalp	Indralupta
Scabies	Pama-Katchhoo
Sciatica	Gridhrasi
Scrofula	Gandamala-Apachi
Sinus	Nadi-Vrina
Small-Pox	Masoorika
Spastic Paraplegia	Kalayakhanj
Spermatorrhoea	Shukra-Meha
Splenic Enlargement	Plihodar
Sprue	Grahani
Stiff Neck	Manya-Stambh
Stomatitis	Mukhroga-Mukhpak
Stye	Anjananamika
Sunstroke	Suryabhi-Ghatjanya,

	Moorchha
Synovitis	Kroshtruk-Shirsh
Syphilis	Firang
Tetanus	Dhanustambh
Teething	Dantoadbheda
Thirst	Trishna
Tonsilitis	Galagriha-Kantha-Shalooka
Tooth-Ache	Dantroga
Tympanitis	Adhman
Ulcers	Vraina
Uric Acid-Diatheses	Sikata-Meha
Urticaria	Sheeta-Pitta
Vomiting	Chhardi
Warts	Mashak
Whooping Cough	Kukas
Worms	Krimi

Courtesy : Panel of Vaidyas; Clinical Application of Ayurvedic Remedies, Sri Satguru Publications, Delhi, 2nd Edition 1986.

Dwivedi R, Singh G., Ayurvediy Rog ka Vargeekaran, Chowkamba Surabharathi Prakashan, Varanasi, 1977.

Subject Index

A

Agni 45-51, 42
Acetylcholine 26-27
Adrenaline 26-27
Amashaya 27, 50, 182
Alochaka pitta 32
avalambaka kapha 32
Ashtanga Hridaya 10
Anabolism 32
Asthayi 42
Ahar rasa 46, 42
Antaragni 50, 149
Amla 232
Ama 51, 78
annavaha 53
Akasha 14, 48
Alashu 245
Asthi 41
Agati 131, 64
Ashita 66
Agantuja 96, 183
Anubhandya 74, 75
Anubhanda 74, 76
Abhyantare 129, 130, 73
Ashyapakarsha 76
Atiyoga 79, 77
Ayoga 77
Algha 23
Anja 24
Ado amashaya 89
Amlika 90
Aatopa 91
Aruna 92
Angaharsha 92
Asthikheda 93
Aaasye-Vyrasya 93
Apraharsha 94
Angasandha 91, 94
Aarathi 92
Angaparsya 95
Atisara 115
Apakti 95
Aranthara death 105
Akalmaranam 107
Ahar shaktitah 143
Amlapitta 38, 124, 185
Amavatta 185
Adibhautika 129, 183
Adhidaivika 129, 183
Adhivalpravritta 134, 182
Amashaya samutha 182
Aparirakshana krit 183
Adhyatmika 182, 183
Aharshakti 143
Apthopadesh 109
Antah-parimarjana 220
Akaladrita 183
Apathya 221

Anuvasana 241
Anupan 257, 258
Akriti 148
Aharam 148
Apana 264
Adhyatma yoga 268, 270
Ashtanga yoga 269
Ayurveda and Yoga 263-291
Ayu 275
Atma 106
Astha siddhi 278
Atrophy 36
Ayurveda, fundamentals of 9

B

Biological rhythms 33
Bhrajaka pitta 32
Bhedaka kapha 32, 46
Brahmanda 12
Bhutagni 47
Bala 212, 23
Brahma 268, 94
Bandha 22
Bheda 88, 99
Bhramsa 93
Bhanga 92, 93
Bhutonmada 184, 185
Bhippa 185
Bahir-parimarjana 220
Brihmana 217
Bali 219
Basant ritu 222
Bhakti 269, 147
Bhakti yoga 269

C

Charaka 10
Charaka Samhita 10
Catecholamines 33
Catabolism 32
Chala 93, 22
Cheshta 93, 22
Convalescence 84
Choshma 91
Chedana 92, 220
Causation of Disease 71-82
Clinical manifestation of Disease 83-107
Case-taking 109-135
Chardi 91

D

Diagnosis, Principles of 173-180
Dosha 212
Doshic rhythm 32
Dehabala 38
Dushyas 41
Dushana 41
Dehadharana 41
Dhatu kshaya 44
Dhatwagni 48
Dhamani 52
Dravya 56, 133
Drava 235, 22
Dhatugati 130, 22
Darshana 110
Dhatu Vriddhi 44
Dehmardana 22
Dhriti 277, 23
Dosha prakopa 76
Defervescence 84
Darunaka 185
Dausana 92
Dhumayana 96
Dhosapaka 101
Dhatupaka 103
Dhaurudra chardi 184
Dhanusthamba 118, 185
Daivibal Pravrutta 183

Doshabala pravritta 182
Daiva vyapshya 219
Dosage 252-255
Drug Administration
- principles 251-261
Diet 66, 258-261, 58
Dhyana yoga 268
Dukha 274
Dhouti 278
Disease, Causation of, 71-82
Clinical manifestations of
Classification of 83-107, 181-206

E

Examination of Patient 109-135
Examination of disease 177-178, 179-180

F

Fastigium 84
Fever 84
Fundamentals of Ayurveda 9-60

G

Guna 233-235
Guru 235
Gatimala 22
Gaurava 22
Garbha vikara 93
Grahani 193, 185
Gulma roga 102, 133, 185
Grudhrasi 195, 185
Gems 219
Gamana 219
Gita 269

H

Histamine 33
Hundana 93
Hridroga 103, 184, 185
Hyperacidity 40
Hemanta ritu 222
Hatha Yoga, Pradipika 269
Hari (Vishnu) 268
Health and Disease 61-69

I

Incubation period 84
Itihasa 11, 185
Interaction of host and environment 86
Incompatible drugs 252
Indriya 275
Investigation of the Patient 139-171

J

Jatharagni 46
Jala 16
Jati 131
Jrumba 93
Jihwa 116-118
Jalodhar 115
Jwar 98
Janmabala pravritta 182
Jivatma 264
Jnana Yoga 269
Jiva 275
Jeevaniya 58

K

Karma yoga 269
Karana 67
Kashyap Samhita 11
Kledaka kapha 32, 45

Kitta paka 42
Koshtagni 48
Ka vaigunya 53
Karuna 276
Katu 232
Kshudra 22
Kshama 23
Khadita 66
Kriyakala 87-101, 208
Karsyavata 92
Karshana 92
Kharatva 72
Kampa 93
Kshobha 93
Kantho dvamsi 93
Karna nada 93
Kandu 94, 95
Kodha 94
Kledha 94, 95
Kruchcha sadhya 104
Kala maranam 106-107
Krimija 184
Kanta kulja 185
Kriusa 148
Kala bala pravritta 134, 183
Kaphaja 39
Kayachikitsa 242
Kriyakala and management 208
Klesam 147
Kruthajnata 147
Kamechcha 147
Kesam 148
Krodha 147

L

Lavana 232
Laghu 234
Leedha 66
Langhana 216

M

Madhav Nidan 11
Madhavakar 11
Malas 44-45, 41
Malina 41
Mandagni 50, 44, 95
Mutravah 110
Mridu 235
Madhur 232
Medha 41, 23
Majja 41
Mamsa 41
Midhya yoga 77
Mudhasanjatha 94
Madhu 222, 67
Mahamarana 106
Madhumeh 114
Muthr 114-115, 42
Matrija 182
Manasa 266, 182
Mantras 219
Mangala 219
Mode of administration - drugs 255
Manasika 129, 146
Moksha 263, 61
Manu 268
Mahabhashya 267
Maitri 276

N

Nishwasa 22
Nidanardhakara roga 76
Namana 93
Nishpradhate 95
Nigandha 102
Nadi 111-113, 110
Netrah 118-119, 148

Nasaroga 185
Nija 135
Nanatmaja vyadhi 184
Niramkarana 218
Niruha 278
Niyama 271, 219
Netram 148
Nasya 245

O

Ovum 182
Ojas 55-60, 42
Obesity 284

P

Prasekar 94
Paka 42, 94
Poothagandhi 94
Pratya khayaya 104
Prasna 110
Pramanatah 140
Pandu 115, 124
Prameha 117
Pitrija 182
Pakvashaya samutha 182
Pishachadikrita 183
Parirakshanadrit 183
Pitruja 182
Prakriti 37-40, 145-171
Panchabhutas 14, 16
Poshaya 42
Poshaka 42
Pramana 128, 141
Panch karmas 217, 241
Pathya 221
Poorva-karma 218, 242
Pashat karma 218
Pranipat 219
Patanjali Yoga Sutra 264
Paramatma 267, 275
Pranayama 269
Parampara 275
Purusha 121, 266
Principles of diagnosis,
treatment 173-180
Pharmacotherapeutics 227-249
Panchakarma Therapy 241
Principles of drug
administration 251-261
Prakrititah 140

R

Rasayana 10
Rasaguna 231
Ranjaka pitta 32
Rajas 40
Ruksha 92, 102, 234
Rashi 148, 68
Roksha 92, 96
Ruk 92
Rishtabhasa 100-101
Rakta pitta 124, 77, 185
Rajyakshma 185
Ruchi Ahar 148
Rukshana 216
Rakta mokshana 245
Rasachikitsa 257
Rhythmic variation of
doshas 32, 33
Rasa Panchaka 231-238

S

Samahanath 142, 149
Saratah 141
Satwatah 142
Shlesmic sannipath 119
Siroroga 245, 185
Samagni 50

Sthula 52
Sahaja 57
Sharir 105, 182
Saghatabala pravritta 183
Shaastrakrita 183
Swabavabala pravritta 183
Samanya vyadhi 184
Sara 235
Sandhanana 92
Satwa 16, 40, 105
Shodhana 215
Shamana 215, 54
Santarpana 218
Srotas—51-55
Swasthya—Ojeskara 61, 224
Shastra paridhana 220, 290
Snehana 217, 244
Sthamba 217, 95
Sirovirochana 278
Swatiayana 219
Sitapadardha 149
Samadhi 263
Siva 263
Shakti 263
Swetaswara Upanishad 269
Samprapti 130-135, 176, 210
Sakhya priti 276
Santosa 276
Sapta Dhatu 41-44
Susatya 104
Soma 278
Sthitha prajna 279
Satya buddhi 279
Sthyai 42

T

Tridosha, Principle of 18-32
Trigunas 15
Tarpaka pitta 32
Tamas 15, 40
Tejas 14, 46
Tikshana 49
Tishnagni 51
Thoda 92
Tadana 92
Tyaga 93
Trusha 93, 94
Tridoshaja 113
Time of administration of drugs 255-256
Treatment, principles of 207-225

U

Udana vayu 28
Ushna 42, 234
Udakavah 53
Upayoga samstha 68
Upayukta 68
Utpada 73
Udgatana 183
Udakmeh 114
Urdavata 185
Upkarmas 216-217
Upahara 219
Upakshanam 276
Upadrava 100

V

Veda 270, 3
Vajikarana 10, 247
Vaghbhatta 10, 72
Vijay Rakshit 72
Vyana vayu 28
Vriddhi 89, 127, 128
Vishamagni 51
Vyadhi kshamatva 210, 58
Vayu 18
Vishada 102
Vuchwasa 22

Vrishya 22
Viprakrishta 73
Vyabhicharika 73
Vyanjaka 73
Vaikrita 73
Vyadi utpadaka 73
Vyakti 88
Vimarga gamana 91
Voshama 91
Vyadha 92
Vimodana 92
Veshtana 93
Vikshapa 93
Vislesha 93
Vunncanana 93
Vak parushya 93
Vushna kaitvam 93
Vutseda 95
Vyrushya 95
Vidhradhi 102
Vishakamba 103
Vamanadhikyatah 115
Vishuchika 115
Vikritatah 140, 74
Vyayama shaktitah 143
Vayastah 143
Vatarakta 185
Vikrata Anga suchaka 185
Vatukam 185
Vyatadidrita 183
Vidyutakshinikrita 183
Vyapath 129
Vyadhi pratyanika
Viharc 224
Vamana 278
Virechana 278
Vasti 278
Visarga kala
Varsha ritu 222
Vishnu 268

Y

Yapya 104
Yukti vyapashya 219
Yoga 263
Yujir 263
Yojana 263
Yokta 263
Yama 271
Yoga and Ayurveda 263-273
Yoga, Therapeutic 274-291
 applications
Yoni 127